MEDICINE AT THE CROSSROADS

ALSO BY MELVIN KONNER

The Tangled Wing
Becoming a Doctor
The Paleolithic Prescription
(with S. Boyd Eaton and Marjorie Shostak)
Why the Reckless Survive
and Other Secrets of Human Nature
Childhood

MEDICINE

at the

CROSSROADS

THE CRISIS IN HEALTH CARE

MELVIN KONNER

PANTHEON BOOKS   NEW YORK

FEB 15 1994

All rights reserved under International and Pan-American Copyright Conventions. Published in the United States by Pantheon Books, a division of Random House, Inc., New York, and simultaneously in Canada by Random House of Canada Limited, Toronto.

Library of Congress Cataloging-in-Publication Data
Konner, Melvin.
    Medicine at the crossroads / Melvin Konner.
    Includes index.
    1. Medical care—United States 2. Medical care, Cost of—United States.
3. Medical policy—United States I. Title.
    RA395.A3K66 1993
    362.1'0973—dc20   92-50463
    ISBN 0-679-41545-9

Book design by Glen Edelstein

Manufactured in the United States of America
First Edition

To the memory of
Abraham "Bobby" Fink, M.D.,
and
Milton Finkel, M.D.,
general practitioners

CONTENTS

I ask God for medicine and put it into you. And I say to God, "Here's my child, give me some more medicine so I may put it into him."
> —Tsau, a blind master healer of the ¡Kung San, Kalahari hunters and gatherers, as recorded by Richard Katz

Day and night, however thou mayst be engaged, thou shalt endeavor for the relief of the patient with all thy heart and soul. Thou shalt not desert or injure thy patient even for the sake of thy life or thy living.
> —From the commandments to medical graduates attributed to Charaka, a Hindu physician of the seventh century B.C.

I will apply dietetic measures for the benefit of the sick according to my ability and judgement; I will keep them from harm and injustice.
> —From the oath attributed to Hippocrates of Kos, a Greek physician of the fifth century B.C.

Keep far from me the delusion that I can accomplish all things.
> —From the physician's prayer attributed to Maimonides, a Jewish physician to the court of Cairo in the twelfth century

With your talents and industry, with science, and that stedfast honesty which eternally pursues right . . . you may promise yourself every thing— but health, without which there is no happiness. An attention to health then should take the place of every other object.
> —From a letter to a young man by Thomas Jefferson, July 6, 1787

No society can legitimately call itself civilised if a sick person is denied aid because of lack of means.
> —Anaurin Bevan, founder of the British National Health Service, 1948

PROLOGUE

IN THE UNITED STATES today medicine and society appear to be on a collision course. Every day, it seems, the front pages and editorial columns of our newspapers tell another tale of woe in medical politics, and some important elections have been determined by what people think about health care and doctors—even though they know little about either.

Some claim that there is no crisis, repeating endlessly and soothingly that America has the best health care in the world. I keep trying to figure out what they mean. It can't be that we have the greatest longevity. Many European countries have longer-lived people than we do, and some groups in our society do not even meet the standards of the developing world in longevity: men in Harlem have lower life expectancies than men in Bangladesh. It can't be that we have the best prenatal care, since we have made no organized effort and so have a rate of preventablepremature birth that is higher than in other countries—for example, France, where pregnant women are *paid* to come to the clinic.

It can't be infant mortality, where we are twenty-third lowest. It can't be child health, since children are far overrepresented among the uninsured, and since we have one of the largest proportions of nonimmunized children of any industrial country. Embarrassed, the Reagan administration stopped counting them in the mid-1980s, so now we have no exact idea how many there are, but we do know that this neglect caused a completely unnecessary measles epidemic in the late 1980s. It certainly cannot be fairness, since more than 35 million people are uninsured—a category that has far more than its share of African-Americans. And it cannot be efficiency, since costs are out of control.

If the boosters of our present system are not referring to any of these measures, what can they mean in claiming America's excellence? The number of surplus magnetic resonance imagers per square mile? The number of unnecessary cesarean sections or coronary bypass operations per year? The number of one-pound premature babies saved—in many cases, for a markedly impaired life—at a cost of hundreds of thousands of dollars each? The number of brain-dead patients kept "alive" on ventilators?

But then, maybe I do know what they mean: that if you are rich—not just middle-class, but rich—and money is no object, then your chances of survival are best here, because we have the most sophisticated technical equipment and procedures. However, we don't even know whether this is so, since so few outcome studies have been done. According to authorities such as John Wennberg and David Eddy, only about 20 percent of currently used medical and surgical procedures have been evaluated properly, as the recent experience with breast implants shows. Consequently, although the poor are certainly, tragically, getting far too little medical care, the very rich often get too much for their own good, suffering iatrogenic—doctor-caused—illness that outweighs any possible benefit. Women of all economic levels receive inadequate treatment for some ailments, such as heart disease, while being overtreated for others—as shown by recent experience with cesarian section and ovariectomy, for example.

The system's ills are pervasive, and all sectors are responsible. Worst is the insurance "industry," a vast parasitic bureaucracy of fifteen hundred private businesses whose tentacles reach deep into the lives of patients and whose burdensome activities demoralize doctors and drive them out of medicine. At their whim, they can refuse to insure anyone who is sick or otherwise looks like a bad risk—male hairdressers, for instance—an egregious practice that has aptly been called the "monstrous game" of red-lining. Worse, people who have faithfully paid their premiums for years can now be turned out on the street when they get sick; a company simply pretends to raise its premiums across the board—say, tenfold— and then informs all those who are not yet sick that they are eligible for 90 percent discounts. Called "policy churning," this practice turns the very core of medical insurance into a cheap confidence trick.

Second worst are greedy doctors and hospitals. Doctors on average are not paid too much, given their onerous training and heavy responsibility; but an important minority either cheat the system outright or (less odious but no less expensive) choose options for care on the basis of hoped-for income rather than medical necessity. Corporate hospital ownership has not reduced costs as promised and has increased the evil practice of patient dumping— rejection at the emergency room door that sometimes causes loss of life—and has generally confirmed and extended the egregious "greed is good" eighties philosophy from which America must now very painfully recover.

Third, we have a malpractice redress system that is an utter failure. A 1991 study in New York State found that less than 2 percent of actual negligent acts by doctors were brought to the point of a lawsuit. Of these, only half were likely to result in awards. Because of the large size of some of these awards—up to millions of dollars—there is a widespread impression that litigation is a good way of controlling physician error. It is not. The vast majority of truly negligent acts by U.S. doctors are not detected and certainly not punished. This is not true elsewhere. In Sweden, to take one example, the mechanism for compensating patients who experience losses due to doctor error is separate from the one for punishing and restricting bad doctors. This allows doctors actually to help patients recover their compensation, independent of the courts. The awards are much smaller—tens to hundreds of thousands of dollars—but far more patients are compensated. Yet ironically, in the United States, the fear of being ruined by a lawsuit is so frightening to doctors that they practice what is called "defensive medicine." A large factor in what they decide to do with patients—tests, procedures, and the like—is the fear of litigation. Some official estimates of the total cost of medical litigation, including defensive medicine, range up to 20 billion dollars annually. But it is very difficult to estimate the cost of defensive medicine, and the total bill for medical lawsuits may be much higher. As with the Savings and Loan debacle, officially claimed losses are only a fraction of real cost.

So in reality there are several crises, and thus several dangers and several opportunities. First, trust between doctor and patient, built up over a century of increasingly good medicine, is breaking down. Besides the colossal rise in malpractice action and the resulting understandable but enormously costly defensive medicine, indicators include the declining prestige of the medical profession in polls and studies, the increasing use of unorthodox healers, and the widespread fear among older people that they will fall into the hands of a doctor who, for selfish or scientific reasons, will not let them die a timely death.

Second, the failure of the medical insurance business to live up to its obligations even to those it purports to insure, much less those it has missed altogether, has reached crisis proportions. This will not be allowed to continue much longer. Because physicians have not been vocal enough in opposing this injustice, people blame doctors, mistakenly thinking that the medical and the insurance establishments are one and the same.

Third, costs are out of control. Although we are the only industrial country other than South Africa that does not have a national plan guaranteeing health care for all, we greatly exceed them all in health costs. The reasons are many. Malpractice actions are one; greedy doctors another. But more important is rampant overreliance on technology—unnecessary treatments and tests—

and the replacement of primary care and prevention with sub-specialized acute intervention. And the cost of bureaucracy alone in the tangled web of private insurance may be as high as a fourth of our health-care bill—five to ten times the proportion in some industrial nations.

That's without even weighing in the devastating damage to the morale of physicians, our most priceless commodity. Physicians, it has often been said, cannot be expected to solve the problems of society. William Osler, that peerless clinician, left many epigrams, but one of his most cogent was "Shut out the future as tightly as the past. . . . Let the limit of your horizon be a twenty-four-hour cycle." He meant that in an acute illness the doctor's obligation to the patient is to think about nothing else: not costs, not politics, nothing but the patient, right now, tonight.

The trouble is, doctors know they are usually nowhere near the root cause of the problem, which they feel powerless to affect, and that sense of powerlessness prevents them from trying to buck the system or change human nature. All physicians know another great name of nineteenth-century medicine—Rudolf Virchow, the pioneering pathologist. Few realize that he was also a key leader in the social medicine movement of his time, a pioneer of public health who had his own aphorism: "Medicine is a social science, and politics only medicine on a grand scale."

What could this rigorous scientist of the body have meant by such an extravagant claim? The answer is in his life. He never stopped fighting to change the social conditions that promoted the great epidemics of his era, even as he sought under his microscope the pathophysiology of how those scourges killed.

So who was right, Osler or Virchow? The answer is, Both were. In the acute instance the physician owes it to the patient to blot out all that distracts from the art and science of vanquishing illness and death. But in the walk-in clinic, in the hospital staff meeting, in the county medical association, in the training of medical students, and in the citizen's role, doctors can engage in social medicine and in the politics that Virchow believed was nothing but medicine on a grand scale. As in his era, some of the great killers of our time have social and cultural problems at their sources.

Coronary artery disease, lung cancer, colon cancer, diabetes, AIDS, and now multiply-drug-resistant tuberculosis—these will threaten all of us unless we get some kind of handle on the social and political forces underlying their rise.

The crisis is not news. An article in the *Lancet*, the leading British medical journal, entitled "Crisis in American Medicine," said the following:

> In terms of gross national product the U.S.A. spends more on health than does any other country. But costs are rising at such a rate that more and more people will find it difficult to get complete health care. This particularly applies to the poor, the old, the African-Americans, and other disadvantaged groups. . . . There are indications, too, that the quality of care has been inferior, especially in terms of antenatal and infant mortality. The whole organisation of medical care in the U.S.A. has failed to respond to changing disease patterns, the move from country to cities, industrialisation, and the increasing proportion of old people in the population.

The year, astoundingly, was 1968. All of these problems have worsened in the ensuing quarter century, not because of lack of knowledge but because of lack of action.

All of us must share responsibility. Few of us take the simple, timely, consistent actions in our lives that constitute comprehensive prevention; yet even fewer are willing to forgo the most drastic and expensive interventions later, in life-threatening illness—even when there is little likelihood that those interventions will work. Is the doctor ordering the angiogram for the patient's good, to meet the patient's or the family's unreasonable but insistent demand, or for self-protection, curiosity, or maybe even money? Is the bypass really needed *now*, or is there still a medical or lifestyle route of management that has not yet been fully tried? Is the patient's quest for health—in essence a spiritual quest—being properly and fully called into play? Last but not least, is the psychological power of the doctor-patient relationship brought to bear to achieve the kind of healing that no other strategy can accomplish?

During my years with the !Kung San, hunters and gatherers of Africa, I witnessed an ancient and supposedly "primitive" form of medicine: healers entering trances in the course of a complex ritual dance, set to an eerie music between the firelight and the desert night sky. They laid their hands on the ill and the well alike, showing with all the energy in their hearts, minds, and bodies that they cared deeply about the outcome. It was about all they had to offer, but it was worth a great deal to their patients. Call it the placebo effect if you like; placebo effects work. Otherwise why would we always insist on placebo-controlled studies? Since long before Hippocrates, wise physicians have recognized that with their behavior alone they wield enormous power.

This is not just speculation about "mind over illness"; it is about something much simpler too: compliance. What good is the miraculous antituberculin drug if the patient can't be somehow convinced to take the whole course? What good is the most exquisite ultrasound study if the pregnant woman goes out and poisons her baby with alcohol or cocaine? What good is the triple bypass or the liver transplant if the patient goes out and destroys the new, hard-won tissues and organs with the same old suicidal lifestyle?

Theodor Billroth, the famous German surgeon, was skeptical of prevention. "The physician," he wrote, "is even expected to do his part in curing the stupidity and indifference of humanity. A beautiful task, but one that can be accomplished only by many generations of physicians, and then only imperfectly."

To this we might reply with an epigram from the Talmud: "It is not up to you to complete the work, but neither are you free to desist from it." Every experienced clinician has had both kinds of patients: those who never cared about themselves no matter how much they were cared about, and those whose lives were completely changed by a caring voice and hand. In addition to there being more to healing than modern science and technology, there is also more to diagnosis. A 1975 British study showed that the overwhelming majority of a physician's information for diagnosis comes from the history—the interview of the patient—alone, with a small additional contribution from the physical examination, and about the same small amount of added help from subsequent laboratory tests. More sensitive doctors, the ones who take time to listen to their patients, may well be more cost-effective ones.

But the purpose of this book is not to present a thesis on health-care policy; rather it is to show how doctors and other health-care workers around the world carry out varied policies for better or for worse. Glimpses are given into a large hospital north of Tokyo and a general practice in a small Japanese mountain town; mental hospitals in Siena and Rome and a genetic disease prevention program in Sardinia in Italy; a storefront counseling center for pregnant women in Bremen and a transforming cardiological practice in East Berlin in post-unification Germany; drug- and prostitution-ridden streets of Sydney, Australia; home-care health services for the elderly in the seaside village of Clifden in Galway, Ireland; a general practice in Jarrow, a small city in the north of England; care of the mentally ill and the dying in the holy city of Banaras, India; an AIDS clinic in Bangkok, Thailand, as well as a brothel in a rural Thai mountain town; and hospitals and clinics in many locations in the United States.

The American settings illustrate how things can go wrong with modern medicine, despite its enormous scientific power. Health care in the United States is in disarray as compared with that in Canada, Britain, and many other industrial countries. Some features of the American system are fortunately unique or almost so; others, however, represent exaggerations of trends that may be seen in lesser forms elsewhere. These include the trend toward rapidly rising costs; increasing specialization at the expense of primary care, in a way uncorrelated, or even inversely correlated, with need; increasing emphasis on high-technology medicine, adopted on a wave of characteristic enthusiasm, often with minimal scientific evidence; and a universal tendency to postpone intervention to the acute crisis stage of an illness, rather than taking steps to prevent worsening of the condition at an early stage, or even before the onset of the disease process.

Although the book will certainly anger some in the medical profession, it has been prepared with the direct and indirect advice of some of the leading physicians working today. I have tried to rely on my own authority as little as possible, referring wherever

I can to much greater authorities in specialized fields. The book as a whole, then, would find support among some leading, and to my mind enlightened, doctors, who are named whenever possible in the text. They are in a minority in the medical profession at the moment, but a growing minority, and I believe that theirs is the voice of the future. Fortunately, theirs were among the voices that shaped the television series *Medicine at the Crossroads*, to which this book is linked. Four years in the making, the series took a bold approach to the problems of modern medical care around the world, focusing on the human consequences of policy decisions in many different countries. It strongly influenced the shape and style of the book.

Inevitably, the book also draws heavily, although usually not explicitly, on my own experience; so it seems appropriate for me to relate some of that experience. I started out as an anthropologist interested in the interplay between anthropology and medicine. As a young man I spent two years in Africa researching my thesis among the !Kung San, or Bushmen, hunter-gatherers of the Kalahari Desert in Botswana, a formative experience for me. Although my specific studies were of infant development and the physiological effects of prolonged, intense breast feeding on fertility, I took a general interest in the people's health and healing practices as well. I was struck by their success in coping psychologically with illness and death, given few of the defenses we consider essential. I even became an apprentice healer in their medicine-trance ceremony—a powerful, moving ritual that mobilizes all the creative efforts of an entire village to give spiritual support to an ill person. This experience taught that there is more to healing than the mechanical fixing of physical things gone wrong.

After some years as an anthropology professor, I decided to enter medical school. Although I did not end up practicing medicine for a living, I experienced firsthand the excitement and tribulations of medical education, and even wrote a book about the clinical years of medical school. I got to know something of what it feels like to be a doctor: to interact with and try to help patients in pain and suffering, suddenly wounded or chronically ill, giving birth or dying, calm or whimpering or stoical or defiant, almost always confused and fearful, counting on the doctor to do something right and smart. No amount of criticizing doctors—and I've done a lot of that, in this book and elsewhere—can erase the basic sympathy I feel for the moral, intellectual, and practical difficulties that doctors live with every hour of every day. I hope that this sympathy, and the attitudes and policies it leads to, has as clear a place in this book as do the criticisms.

The trouble with medicine is not trouble with doctors but rather with a vast social and cultural system. That is why anthropology is at least as relevant to this enterprise as medicine is. What is needed is not a finger pointed in blame, but an analysis of a system—of a society and culture of medicine produced by advanced industrial states. One of the reviews of my book on medical education was called "The Tribe That Wears White." That says part of it, but is too restrictive.

The tribe under study in *Medicine at the Crossroads* is all of us—doctors, nurses, hospital administrators, government or insurance-company health bureaucrats, malpractice litigators, pharmaceutical and medical-instrument company executives and salespeople, advertisers and public relations representatives for drugs, medical technology, and hospitals—and above all, perhaps, patients. The last category sooner or later includes all the others, plus everyone else in our society. And patients are centrally involved in providing leverage for all that happens in medical systems, for good or ill.

For this reason it is not irrelevant to mention my experiences as a patient and a family member of patients over the past few years. About five years ago my brother's wife, then in her early forties, had a rare type of major stroke in her brain stem; I was involved in her care, which was long, complex, and difficult, including everything from major brain surgery to alternative rehabilitative medicine. Ultimately her improvements were great and are still ongoing. Less than a year later my wife began her battle with cancer, so far quite successful, but also long and difficult. Two years after that my mother, at eighty, was drastically incapacitated by a stroke; by the time of her death three months later I had had a new kind of education about the medical care of the elderly and the allocation of resources to the dying.

Then my own long-standing illness, disc disease in the lower back, finally reached a stage at which even weeks of complete bed rest, which had worked for me when I was younger, could not resolve an acute crisis. I had surgery for repair of two ruptured discs, followed by a long convalescence. I had been familiar with chronic pain, but this was a new level of pain that served as another kind of education. And my own central role in maintaining the health of my lower back in the future, through exercise and other preventive care, has made my theorizing about prevention very practical and real.

Last year my four-year-old daughter was bitten by a poisonous snake while her mother was out of the country, and I stayed with her in the hospital around the clock for a week that included two operations. I had attended her birth and the births of her brother and sister. While a man can understand only so much and no more about childbirth, these experiences, and delivering thirty-five babies while in medical school, gave me at least a feeling for what happens at this crucial moment of life. Two of my children were delivered by nurse-midwives, so I have thought long, hard, and personally about questions relating to the "medicalization" of pregnancy and childbirth. Perhaps, too, my parents' lifelong deafness sensitized me at an early age to the conundrums of illness and handicap. And as a father I have had the basic education in pediatrics that all involved parents get as their children grow.

I do not recount this history to impress the reader with my personal medical suffering. Indeed, I have been lucky, since the outcomes of most of these episodes have so far been favorable. Rather, I mention them to make it clear that I am personally acquainted with the things I am writing about. I know what it means to be on both sides of the stethoscope.

My experience has been like that of many physicians in such situations: to be greatly impressed with the technical power of modern medicine, and not so impressed with the human side. Even with my knowledge of the system and its problems, my friends in high places, and my ability to pull the strings, I had to struggle constantly to get a human response out of some physicians and institutions. This deficiency of modern doctors has become a truism, and many medical schools have instituted new programs to remedy it. But programs alone do not solve such problems; only people solve them—doctors and patients alike.

I certainly do not have all the answers, but I think I have a number of the most important questions. This book raises them, in as complex and penetrating a way as I know how to, given my training and experience, in the context set by leading physicians and others studying health, and greatly enhanced by the facts and ideas uncovered by the research and production teams fielded around the world for the television series.

If I could summarize my conclusions in a few words, they would be that I prefer personal medicine to the impersonal kind that has become common; low-tech primary care to high-tech specialized care wherever safely possible (more often than we think); prevention and early intervention to late-stage crisis management; patient and family involvement in decision making to medical authoritarianism; a dignified death a little sooner to an overmedicalized one later; a true system of accountability for doctors and compensation for injured patients to chaotic malpractice litigation; careful measurement of the outcomes of medical and surgical procedures to the haphazard system of trial and error we have now; rational and continuous monitoring of the health of a population and outreach for treatment and prevention to the passive stance of a medical system that waits for an illness to present itself; not-for-profit medicine to the cash-register variety; and universal health insurance to the ragged health safety net that exists in the United States.

I fail to see any positive role for private insurance companies in providing that safety net, and would be happy to see the Canadian health system—but at our present higher level of funding, to bring the underserved up to par—become a model for health-care delivery in the United States. But there are problems that transcend national boundaries. Surgical operations and diagnostic procedures are subject to inadequate evaluation almost everywhere.

Drug companies hawk their wares using methods that typically obfuscate, rather than clarify, the choices that are best for patients. Prevention is pitifully neglected. Doctors and patients alike wait till the last minute and then expect a quick fix, one that can often cost a fortune and still not work. Almost all of us overestimate what modern medicine knows and can do, and few of us are prepared to face a fact that people in past generations simply could not ignore: all of us must die sometime, and if in the process we consume too many of the resources of those who will go on living, we may deny them the quality of life we ourselves have enjoyed.

Medical training is still biased against primary care and general practice, against prevention and early intervention, against the simplest tactics of nutrition and exercise, immunization and monitoring, house calls and home help. Unnecessary operations by the tens of thousands, including cesarian sections, pacemaker implantations, coronary bypasses, hysterectomies, and prostatectomies, occur throughout the industrial world whether a profit motive exists or not. Drugs without merit, and many more that have no merit beyond drugs already available, are developed at enormous expense passed on to patients. And doctors who devote themselves to the simplest, most effective measures of primary care and prevention are looked down upon by their colleagues and by medical students as nonscientific second-class citizens. In fact, they—not the overpaid superspecialists—are the true heroes of modern medicine, and we as patients and citizens should do all we can to see that they are well rewarded and encouraged.

Each of us has a personal responsibility, too, to see to our own care, to the monitoring of our own symptoms and illnesses. The notion that every person is really a patient who doesn't know it yet is not just a joke among doctors, but a quite profound truth. There is no life without illness, no day without healing. What we can do best is what doctors and medicine cannot do for us at all: develop an active sense of the balance of health and illness within ourselves, and develop tactics for tilting that balance more and more against illness. Perhaps then we will be able to recognize that doctors are neither gods nor demons but human beings like ourselves, doing the best they can to help in any way they know how. A society that takes its own responsibilities seriously, and that sympathizes with and respects its doctors, is likely to find doctors who do the same in return.

MEDICINE AT THE

CROSSROADS

ONE

THE CODE
OF SILENCE

B ETWEEN DOCTOR AND PATIENT there has always been a certain amount of mystery. Among hunting-and-gathering people, such as the ones I lived with in Africa's Kalahari Desert, the doctor-shaman has little more to offer than mystery—expressed in a kind of pageantry of dance and trance—and comfort. All he and his fellow healers can do is dance all night in a ritualized, monotonous way, until the trance is effected. Then they will lay hands on the sick, tremble and moan in an intense crescendo, and finally shriek piercingly as, according to the belief, the slivers of illness-causing substance tear out of the sick person, through the arms and neck and head of the trance-dancer, and out into the vast night—back to the spirit world where they belong.

It is all they can do, yet it proves to be a lot, psychologically, convincing the patient that serious powers are being mobilized in healing, that weighty effort is being undertaken, risks are being run. In Western countries today we like to think we have ruled out mystery. But in truth, as we approach the dazzling technology of the modern medical center, and read of the wizardry of modern doctor-scientists—with their lasers, computer-produced images, and gene control—we too are in the firm grip of mysterious forces. Of course, we say, smiling; but unlike the shamans of the past, *our* magic is real. Which would be a fine reply were it not for the fact that the vast majority of us, including doctors, routinely overestimate the power of the technology; and the additional fact— endlessly proven by placebo effects—that mystery alone often heals. Studies have shown that the patient's state of mind affects the course of serious physical illness. Psychological interventions, including counseling and psychotherapy, have been shown to reduce the recovery time from heart attack and surgery and to lessen the suffering of patients in radiation treatment for cancer. Even a pleasant view through a window, as opposed to a view of a blank wall, leads to decreased use of pain medication in the hospital following surgery. In spite of the reduction in mystery that science has brought to medical practice—except of course for the aura of mystery surrounding technology—there remains a vital element of belief on the part of both doctor and patient that can apparently influence the outcome of an illness.

The Hippocratic tradition of ancient Greece was much closer than we are to the shamans that preceded it, so it is not surprising that Greek physicians cultivated mystery. Consider this passage from *Decorum*, attributed to Hippocrates, who practiced and taught medicine on the Aegean island of Kos in the fifth century B.C.:

> In fact it is especially knowledge of the gods that by medicine is woven into the stuff of the mind . . . For in medicine that which is powerful is not in excess. In fact, though physicians take many things in hand, many diseases are also overcome for them spontaneously . . . The gods are the real physicians, though people do not think so . . .

But there were also specific recommendations—apparently with a view toward making the physician seem even more godlike:

> On entering bear in mind your manner of sitting, reserve, arrangement of dress, decisive utterance, brevity of speech,

composure, bedside manners, care, replies to objections, calm self-control to meet the troubles that occur . . .

Perform all this calmly and adroitly, concealing most things from the patient while you are attending to him. Give necessary orders with cheerfulness and serenity, turning his attention away from what is being done to him; sometimes reprove sharply and emphatically, and sometimes comfort with solicitude and attention, revealing nothing of the patient's future or present condition. For many patients through this cause have taken a turn for the worse, I mean by the declaration I have mentioned of what is present, or by a forecast of what is to come . . .

The essay goes on to advise bluntly, "Never put a layman in charge of anything," and concludes that "the physician must mark off the parts about which I have spoken . . . For things that are glorious are closely guarded among all men."

It seems an odd addendum to the Hippocratic oath: Keep medical mysteries mysterious. Although there is clearly a motive of secrecy for the sake of the guild and its practitioners, the reference to the patient's welfare seems genuine—take care especially that you do not reveal very bad news, "for many patients through this cause have taken a turn for the worse." In the United States today, a doctor who followed this advice would be on shaky ground legally; over the past few decades truth telling has become so routine that it is virtually inescapable, however bad and potentially unsettling the news. Until 1960, when the medico-legal doctrine of informed consent was emerging, most American physicians still practiced Hippocratic decorum; but after that time the patient had to be included in every decision with full knowledge of the facts— which in effect made the patient part of his or her own health-care team.

Yet of course there is still a chapel in every sizable hospital; and doctors and nurses perform at least some rituals as much for the sake of mystery as for any compelling medical reason. As for patients, they sometimes tell you in plain English that they do not want to know bad news, or at least that they are sure they will beat the odds. At such a juncture a certain diffidence is advisable,

however modern you may be, however convinced you are of the
bad outcome. One of my teachers in medical school had been a
Jesuit priest before he became a doctor. "It is not the job of the
physician," he used to say wisely, "to take away the patient's
hope."

One of the most impressive experiences in anthropology is to go
to the other side of the world in search of the exotic, and to find
concealed within it a sort of mirror. Just as in Europe the ill among
the faithful have always traveled to places like Lourdes in search
of unearthly healing, so have many Japanese over the centuries
flocked to Buddhist temples to feel the sacred breeze from prayer
scrolls fanned by the hands of the temple priests. Like the waters
of Lourdes, this gentle breeze is said to be healing. But although
it is very unlikely that Japanese physicians of the past followed
Hippocrates, they preserve in their own tradition a strict code of
silence that fulfills to an extreme degree the secrecy commandment
of *Decorum*. Most, and until recently all, practitioners have systematically and quite proudly lied to their patients rather than tell
them the worst.

Take a typical example: Dr. Suda, a surgeon at a leading hospital,
the Saitama Cancer Center just north of Tokyo, has only a few
minutes to meet with each patient. He shows his patient an X-ray
study of her stomach that reveals an ulcer. She will need an operation to make her better. But then he blankly tells the woman
to leave the consulting room so that he can talk to her husband.
As the door closes behind her, he tells her husband the truth. His
wife has a serious cancer; the surgery will not cure her, only
prolong her life a little. This is not sexism—two men infantilizing
a woman by sequestering bad news—because had the cancer been
the husband's, his wife would have gotten the truth, while he
would have been left to guess at the facts or believe the story.

Nor is this some simple guild rule, with doctors shutting patients
out purely to elevate their own importance. Rather it is an osten-
sibly noble collusion among doctors, patients, and family members
to shield the one who is sick from the harshest truths. As medical

anthropologist Margaret Lock points out, it would be quite un-acceptable to tell the patient the truth, since the truth would be considered an assault intended to cause alarm. The Japanese "be-lieve very strongly that one has to try and bolster the feelings of the patient up to the very last minute—"

> that if the patient is psychologically strong, if they keep their mental state in good shape, then there is a chance that they can overcome the illness for much longer. There's a word in Japanese, which is *gambate*—the patient must work hard to try and overcome it. They feel quite strongly that if they actually give this diagnosis of cancer, if they actually tell the patient that they've got cancer, that this is going to reduce their abil-ity to fight this illness. Because in the minds of most people, cancer is a death sentence.

Utter insistence on the hope of a good outcome is a tradition arising originally from Buddhist religious belief; an optimistic mood may make the difference between life and death. Whispers behind the patient's back, far from being treacherous, are instances of tender concern. The truth will make itself plain soon enough; meanwhile all who really care will help nurture hope, since hopelessness, all agree, would clearly shorten life.

Not every patient will really be convinced. Friends and relatives have been told tales before, and have died in short order from their "ulcers" and other "minor" conditions. Some patients wel-come the lie, some resent it, some even laugh at it—like Mrs. Fusako Otani, an irrepressible, charming woman at the cancer center who chatted to all who would listen about the likelihood that she had a fatal cancer. Soon she was seen by the staff as undermining the lies they had been telling all the other patients, and the physicians and nursing staff had to call a meeting specif-ically to discuss the challenge she posed to their strange structure of falsehood. Indeed, in addition to the usual process of case-by-case treatment review in meetings of health-care professionals, the cancer center staff had routinely to review together the lies they had told to different patients, in order to achieve and maintain consistency.

To Anglo-Saxon eyes, withholding the truth looks outrageous. Our gorge rises in a swell of civil-liberties logic—what could be more threatening to a person's rights than not knowing things at once so personal and momentous? Yet it was not many decades ago that Western physicians concealed the truth from patients as long as they could, often whispering the truth to the next of kin— and indeed in some countries, like Spain, they still conceal it. Gradually, because of a strong sense of rights and general litigiousness, Western, especially American, physicians found it more and more necessary to reveal the truth to the patient. Science had become the key to health and illness, and patients theoretically could master some of this science, and then take responsibility for helping the doctor fight or manage the illness. The doctor would be in part a teacher of human biology, and indeed would try to dispel mystery, not cultivate it.

At least in theory. In reality mystery remains, but it has a different location: it lives on the frontier of technology. Computed tomography, magnetic resonance imaging, laser surgery, laparoscopy, television-assisted microsurgery, lithotripsy, radioactive isotope tracing, radiotherapy—these are only a few of the state-of-the-art methods that doctors love and patients increasingly demand. These methods often work, but they cost a great deal of money, and they are certainly not always cost-effective. However, they do pretty much guarantee mystery—in fact, the way they work is usually beyond the technological grasp of the doctors who make use of them. Only some engineers and physicists understand them. Doctor and patient stand together, grateful and humbled, before what almost seem to be technological gods.

Medical systems around the world differ greatly, but all modern ones have this in common: a relentless pressure to adopt new technology. Although the Japanese have their code of silence, their patient-processing assembly lines, and their struggle with health-care costs, they also have their counterpart of the old-fashioned country doctor. One such physician is Dr. Hideo Ozawa, who has spent forty years among rice planters in a northern mountain district. He is an old man now, but he has practiced in this village since he was fresh out of medical training. He is the sole doctor here, and all of the townspeople, at least theoretically, are his patients. Some who now could be considered older adults were born into his hands, and he has tended five generations in some families. He knows his patients and their relatives as friends, has ceased to charge fees to some of them, and knows the context and meaning of virtually every illness. His dedication exemplifies the statement of another Japanese country physician: "When an old person dies, you cry with their family."

And yes, he makes house calls—lots of them. He even gives advice to patients he passes on the sidewalk. But increasingly, the patients he visits are very old, beset by chronic illnesses that are slowly becoming terminal. He follows them, examines them, chats with them and their families, gives what corrective medicines he can, and, certainly, palliates their pain. They seem glad to have his care while they are dying.

But more and more, his patients are only the old. It is not that there are no young people in the town, nor even mainly that the young suspect his admittedly aging skills. Rather, like people throughout the industrial world, they get in their cars and drive for hours to a big-city hospital—like the Saitama Cancer Center, for instance, which sees many patients without cancer (in addition to the ones who merely *think* they don't have cancer). There they sit or stand in crowded waiting rooms, always for hours, some-times for an entire day, to spend three to five minutes with a doctor they never have seen and may never see again. Why? Because they believe in the big-city hospitals, in the famous-name medical cen-ters, and perhaps above all, in the magic of the technology. Yet the Japanese report the lowest levels of satisfaction with their doc-tors of any industrial nation in the world.

The Japanese are not unique, of course; on the contrary they exemplify problems that affect medical care in all modern coun-tries: confusion about how much money to spend, and about where to put the emphasis; excessive faith in science and tech-nology—some faith is certainly justified, but ours is still excessive; and a decreasing emphasis on the traditional—or indeed *any*—doctor-patient relationship. We are a long way from the !Kung ritual of healing, in which the earthly passion and transcendental risk of the healer create a "doctor"-patient relationship that in itself is believed to be healing. And yet some voices are being raised in Western countries on behalf of reviving such a relationship.

One of these is that of Dr. Bernie—he prefers the nickname— Siegel, a former surgeon on the clinical faculty of the Yale University School of Medicine. After treating countless cancer patients with the knife, he became convinced that the patients themselves had an even more important instrument: the will to live. Looking back over his surgical career, he thought he could see a pattern in which patients who gave up on their own powers and placed their future entirely in the doctor's hands frequently died, and others who seemed to take their destiny in their own hands frequently lived. Siegel changed careers and became an inspirational writer and speaker, dedicated to rousing patients' self-interest on their own behalf, encouraging them to challenge their doctors and fight for their lives. To emphasize his change of direction, he even shaved his head. A dramatic presence by any measure, he fills auditoriums with seriously ill people, and very obviously he inspires them.

Few medical scientists take what Siegel says at face value. Among his critics are Dr. Leon Eisenberg, a distinguished professor of psychiatry and social medicine at Harvard Medical School, and Dr. Sherwin Nuland, a respected professor of surgery and former colleague of Siegel's at Yale. They and others point out that there is little scientific evidence to support Siegel's specific convictions. All agree that patients must play a role in their own healing— taking their medicine on schedule, returning to the doctor for follow-up visits, changing their diet and other habits as recommended. But this is a far cry from the sort of mind-over-illness magic that Siegel preaches. No one doubts that there is some important relationship between mind and body—animal experiments prove that there is. But what is it? What frame of mind should you be in to better fight your cancer? Should you be angry or calmly accepting? Should you fully express your emotions of grief and fear or find a serene path through meditation and faith? Should you seek support widely or stand on your own two feet? No one, including Dr. Siegel, knows. Certainly it is likely that when the results of scientific studies are in, the advice we will have to give will be more complex than Siegel's simple exhortations.

And there is a dark side to his counsel. When I wrote in a national magazine in the United States criticizing Siegel, I got many letters. One, it is true, was from a woman who had consulted Siegel personally while fighting her cancer; she believed he had helped her and was very angry at me. But most of the others thanked me for lifting a burden of guilt from their shoulders. Either they or a loved one had fought cancer—sometimes unsuccessfully—and the main feeling they got from Siegel was one of guilt and blame. One woman had felt after reading Siegel's book that her brother's death was partly her fault—perhaps she had not loved him enough. Others felt that they were somehow responsible for their own cancers. This was not surprising; one of the questions urged on cancer patients in Siegel's best-selling book, *Love, Medicine, and Miracles,* is "Why did you need this illness?" I'm not sure what Siegel means by love, but I would not want anyone *I* love to face that question—which by the way is scientifically meaningless—while in the midst of a serious illness.

Far better than Dr. Siegel's exhortations, I think, are certain subtle and wise accounts by people who are seriously ill—for example, Alice Stewart Trillin's 1981 essay, "Of Dragons and Garden Peas: A Cancer Patient Talks to Doctors," and Arthur Frank's recent book, *At the Will of the Body,* about his experience of two life-threatening illnesses simultaneously. On the matter of mind over illness, Trillin writes:

> The trouble with this explanation of cancer is the trouble with any talisman: it is only useful when its charms are working. If I get sick, does that mean that my will to live isn't strong enough? Is being sick a moral and psychological failure? If I feel successful, as if I had slain a dragon, because I am well, should I feel guilty, as if I have failed, if I get sick?

Most seriously ill people fight their illnesses bravely. They don't need to shoulder a burden of guilt if and when they fail.

What about the stories of miracle cures—whether through meditation, "empowerment," attitude, massage, or faith healing? The late Norman Cousins, a distinguished writer and editor who took a leading role among the new psychological healers, believed he had cured his own potentially fatal illness with laughter and vitamins. In his very popular book, *Anatomy of an Illness*, he described his bout with a severe collagen disease called ankylosing spondylitis, which affects many parts of the body. Feeling that the doctors were handling his case badly, he checked out of the hospital, stopped all his medicines, and put himself on a regimen of Marx Brothers movies and vitamin C. He improved, eventually recovered, and became a sort of guru of psychological healing like Bernie Siegel, but with a somewhat less far-out approach. He got thousands of letters from doctors in response to his story, and even became a professor at the UCLA School of Medicine. For a decade until his death he was an important, supportive psychological adviser to seriously ill people. Over and over again in this experience he met patients who considered their relationships to their own doctors to be nonexistent, cold, or counterproductive. These people sought and accepted a relationship with Cousins that filled, for them, a very disturbing gap.

What really happened in Cousins's recovery will never be known, but there are possibilities other than his own explanation. First, his putative disease is rare and never easy to diagnose; he may well have had a different disease that was self-limiting. Second, the medication he had been taking in the hospital may have done most of its work before he turned his back on it. Although discouraged, he may actually have left the hospital in pretty good medical shape. Finally, many multisystem diseases have erratic courses—they come and go, worsen and improve, hang around longer or less long almost as if by whim.

And then again, it could be that the laughter and vitamin C did the trick. This is not impossible. There is an enormous amount that doctors and scientists do not know about disease, and occasionally a sick person may try this and that and stumble on something that works. Aspirin, digitalis, and some other important drugs originated in folk wisdom and only *later* were adopted by the medical profession—which proceeded to take full credit for these old home remedies. As for laughter, well . . . maybe. And maybe too for warmth, supportive relationships, stiff upper lips, prayer, crying it out, laying on hands, and anger. And perhaps decorum, the Hippocratic code of silence, can either help or hurt depending on the individual.

In fact there have been hundreds of experiments with animals and studies of people showing that psychological factors—things in the mind—affect the body, including the immune system—the molecules and cells we mobilize to fight off illness. Unfortunately these experiments have not fallen into any pattern that is useful for guiding the doctor-patient relationship, or the kinds of mental states that help the body defend itself. We can say that there is such a relationship, but we don't know what it is or how it works. Still, these experiments are or have been used by Siegel, Cousins, and others to justify very specific recommendations for seriously ill people to follow.

Perhaps a fairer approach would be to say this: Almost every patient needs to believe that his or her doctor really cares, at least a little; that the doctor's effort is a serious one, mobilizing powerful resources on the patient's behalf; and that if the treatment fails, it will not be because the doctor omitted some reasonable approach that might have worked—not, in other words, because the doctor did not care. One does not have to go to Siegel's extreme to recognize that all of us, when we are ill, need a doctor who will address the substantial part of our pain that is not physical. Dr. Eric Cassell, a practicing internist who also teaches at the Cornell University School of Medicine in New York, has for many years eloquently called his colleagues' and students' attention to such matters. In an important 1982 article in *The New England Journal of Medicine,* "The Nature of Suffering and the Goals of Medicine," in his 1991 book of the same name, and in his other writing and lecturing, he has steadfastly resisted the tendency of the modern physician to treat all illness as mechanical breakdown. In his summary of the article, he wrote:

Suffering is experienced by persons, not merely by bodies, and has its source in challenges that threaten the intactness of the person as a complex social and psychological entity. Suffering can include physical pain but is by no means limited to it. The relief of suffering and the cure of disease must be seen as twin obligations of a medical profession that is truly dedicated to the care of the sick. Physicians' failure to understand the nature of suffering can result in medical intervention that (though technically adequate) not only fails to relieve suffering but becomes a source of suffering itself.

One of Siegel's recommendations is "Get angry at your doctor." He harangues his audiences to refuse to take the doctor's clinical aloofness, the doctor's eagerness to get on to the next patient, lying down. He urges people to come armed with questions, to pry out the facts, to refuse to tolerate bafflement, to force the doctor to break the code of silence. He tells them to learn as much as they can about their illnesses. Up to a point this is not only good but wonderful advice, and it has the potential to improve patient care in many medical systems throughout the world.

For example, Dr. Julian Tudor-Hart, a leading general practitioner and health authority in Britain, has proposed a new model of the doctor-patient bond, which he calls the "patient-as-colleague" model. The image is one of doctor and patient standing side by side, as it were, perusing the same facts together, exchanging views, planning treatment and prevention—in a word, collaborating. Tudor-Hart's idea—which, unlike Siegel's, contains no psychological speculations—could certainly stand as a goal for the doctor-patient relationship of the future.

Doctors can write the prescriptions, but they cannot come to the house three times a day to watch the patient take the medicine. They can teach exercises that will protect the weak back or knee, but they cannot stand over the patient to make sure the exercises are done. They can sermonize about cigarettes, fatty foods, and alcohol, but they cannot physically stay the hand that is reaching out for these things. This is an ancient conundrum, and the ancient solution was—mystery. There was something so compelling about the power of the physician, something so frightening and yet empowering about the physician's orders, something so comforting yet awe-inspiring about the physician's perceived link to the supernatural, that little or no understanding was needed to ensure the patient's compliance. And, since the theories of illness were mostly wrong, patients would have gained little by struggling to understand them in any case.

Today patients can be brought in both as students of the illness and equals in the process of treatment or cure. The doctor's role becomes one of teacher as well as healer. But as Siegel, Cousins, and Tudor-Hart all agree, today's physicians are very poorly equipped to fill any of these roles—teacher, colleague, or in the broad sense, healer. They are not taught any of the skills involved, from sympathetic listening to speaking in everyday language, from calming patients' unnecessary fears to inspiring them to play a major role in their own recovery. Despite studies showing that patients have their own theories and models of illness, derived from ethnic or personal backgrounds, and that these theories strongly influence whether the patient will comply with or even comprehend the doctor's advice, doctors are not taught to ask about or attend to such things, or to try to compensate for them.

Among the results are confusion, skepticism, noncompliance, and anger. Siegel strongly encourages the skepticism and anger. One result is patients who almost never believe what the doctor says. For example, one woman who had been in a serious auto accident felt inspired by Siegel to demand more and more information from doctors, amassing a large collection of X-ray films and studying them extensively at home. She developed her own theories of lingering symptoms and angrily went to one doctor after another—twenty-eight in all—in a search for answers.

It was evident from her questions that her grasp of the medical facts and processes was very poor, and that she was really looking for confirmation of an idiosyncratic, speculative, and very improbable theory of some of her symptoms. True, it is possible that one plain-speaking doctor, coordinating all her different examinations and capable of inspiring her trust, might have set her mind at ease and diverted her from an essentially pointless quest. But some of her twenty-eight doctors were certainly patient and decent people frustrated by her unwillingness to listen. Such patients burden an already badly stretched health-care system, and incidentally do themselves little good in the process.

However—unfortunately for simplicity—this is not always the result. Sometimes patients *are* the best judges of their own illnesses. One breast cancer patient I knew was especially diligent about self-examination. She found a pea-sized lump in her chest some years after mastectomy. Her surgeon had trouble feeling it, but when he did he sampled it by drawing some of it into a needle. A pathologist pronounced the sample normal, and the surgeon told her to stop worrying. She did not stop worrying, and continued to pester the doctor ("Whatever it is, I want it out!") until he acceded to her demand. When the little lump was excised and sent to the pathologist whole it was identified as a recurrence of her cancer; the timely removal and radiation treatment that followed probably saved her life—and the surgeon, not unexpectedly, praised her persistence. But she never trusted him again.

The patient-as-colleague model has the greatest likelihood of fostering good rather than counterproductive second-guessing of the doctor. In the absence of this kind of open and trusting relationship, patients respond in one of three ways. First, they overuse and even abuse the system of health-care delivery. Getting a second opinion or even a third may be reasonable; going to twenty-eight different doctors and not believing any of them uses up resources that are badly needed by other patients—some of whom can be really helped by visiting those doctors and having those X-rays and other procedures.

Industrial nations are progressing toward a greater and greater sense of health care as communal property. Except for the extremely rich, all of us will be drawing on pooled funds for our treatments, especially the more expensive ones. And where there are pooled funds, there is mutual responsibility for careful use. In most countries doctors realize that economizing is not only a financial but a moral responsibility, and in the future one of the main goals of the doctor-patient collaboration will be to guide this economizing. In other words, some patients will have to be convinced that the next test, the next consultation, may not be really worthwhile. The more they know about medicine, and the more they trust the doctor, the less likely they are to insist on having expensive, inappropriate care.

The second response patients make to failed communication with doctors is to pursue "alternative medicine"—unorthodox methods of healing. These range from faith healing to nutritional fads, meditation to chiropractic, herbal remedies to therapeutic massage. A few of these methods have received scientific support for certain purposes—for example, meditation or relaxation for reducing blood pressure, at least transiently; vitamin C for reducing the duration of colds; and, in some studies, chiropractic manipulation for low-back pain. Most methods as applied for most purposes have not. Yet recent studies have shown that there have been enormous increases in the number of people who resort to such methods, that they cut across national boundaries and socioeconomic and educational levels, and that few mainstream doctors appreciate how widespread the use of such methods has become.

According to a 1988 study in northern New Jersey, seventy-three different alternative healing practices were used by well-educated patients. In another American study of 660 cancer patients, more than half were using alternative healing methods; of these, 8 percent had never had mainstream medical care for their illness and 40 percent abandoned mainstream care some time after starting alternative healing.

As for Britain, in 1981 there were an estimated 13 million visits to a total of 7,500 alternative healers—a "healer" pool almost a third the size of the pool of general practitioners, who deliver the great majority of basic mainstream medical care. In France the use of alternative healers has become so common that the government has had to establish a foundation to study "soft medicine," and five universities offer certificates in it. In the Netherlands an increasing public demand for alternative methods has led to 7 percent of the population visiting unorthodox healers yearly, with 18 percent having consulted one at least once. Demand for this sort of shadow medicine is also growing in Australia and New Zealand; the trend appears to be worldwide.

It is as if the advance of science and technology themselves, crowding the humane and the sacred out of mainstream medicine, has forced people to look elsewhere for the kinds of relationships with their doctors that they crave. Although they are frequently deluding themselves about the efficacy of alternative treatments, and although some of these methods are simply dangerous, a few can be of benefit in limited circumstances. Many mainstream doctors are learning to take a tolerant attitude toward their patients' efforts to find alternative healing. As long as the unorthodox methods can be combined more or less smoothly with the orthodox ones, rather than interfering with or substituting for them, patients should get all the help they can get—including psychological help, which is too often wrongly denigrated with the misleading qualifier "merely."

In fact, one of the main reasons people go to alternative healers is that unorthodox practitioners are far more effective in communicating with their patients than modern mainstream doctors are. In one study of chiropractors, for example, they were more effective in helping patients with low-back pain than orthopedists were. But this was not because of their particular manipulations or other procedures; rather, it was apparently because they had more success in getting patients to do their preventive back exercises. Why? Because they spent more time explaining the treatment to their patients, more time teaching the exercises, and more time establishing trust. If it is objected that the time of orthopedic surgeons is too valuable for talk, consider the cost of back operations for the patients who do not stick to their exercises.

The third way patients dispose of their resentment and anger—at least in the United States—is by registering a claim of malpractice. Such claims have skyrocketed in a single generation, far exceeding comparable legal actions in any other industrial society. As has been aptly said by Robert White, Jr., an American attorney who works for a medical insurance company and advises doctors on how to avoid lawsuits, "We are in the malpractice equivalent of Beirut"—an image of relentless and often pointless crossfire. Physicians make mistakes, of course, but few are negligent. Many malpractice claims cite physicians for what are really expectable or normative errors—things that happen not because the physician was careless, or stupid, or greedy, but simply because the physician was human.

In addition, there are what used to be called acts of God—bad outcomes that don't involve *any* sort of error, that could not have been prevented even if the physician *were* perfect. Malformed newborn babies, to take an especially tragic example, are usually in this category. Yet many malpractice claims after untoward outcomes of birth have stretched the facts to try to blame some act or omission of the physician for the tragedy. The result is that obstetricians have among the highest rates of malpractice claims of any medical specialty in America, and consequently they are leaving the specialty by the thousands.

White's advice to physicians often boils down to maintaining a good doctor-patient relationship. "We need to teach doctors that you have to care about your patient, and express that caring attitude to the patient. Because the fact of the matter is, we don't sue people we like." There are also other reasons. The United States is the most litigious of modern nations, and its people reserve their right to take to the courts for satisfaction when things go wrong with their lives.

If in the course of a medical mishap they forget about this right, there are plenty of malpractice litigators around to remind them of it. Juries confronted with a disabled person claiming physician negligence empathize with the person's need for compensation, and are not deterred by a sense that the physician and the insurance company are unable to pay. The result is often a multimillion-dollar settlement—of which the lawyer gets up to half. But ironically, studies have shown that only a small fraction of doctors' acts of negligence result in malpractice claims, and many of the actual claims—including the successful suits—do *not* involve negligence. Thus the system neither does justice to the injured nor effectively identifies negligent doctors, the size of the settlements notwithstanding.

Yet the fear of being sued punishes every single U.S. physician. Since the fact is that the quality of the medicine being practiced does not correlate well with the chance of being sued, it follows that every physician must anticipate a legal action. Adequate preparation involves leaving no stone unturned in the effort to diagnose and treat the patient. Some of the stones cost a great deal of money to turn over and have very little likelihood of uncovering something new, but you turn them over anyway, with the patient's lawyer in mind. This is called defensive medicine, and it accounts for a substantial minority of the tests and procedures done by U.S. doctors. It must also be added that successful defense against a suit is always a Pyrrhic victory for the physician. The cost in time, effort, emotion, money, and damage to morale is very great. The fear of lawsuits undermines the doctor-patient relationship by eroding the doctor's trust in the patient. And the publicity gained by jury decisions and settlements adds to other patients' mistrust of their doctors. It is thus a strange irony that in the era in which medicine's effectiveness is greater than it has ever been, the mutual trust between doctors and patients has largely broken down.

Although this breakdown of trust is a relatively new phenomenon, and the code of silence an old one, there is an often unrecognized role played by medical training in the estrangement. The very first experience young people have in medical school is often the anatomy laboratory. These fresh-faced acolytes, having attained stage one of their dream—before holding a stethoscope, a reflex hammer, or a patient's hand—are sent into a room full of strong-smelling formaldehyde-soaked corpses. Something deliberate and important is happening here besides learning the structure of the body; it is part of what has been called the "latent curriculum." Students and teachers alike know that this is a crucial step in the initiation process, a way of immediately separating even the youngest people in medicine from all who are on the outside. It is the first real *we-they* experience, the first event that makes medical students conscious that they are not like other people, and will never be again. The mood in the lab alternates between studious high seriousness and rather sick joking—perfectly understandable given the stress of an experience which none of them are supposed to reveal is stressful.

From my own anatomy lab I recall the group of students who named their cadaver "Shop," so that at the end of each long afternoon one of them could say, "Well, it's time to close up Shop." Other remarks ranged from "Chopped liver, anyone?" to "I don't think this guy's gonna be playing tennis this weekend." Except for a solemn but cursory speech by one of the professors at the outset, no attention was given to the psychological side of this learning process. But clearly each and every one of us was learning more than anatomy. We were learning to feel comfortable slowly and carefully dismantling the bodies of dead people. We were learning to hold sophisticated scientific discussions while holding parts of those people in our hands and blinking away the sting of formaldehyde in our eyes. We were learning not to think of them as people but as a more or less organized structure of organs and tissues.

In short, we were having our first lesson in keeping emotional distance. This patient would not nag at us with questions, show fear or anger, or cry out and get teary-eyed when something really hurt. By some lights we were dealing with the very best patient we would ever have: no psychological complications, no back talk, and total cooperation with all the procedures we needed to carry out. In some sense, cadaver dissection became a model for future relationships with patients, in which we would try to keep our scientific wits about us, suppressing all emotion while "dissecting" and solving the patient's problem as quickly as possible.

If we became emotionally capable of treating the live patient as something like a dead person—an intricate structure going somehow wrong, a puzzling, endlessly fascinating, broken machine— then our minds could win the contest of diagnosis and treatment, win the fight against the disease, without interference from our feelings. Our modern version of Hippocratic decorum could be seen as a systematic attempt to manage away feelings, our own as well as the patient's. And the spectacle of a circle of doctors standing around a critical-care patient with tubes in every orifice, unable to speak around the tubes even if conscious, the target of all modern science's magical, often effective, yet dehumanizing power—well, there is something here that recalls the group of first-year students gingerly encircling their cadaver.

The we-they distinction in the anatomy lab becomes an us-versus-them confrontation in clinical training. It's not that student doctors start out thinking of patients as the enemy; rather, the process of clinical training with its extremes of sleep deprivation, mountains of paperwork, endless new science to learn, and a deliberately excessive patient load instills in the young doctor a sense that his or her own survival is at stake. Eventually, as they often put it, you have to go on "automatic pilot," processing the patient through the stages of treatment as quickly and efficiently as possible. There is little time for courtesy and no time for feelings—on either side. There is a tendency to "turf" the human side of care to nurses, chaplains, psychologists, and social workers. (As one authority on nursing said, "Among other things a nurse's job is to make sure hospitals don't scare patients to death.") This approach has been supported by some leading medical educators, who believe that a doctor can be just a very high-grade technician, a sort of physiological engineer, leaving the human dimension to other professionals. But although these others can be very good at it, they cannot completely assuage the pain of having an overstressed, uncaring doctor.

More important, there is on the part of the young doctor an absolutely essential, self-preserving anger, and much of this anger is directed against patients. It is the patient who rousts you from your desperately needed sleep. It is the patient who is "trying to die" in the emergency room despite your best efforts to postpone this finale. It is the patient who often does not appreciate your efforts. And it is the patient who so often goes out of the hospital to return to the habits that brought on the illness in the first place. Getting Rid of Patients—"GROP"—through discharge or "turfing"—transferring them to some other, more specialized medical team—becomes one of the main goals of daily medical life. Doctors change inside during training—increasing cynicism is documented. From the 1961 book by Howard Becker and his colleagues,

Boys in White: Student Culture in Medical School, to Terri Mizrahi's
1986 study, *Getting Rid of Patients: Contradictions in the Socialization
of Physicians,* careful observers have described and measured the
effects of what has been called the "punishment theory" of medical
training. As one young doctor told Mizrahi in the early eighties:
"You start regarding patients as the enemy and you really don't
care." As we will see in the next chapter, the basic facts and effects
of training were no different in 1991. Some predicted that the great
influx of women into medicine—they changed from around 5 percent to around 30 percent of medical school classes during the
1970s—would humanize the profession. But so far these women
have basically had to adapt to male medical culture rather than
change it. Still, their era has only just begun, and it is possible
that as they rise to positions of influence and increasingly take
charge of medical education, they will make both medicine and
training more humane. But at present training is a hardening and
distancing experience.

Although when you go into practice the patient load is usually
manageable and the sleepless nights are few and far between, you
have built a transparent wall between yourself and patients, a wall
made of science, decorum, and silence. You care about your patients, you really do your best for them, but they are on the other
side and that is where they stay.

Tudor-Hart's patient-as-colleague model has been adopted by
some American physicians as a response to the threat of malpractice suits. The idea is that if you let the patient in on all the
information you have, if you make the patient feel as if the two of
you are making all the important decisions together—or even that
you are turning these decisions over to the patient—then you can
scarcely be asked to shoulder the blame yourself when things come
out wrong. The patient's lawyer can still ask whether you let the
patient know all the risks of the procedure, but you will have an
answer: *Yes. We discussed the risks and the alternatives in detail. In
fact,* you could even say, *the patient, given all the relevant information,
was the one who made the decision and chose the treatment.*

Dr. John Wennberg of the Dartmouth Medical School, an authority on the outcomes of different medical and surgical procedures, has made an interactive videodisc to help provide this information to patients facing the choice of prostate surgery. Called *Prostate Options,* it describes the experience of patients who have had surgery for prostate cancer, as well as those who have chosen radiation and other options—including the option of not doing anything. Although it is quite technical, at least some patients appreciate it, and it gives the physician a sense of not being alone in the decision making. A lot is at stake; surgery frequently causes impotence, and can cause incontinence and other serious side effects. Since the differences in survival time are measured in months, the choices are not obvious.

One of the surgeons who uses the film is Dr. Ian Nisonson, a Florida urological surgeon. He not only insists that each patient see the film, but spends literally hours talking with the patient and his wife, clarifying the disease and the treatment choices. This is not just a matter of avoiding malpractice suits, though he certainly is wary of them; the sense of relief he gets from collaboration with the patient is profound:

> There are times when I'm stymied. It is not because I don't know the literature or understand the facts. It is in fact because it is a toss-up, it is a fifty-fifty toss-up . . . After all, when you really think about it, it is the patient's body that is being helped, cured, or violated, depending on how you want to look at it, and therefore they have the absolute right to make a decision. And sometimes it's comforting when you explain the pros and cons to have the patient and the family say, "You know doctor, I understand what you're saying and I realise that I have to make the decision, because it's me."

Yet even videodiscs and hours of conversation cannot give a patient a medical education, and may lead to false confidence in very partial knowledge. Also, not every patient wants to delve into those details. Some are greatly discomfited by them, feeling that they may not quite grasp what is going on. They may need a little of the old medical mystery, the sense that the doctor is in control and giving the best possible care. Dr. Nisonson also points out that without some trust in the doctor there is no placebo effect—that almost magical patient improvement that comes even with sugar pills. But at the very least the patient must take the doctor's point of view occasionally, if only to avoid developing unrealistic expectations.

Few patients understand how many decisions are a toss-up, and how bleak and forbidding the landscape of disease can look even to those who know more about it than anyone else in the world. Doctors, scientists, and journalists have given us all—including themselves—such a hard sell about the advances in medicine that only the most sophisticated ever go to a physician anymore without overestimating what that physician can do. One of the best antidotes for the loss of trust between doctor and patient would be for patients to appreciate the limits of medical knowledge.

Think of medicine not as a sleek space shuttle rocketed into the perfect clarity of the stratosphere, but as a small and rickety aircraft taking off from a backwoods airstrip. Imagine that the ceiling is very low, and that not long after takeoff we are flying in the clouds. There is equipment for instrument flying, of course, but it is not as effective as it looks. You can learn to copilot, or you can sit back and let the doctor take the controls; but either way, for much of the time, you will not know where you are or where you are going.

Today in Japan there is a growing minority of physicians who want to break with the ancient code of silence and to enter into the patient-as-colleague collaboration style of doctor-patient relationship. But the danger of abruptly going to the other extreme is already clear in some cases. Dr. Yasuhiro Higashi, a respected cancer surgeon, after removing the breast of a young patient with a malignancy, met with the patient's family in a seminar-room setting. He had already been frank with the patient, and now he was planning to share the details with her husband, her two younger sisters, and her aunt. He sat them around the table and proceeded to give a lecture in a style appropriate—and no doubt developed—for medical students and doctors-in-training. It is unlikely that they could have understood much of what he said, or of the technical diagrams he drew on the blackboard.

Then, astonishingly, he did something else that he would have done with medical students: he opened a plastic container holding the breast he had just removed. Pushing it forward on the table, he continued lecturing while pointing to the breast, trying to explain the illness and treatment for the relatives of the young woman who had had to give it up. He did not seem to notice the tear being wiped away by one of the younger sisters, or the frightened look on her face. In Japan, a culture that tends to conceal emotions, this small degree of expressiveness said something powerful, but the surgeon did not react.

Surely the collaboration among doctor, patient, and relative does not have to go this far; surely *some* degree of Hippocratic decorum is acceptable—appropriate to the modern age and compatible with truth telling. Withholding information is not the only imaginable kind of failed communication between doctor and patient. There are also failures of physician sensitivity, failures of compassion.

But then, the code of silence never worked quite the way it was supposed to. The action of Tennessee Williams's great play *Cat on a Hot Tin Roof* centers partly on Big Daddy, a Southern family patriarch who has been lied to about his cancer—back in the days before informed consent. Part of the action of the play revolves around his growing suspicions about the benign diagnosis, and his ultimate discovery that he is dying. His response is not, as the code predicts, to get worse, fold up, and die faster. On the contrary it is first to excoriate those who have lied to him for their "mendacity"—the word is fairly thundered by Big Daddy at all and sundry—and later to go up on the roof of his mansion and glory in the farm he has given his life to building: "Twenty-eight thousand acres of th' richest land this side of the Valley Nile!" Big Daddy's doctor is actually present in the play—as a foolish, almost pitiful figure who disappears from the scene when the emotional going gets rough; he is a minor character dwarfed by the sheer human magnitude of his patient, and by the unforgiving power of the illness. He can offer diagnoses or lies, but he quickly and clumsily bows out on any search for meaning.

In Japan, too, drama has flowed from the doctor's code of silence. The central character in Akiru Kurosawa's classic film *Ikiru* (*To Live*) is told he has only an ulcer, but he deduces that he must have stomach cancer, a common cause of death in Japan. As he confronts his grief and pain, he slowly begins to try to find the meaning of his life—a middle-aged minor bureaucrat with an average, distant, unsympathetic family. After an unsuccessful expedition late one night to try wine, women, and song as an answer, a single obsession dawns on him: he is going to take an abandoned, junk-filled lot in his neighborhood and turn it into a playground. Sometimes doubled over with pain, he works his way through the local government bureaucracy, quietly browbeating one petty official after another—after a lifetime in the system, he understands bureaucracy—until his persistence pays off, and the transformation occurs. After his funeral, fellow bureaucrats memorialize him, trying to find words to praise the dull life he led. But their comments are belied by a closing shot of the hero rocking back and forth on a swing in the darkness, smiling beatifically at the small, impressive achievement that gives meaning to his death—and that will go right on giving it meaning.

The code of silence underestimates people in at least two ways. First, it is based on the dubious assumption that harsh truths always worsen their illnesses. Second, it fails to give them their own lives to live, and their own ways of giving meaning to their dying. Yet the patient-as-colleague model has its own drawbacks if carried to an extreme. Most patients need neither fairy tales to protect them from the facts of their condition nor a medical education to intellectualize those facts. What they need is a fairly succinct but compassionate account of the truth from a doctor who is prepared to help them through the darkness, either toward health or toward death—a place where, after all, we are all going— and to show that, at least a little, their feelings are understood. It would seem easy enough to combine these abilities with the skills needed to manage patients' diseases. It is what Anatole Broyard, when terminally ill, called for eloquently in his essay "Doctor, Talk to Me." It is also what doctors themselves wish they had more of when *they* get sick. So why is it so difficult to find such doctors?

TWO

THE TEMPLE OF SCIENCE

THE JOHNS HOPKINS University Hospitals in Baltimore, Maryland, make up one of the very best medical complexes in the United States, and so in the world, bringing the full spectrum and power of modern medicine to bear on the health crises of ordinary people. Unlike at many hospitals today, no one who walks through its emergency room doors is turned away. In one old foyer, a two-story-high statue of Jesus Christ beckons all who enter with a kindly gaze and inviting open arms. If his pose is meant to be symbolic of *this* hospital, it is surprisingly close to the truth.

As countless sufferers have crossed the threshold of cathedrals or mosques or synagogues, desperately seeking a remedy for illness, so we cross the threshold of great and powerful hospitals. They are our modern cathedrals, embodying all the awe and mystery of modern science, all its force, real and imagined, in an imposing edifice that houses transcendent expertise and ineffable technology. And best of all, they often do what they are supposed to do; they work. There are other great hospitals in other cities, but Hopkins has a special place even among the awesome. Medical school admissions officers in certain other top medical centers sometimes express bafflement at the number of students they admit but lose to Hopkins. The reason is simple: Hopkins has an added mystique—its unrivaled clinical tradition. Here William Osler, arguably the most illustrious physician in American history, not only plied his trade but spread a gospel that his turn-of-the-century colleagues found compelling. Henceforth, he proclaimed, medicine would be wedded to science. Hospitals would house laboratories and yet also be laboratories, and science would never stray far from the bedside.

Osler emphasized rigorous observation and recording of data. Students, acting as "clinical clerks," were assigned beds on the wards and were responsible for taking new patients' histories. With Osler in attendance, each case had to be reported before the class as the students sat or stood in a semicircle around the bed of the patient—a drama that in its modern guise still makes medical students tremble.

Though most identified with Hopkins, Osler was born in Canada and is in fairness also claimed by Britain, where he later occupied the Regius Chair of Medicine at Oxford and was even made a baronet. So he influenced medical traditions, and especially medical teaching, in all three countries. Osler himself, who is more frequently quoted today than any other nineteenth-century physician, once wrote, "I desire no other epitaph . . . than the statement that I taught medical students *in the wards*, as I regard this as the most useful and important work I have been called upon to do" (emphasis added). This from a man who had helped delineate the nature of coronary artery disease and wrote a textbook of medicine that still serves as a model, among many other achievements.

Today at Johns Hopkins, on the medical wards that bear his name, medical students, interns, and residents are taught and teach others according to the tradition that stems from Osler. "Live on the wards" is one of the most memorable of Osler's many aphorisms. Hence the term "resident" applied to house officers, and the command that they frequently stay in the hospital overnight. A professor in medical school once asked me what I as an anthropologist would think of a graduate student who insisted on going home from fieldwork every night; my answer was, not much. It is in effect the same as Osler's dictum. Immerse yourself in illness; live with it, smell it, breathe it, be jostled out of your nightly stupor thinking of nothing but illness. You must wrestle with it as Jacob in Genesis wrestled with the angel; only then will you be fit to spend the rest of your life eye to eye with it.

Hopkins house officers are among the smartest and best-educated young doctors in the world. Each has beaten out many other excellent doctors who would have wanted his or her place. In their third and fourth years of medical school, they had already begun to live on the wards, and they have been chosen for Hopkins because of their pragmatic skills as well as their academic excellence. Surrounding them, teaching them, supporting them, even covering for them when they fumble, are many of the world's best and most highly trained nurses—the people who run hospitals minute to minute and day to day. If house officers do manage to learn to be humane, it is likely that they will learn it from the nurses.

Supervising them are some of the world's leading physicians and scientists. Most of these are specialists who have developed and mastered knowledge and techniques that in their field are unexcelled in the world. Victor McKusick, for example, is senior enough to have been taught by some doctors who studied with Osler. He is the world's most respected authority on human genetic diseases—his encyclopedic textbook is the bible of the field—as well as a practicing internist and a dedicated teacher of young physicians. Dr. McKusick espouses the medical ideal of *aequanimitas*—equanimity—the title of one of Osler's famous speeches. McKusick even designed a necktie bearing the Latin word as a repeated motif; it is worn with pride today by many Hopkins physicians.

Aequanimitas means poise in the face of crisis, grace under pressure. If you (to paraphrase Kipling) can keep your head while all about you are losing theirs and looking toward you, then you may well turn into a good doctor. If, because of personal trepidation, a headstrong nature, excessive emotionalism, or inadequate knowledge, you cannot keep your head, your calm, then you will make a botch of all that must be smooth and precise and competent. And if that is the case, you cannot serve in the temple.

Today some claim that the ideal of *aequanimitas* encourages hardening and callousness, distancing doctors from their patients and rendering medical care impersonal. In an eloquent essay titled "Against Aequanimitas"—which deserves to be read at least as often as Osler's original—Dr. Gerald Weissman, a senior professor of medicine at New York University School of Medicine, takes on medicine's greatest cultural icon. Osler, it turns out, was an arrogant representative of the upper classes; he was contemptuously patronizing toward his patients and favorable to the Social Darwinist ideology of his era, and he actively prevented women from entering medicine—a woman "without urgent domestic ties," he believed, "is very apt to become a dangerous element unless her energies and emotions are diverted in a proper channel."

He told medical students in his most famous speech, *Aequanimitas*, that "imperturbability is a bodily endowment" that some of them would never attain. Yet he said:

> The first essential is to have your nerves well in hand. Even under the most serious circumstances, the physician or surgeon who . . . shows in his face the slightest alteration, expressive anxiety or fear, has not his medullary centers under the highest control, and is liable to disaster at any moment.

It seems to be an early-twentieth-century version of Hippocratic decorum. Dr. Weissman doubts that this advice will produce medical students who "will become caring, compassionate, or humane."

> If the goal . . . is to lead to *aequanimitas*—to teach control over our "medullary centers"—I want no part of it. The passion of the physician may be the best part of what we have to offer our patients and society.

This from a man who has soberly and successfully treated patients with all varieties of illness, and taught medical students how to do the same, for decades.

Dr. Julian Tudor-Hart challenges the Osler legacy on somewhat different grounds. He respects the concept of the twenty-four-hour cycle but rejects Osler's ability to ignore the social conditions that produced the illnesses he studied and labored over. Osler, for Tudor-Hart, was the serene scientist who deigned to step down from his social pedestal long enough to minister briefly to the poor sufferer, bringing the alleged power of science (actually very small in his day) to aid the victim in a crucial moment. Even with today's knowledge, Osler's idea of science is very inadequate, eliminating the sciences of epidemiology and preventive medicine from the picture. But back then, the science was quite laughable, and so Osler's approach was not so much scientific as *scientistic;* and unfortunately, although science is much more powerful today, Osler's habit of exaggerating its power has come down to us little changed.

Perhaps this exaggeration was where he got some of his dubious *aequanimitas.* In any case, one can see the same process operating among young hospital doctors today. But defenders of the process say that doctors-in-training will have time enough to learn humane medicine when they have gone out into practice. In the teaching hospital, the crucible that forms them, they must first and foremost learn how to apply the science of medicine. In a departure from Osler's preference, they study mainly under specialists, who focus the utmost scientific sophistication on specific organs and problems. This, medical educators believe, will best foster a scientific orientation in young doctors.

Most house officers and medical students agree, but in the reality of training they often feel overwhelmed. First- and second-year medical residents may be on call every third night. That means they serve a thirty-six-hour shift, sleep for a night, serve twelve hours, sleep, and serve thirty-six again. If they have not finished their work by the end of a shift, they stay and finish it. Some programs at other institutions may have lighter schedules, but not by much. Somehow the residents must also fit in clinics where they see a long roster of outpatients—those not staying in the hospital—and attend lectures and seminars to further their formal knowledge of medical science and enable them to stay on a constantly moving frontier.

They rarely complain (*aequanimitas* again), but if a dour look should cross a house officer's face in the presence of a professor, the senior physician will smile and say, "This is the army"; and it is. Hopkins house officers call themselves "the Osler marines." The next time it crosses your mind that doctors are overpaid, turn back to your youth. Now imagine the countless days and nights of study—twenty years of school, the last eight at your expense— followed by three to five years of this house-officer schedule, at a salary of twenty-five thousand a year. When you are in your last year of medical school, still paying twenty thousand or so for the privilege of being there, and with residency still ahead of you, your college roommate of comparable ability who went to business school or law school may already be earning a six-figure salary. Few if any professions have a training process as long or as difficult as that in medicine, yet the ordinary doctor will not earn six figures for many more years, if ever.

If we enter the temple in the middle of a typical night, through the emergency room door, we will find ourselves in the midst of what seems at first to be chaos: stretchers rolling in all directions, blue-suited police officers rushing past nurses and doctors in white, the clatter of instruments and IV poles and drug carts, the rooms abuzz with arcane phrases like "This one's got four-plus ethanol," and "Get me a set of skull films," and "Hang the D-five-W!" and "Just breathe in through your mouth, dear, you're gonna do fine," and "I want some lights on *now!*" On one hand an amazingly calm young man is being treated for a gunshot wound, while chatting pleasantly with the doctors. Piercing screams in the background prove to be coming from a woman giving birth—here in the wrong, but not the worst, place—and when her baby emerges into the stark fluorescent light we can feel a softening in the circle of hardened medical soldiers, and see the most tender look cross a nurse's face.

The scene may strike us as horrific enough to be hell, or at least purgatory, but there is one thing missing from that time-worn analogy: here, people are helped. Almost before we get our bearings the bullet is gone from the young man's body, and wonderful fluids protect him from the ancient scourge of wound infection. Before we have time to become accustomed to her screams, the woman laboring on the narrow, rickety stretcher has become the mother of a well-delivered baby. The questions of why the young man has been shot, and why the young woman gives birth so precipitately—an obstetrics term that evokes a vertiginous fall from a high place, a fall without any preparation—have a legitimate place in our discourse about health. But they have no place in the spare, utilitarian talk of the white-coated soldiers in the emergency room. They remove the bullet; they birth the baby.

Osler again: "Shut out the future as tightly as the past . . . Let the limit of your horizon be a twenty-four-hour cycle." Young physicians under this kind of pressure must relentlessly set priorities. But Osler's advice was not merely for a default condition in which there is no time to think beyond today. It was rather a philosophy of how to think about disease and treatment; shutting out the rest of time and space was necessary not just for efficiency but for clarity. It is you, the patient, the disease, and *aequanimitas* all alone together in the middle of the strange night-world that form the crucible not just of cures but of doctors.

Outside the emergency room, in the equally harsh, spare waiting room, patients with lesser or less pressing illnesses sit for up to ten hours in order to get attention they cannot get anywhere else. These are the uninsured, some 35 million strong in the United States. These people exist because of America's peculiar system of payment for health care. Most health insurance is provided through employers, who purchase coverage for their employees from one of approximately fifteen hundred different private insurance companies. However, employers are not required to purchase insurance at all, so millions of fully employed people toward the lower end of the social scale have no health-care insurance, just as if they were unemployed. Theoretically, people who are poor enough (unemployed and without resources) qualify for Medicaid, a government program that pays their medical bills. However, in reality this program pays for very little of what would constitute good medicine, especially neglecting timely intervention before things go seriously wrong.

The American government claims that Americans do not have and would not tolerate rationing, but this is a simple falsehood. We have rationing now, and one of the ways we do it is by making the uninsured wait—losing hour after hour of earnings at work or time when their children need them. They may or may not complain, but they also sometimes go home without treatment, or more often fail to come when treatment might prevent drastic decline. Dr. Kenneth Covinsky, an emergency room resident, speaks frankly about these people: "This is really acute medicine, and there's a lot of very ill patients that come down here, with illnesses that haven't been managed in the normal outpatient setting. A lot of the people here don't have access to doctors. They come here whenever things get totally out of control. But if they were seen regularly a lot of these things could be better controlled. They wouldn't appear nearly as dramatic and exciting, but patients would be a lot better off."

The point is they needn't have become this sick. These are the walking wounded he is talking about, the people who make up most doctors' practice. They are elderly people and children, people with limbs broken and bound and people doubled over the pains in their abdomens. Many wait patiently and wait and wait and eventually are cared for. Is the hospital right in thinking these people should feel grateful to it, or are its critics right in saying that this is just not good enough? An intern, Dr. Alicia Fry, who is at about the middle of a thirty-six-hour shift, comes down to meet a patient: the Reverend Lilbert Campbell, age eighty-six. She will later learn that he is a retired janitor and only a part-time cleric, but she will continue to treat him as if he were the Episcopal Bishop of Baltimore. Dr. Fry is a pleasant, pretty, soft-spoken woman who looks like the recent medical school graduate she is, but functions as though she had weathered years of rough experience. Rev. Campbell is a sweet, weak, alert, elderly man who quickly rebounds from his astonishment that this puppy can be a doctor, and places himself wholeheartedly in her hands.

This is a safe bet. Gently and deftly she enters a dialogue with her patient, and then with his son and daughter-in-law. She touches people, not just metaphorically but actually, hands-on. She apologizes convincingly for things she has to do that cause discomfort. She draws people out; she listens; she conveys real concern. She keeps her sense of humor, and she shares it with her patients. None of these humane and human gestures impairs her efficiency; in fact, they all enhance it.

Dr. Fry soon learns that Rev. Campbell has been dizzy, has had a feeling of tightening in his chest, has been taking a drug to counteract high blood pressure, and has passed blood in his stool. He is an old man with many medical problems, but she does not take any of them for granted. She begins examining him in the emergency room, but soon takes him up in the elevator—personally, with her own hands on the stretcher—to the bed where he will stay on her service. From that base he will be followed and studied, with a view toward finding treatments that will make his life both more livable and longer.

Yet she knows that he has not been followed properly—with early detection and timely follow-up treatment, the way a well-to-do eighty-six-year-old man might be—and there are narrow limits to what she can do. And despite her gentle dedication, there are other limits, the ones on what *she, personally,* can do: "As an intern," she says resignedly, "you're in the hospital all the time. You deal with acute problems. You're very scared at the beginning. You're scared to death, the first time you have to take responsibility for a patient's life. I don't think it's the ideal way to train. It's very tiring. It makes you a little bitter, I think. You start to look at patients not as patients, but as a 'long hit' or a 'short hit'—are they going to be a lot of work or are they not going to be a lot of work." She laughs nervously at having talked to a stranger in this rough-and-ready resident slang. But she does not let the moment pass. "I think the intensity of the program fosters that attitude. It's hard to keep your perspective."

*   *   *

Another intern, John Townes, is on call with a medical student, Sanjay Marwaha. They are beeped down to the emergency room to meet Isabel Humbles, a thirty-nine-year-old woman who looks fifty. Rather overweight, with a swollen abdomen and face, she is lying on a stretcher, moaning in considerable pain. With the help of some other residents, Dr. Townes finds out that Ms. Humbles has advanced cirrhosis of the liver, causing her abdomen to swell and distend painfully. She is a chronic alcohol and drug abuser. She explains that she stopped taking her prescribed medicine three weeks ago. "I wasn't at home and I didn't have it with me." She has not seen a doctor in quite some time.

A sense of futility floods Dr. Townes's voice as he talks about his patient: "This woman has liver disease—cirrhosis, basically—from alcoholism. She's got massive edema. She has swelling in her abdomen which is compressing her lungs, and she's having trouble breathing. She's got intense abdominal pain, gastrointestinal bleeding, she's not urinating anymore, she's not oxygenating well. Thankfully she still has a blood pressure, and she's mentating okay. But she is extremely ill, and before I take her up to the floor where I'm gonna be by myself, I want to make sure she's stabilized—that we know what's going on.

"Sometimes this kind of thing can make you mad in the middle of the night, because you obviously have to take care of this person who's so sick, and it's a lot of work. But this also can be the thing that makes you want to do it, because you can take a person who's so sick and you make them better, make them feel better. So I have mixed feelings about it."

Clearly the modern hospital invests enormous resources in salvage—emergent or urgent intervention in people who stand or lie at the end of a long path of neglect. Conversely, neither it nor any other health institution invests very much in either primary or secondary prevention—measures designed to prevent illness before it starts, or to prevent it from worsening by acting early in its progression. Since almost all of medical training occurs in these high-technology hospitals, each new generation of doctors sets priorities similar to their predecessors'. Completing the triangle are the poor, who have nowhere to turn except the hospital and its doctors-in-training when their lives are on the line.

How did the system acquire this structure, and why is it so difficult to change? The answers lie in the history of the hospital, and of its relationship to the rest of society—in an era when the forces creating disease were barely understood at all. The first evidence we have of a place where the ill were sequestered and under the care of specially designated healers occurs four thousand years ago in Egypt, although little is known about its function. In ancient Greece the temples to the god of healing, Asclepius, were centers of spiritual but also of practical healing; Hippocrates, we believe, worked and taught in the one on the island of Cos. A certain king Asoka in third-century-B.C. Hindustan established eighteen centers for treating the ill, staffed by physicians and nurses at the expense of the royal treasury. Such centers were also found in first-century Rome; physicians at Pompeii set up convalescent homes for their wealthiest patients, and the Latin word *hospes*, or host, gave rise to our word *hospital*.

The widely believed notion that doctors could do nothing to help their patients until the modern period is a false one. Somewhat effective methods of wound treatment and pain control go back to ancient times, and some of the drugs we use most widely today—aspirin, for example, and digitalis for heart disease—had their origins in long folk healing traditions. At the very least the ill could be told what to expect from the course of the illness, protected from the elements, made at least somewhat comfortable, and also be bathed and fed. None of this is trivial when you are ill and have no other options. Not surprisingly, centers for such care continued to spread.

By A.D. 1000 there were hospital-like institutions in China, run at state expense. At the same time, such institutions were well established by the Christian churches of Europe and Byzantium, and by the Moslem regimes in the Middle East, North Africa, and Spain. Christianity had fostered an intense growth of hospitals, as well as orphanages, hospices, and old-age homes. At the instigation of Constantine, the newly Christian emperor of Rome, the church's Council of Nicaea in A.D. 325 decreed the construction of a hospital in every cathedral town. The church funded these institutions, which maintained a resident staff. According to George Rosen, a physician and medical historian at Yale, Pantocrator, a famous hospital in Constantinople built in the twelfth century, housed five departments with a total of fifty rooms: ten rooms each for men and women with various disorders, eight for acute cases, five for surgical patients, twelve for gynecological problems, and five for emergencies and miscellaneous illnesses. There were five surgeons, two physicians, and two nurses or attendants in *each* of the five departments, and there were medical students in training. There was also an outpatient clinic for the walking ill, as well as a pharmacy, baths, and even a mill and a bakery.

Islam built on those efforts. A hospital founded at Baghdad in the year 970 maintained separate wards for patients with different conditions, had a staff of twenty-five physicians, and was used for teaching medical students. One founded in Cairo in 1283 had separate wards for wounds, for fevers, for women, and for eye diseases; it employed a medical director as well as both doctors and nurses. According to medical historian Roderick McGrew, "the wards for the insane were particularly famous for the luxury of their appointments and the kindness of their care. Islam, like Christianity, emphasized the community's responsibility for those who needed help. The hospitals they built reflected this commitment as well as a high level of medical and administrative skill." Moslem physicians in Arab and non-Arab lands, as well as Jewish physicians trained and practicing in Moslem institutions, were probably the best doctors in the world at that time.

In Europe, hospital growth got a boost from devastating epidemics of infectious disease. By 1225 there were an estimated nineteen thousand "leprosaria," or leper asylums, in Europe—highwalled compounds built to set lepers apart in most major towns. As leprosy declined in importance they were used to house the victims of bubonic plague, an even more disastrous epidemic, and of other infectious diseases, mental illnesses, and various ills afflicting the indigent. They were now more like hospitals as we know them. With the increasing strength of the merchant classes, church-funded hospitals began to receive more extensive financing from guilds and town corporations; people in business saw this not just as a moral responsibility but as a route to stability and prosperity—much the same perspective that has led every industrial country except the United States and South Africa to guarantee health care for all today. So the poor in the medieval towns were not forgotten: Frankfurt am Main, for example, appointed a physician and two surgeons in the late fourteenth century to care for indigent patients; and in 1439 Sigismund, the Holy Roman Emperor, already saw a need for hospital reform, and recommended that every town hire a physician to care for the poor free of charge.

Interns like Dr. Fry and Dr. Townes, as well as more senior, slightly less harried residents must somehow find time in their schedules for what are known as outpatient clinics—situations in which the walking ill come in by appointment to have their medical problems followed. These are not routine checkups; by middle-class standards most patients who come to these clinics unquestionably need to see a doctor. But when they compete with patients inside the hospital, they just don't cut it for a resident. The most likely honest response is *Let me do my real work.* Doctors cannot reasonably be criticized for giving these clinics short shrift; the system they live and train in enforces such neglect.

And their teachers recognize it. Dr. Daniel Sulmasy, a young attending physician who teaches residents, says, "I think that sometimes we have too much of an emphasis on the very, very sick patient. It used to be said that the best way to learn medicine is to care for absolutely the most sick patients, the way we do in the inpatient unit. But I think that's simply not true. Learning to care for somebody with exfoliative dermatitis, where their skin's coming off in sheets, doesn't prepare anybody at all to know what to do when somebody comes in with eczema." In English, this means that the doctor who has saved the life of a hospitalized patient with a near-fatal condition is still unprepared for the day-to-day medical care that must be delivered by any primary physician. He knows what to do if your skin is falling off, but not if you wander in some morning with a rash. Only a small fraction of all patients who come to doctors end up in academic hospitals associated with medical schools. Those hospitals are staffed by harried residents supervised by specialists. The specialists must constantly deal with problems that the residents may never see after they finish their training; and during that training the residents never see the kinds of problems they will spend most of their lives dealing with.

Dr. Sulmasy cites another problem: "I think that there is a lot of frustration for physicians in dealing with chronic illnesses that are frequently not going to be cured by what's being done. I'm reminded of the ancient medieval aphorism about what the goals are for medicine: *To cure sometimes, to relieve often, and to comfort always.* And I think those are still truly what the goals of medicine are and ought to be—although we've distorted them to the point where we think we can cure frequently, relieve a lot of the time, and sort of comfort when we get around to it."

This version of the epigram strikes a familiar chord to anyone who has spent time in a hospital, on either end of the stethoscope. Naturally, it occurs to us to ask what still more senior teachers and supervisors have in mind. Dr. Jack Stobo is one such senior Hopkins physician; as chief of medicine he has responsibility for supervising all the other physicians we have heard from. Yet he is not really pleased with the training he is giving them.

"The way we educate physicians," he says simply, "is out of sync with the problems they have to face when they go into practice. Our education still lags behind the reality. A number of the problems that end up in the hospital—somewhere around a half— are preventable. That is, by the time the patient ends up on the inpatient service, they have a problem which, if appropriately addressed in the clinic or if appropriately addressed with preventive measures, that hospitalization could have been avoided, and the degree of illness that the patient manifested in the hospital could have been avoided."

Dr. Stobo also notes that recent changes in reimbursement policy for medical care, combined with certain medical advances, have eliminated many important diseases from hospital beds. At today's prices for hospital care, you just can't admit the routine pneumonia or moderately unstable diabetes patient as readily as you used to. Such patients are increasingly tested and evaluated as outpatients, in clinics where the patients come and go on the same day. This means that the resident who mainly trains on the inpatient wards will today have an even narrower range of experience than the residents of only a decade ago. "So we made a decision three years ago to try and move more and more of our teaching from the inpatient service to the clinic. Overall, our progress has been much slower than I had hoped." Because of the dual role of the residents—not just to learn, but to bear the burden of care for the acutely ill poor—walk-in clinics just do not get much attention.

But under the circumstances he is sympathetic with the house staff. "The response of the house staff to the patient with substance abuse, in terms of their feeling helpless, frustrated, and in some cases angry, is perfectly understandable, given the training in dealing with those patients. If the residency training program at Johns Hopkins doesn't become actively involved in teaching prevention to its house staff, we will be abdicating our responsibility to our patients." This outlook is part of a growing nationwide trend in medical education, and important conferences have been held to discuss ways of incorporating a substantially greater exposure to "ambulatory" or "outpatient" care into the training of medical students and residents. There are parallel trends in the teaching of nutrition and other aspects of prevention. Yet in most places, as at Hopkins, progress is much slower than had been hoped. And since Hopkins is one of the places that sets the standard for the others, it is not providing ideal leadership.

We must move still further up the ladder of medical authority to find out how to speed the application of widely accepted wisdom, not to mention common sense. Says Dr. Robert Heyssel, former president of the Johns Hopkins Hospitals: "Basically we, and I think most hospitals in this country, have been focused far too much on acute medical care over the years. It's where we started really, as a hospital taking care of mainly acutely ill patients. The world has moved on, and while there's still a lot of need for that, it's very clear that prevention, and handling chronic disease appropriately, is a far more cost-effective way to do things, and basically better for people.

"We skew the residents', and in fact the medical students' experience, badly now, in that most of the simple and reasonably common acute illnesses never get in the hospital any longer. Most of the diagnostic work is done as an outpatient, so the resident doesn't even participate necessarily in that, and what you have in hospitals like this is one or two groups of illnesses, it seems to me: either very complex illness requiring an enormous amount of resources to take care of—cardiac illness, cancer, and other things—or in the case of this community, a very large burden of disease that is caused by behavior and social pathology in the community."

Dr. Craig Basson is an earnest, stolid, dark-haired young man who is also an intern on the Osler service. His middle-aged patient, Helen Supik, is a diagnostic puzzle—in addition to being a very sad case. Her daughter Carla, a nurse, seems discouraged: "When I brought her here initially she was still coherent, but within two days she couldn't move her arms or legs, she couldn't see, and was mentally declining. She's had numerous tests done, and we've really not learned much about what's wrong." Despite her nurse's training, she was not prepared to have a medical catastrophe come this close. "The first week I felt like I was in a nightmare, that *this really isn't happening*, because how can somebody be healthy one day, and literally paralyzed, blind, and confused two days later? The next thing they're talking about doing is a brain biopsy; but I don't think they're real hopeful about that."

Dr. Basson is asked if what she is getting has been the proverbial "million-dollar workup": "Well, she's had the more-than-million-dollar workup at this point. She's had multiple X-ray studies of her head, including standard X-rays, CAT scans, MRI scans. She's had the multiple invasive procedures—she's had a few spinal taps, she's had a liver biopsy, she's had skin biopsies, as well as a whole host of other X-ray studies—CAT scans of her whole body really.

"Some of her physical findings are quite remarkable, at a very basic level. Things like her rash are indicative of certain kinds of blood vessel diseases that are important to be able to identify, and for the students and the interns right away that's an important lesson to learn. But even some of her neurologic findings many of us were confused by, till some of the senior neurologists came by and explained to the interns, the residents, the students, and the attending exactly what they meant. And so she's really been very educational for all of us."

Talking to his colleagues on morning rounds at the bedside, he is more blunt: "I think at this point, you know, we've gone around and around, and I don't think any of us have a clue as to what's going on with this lady. I think we're all in agreement that the brain biopsy is likely to be low-yield anyway, but it's the only thing we've got left." That is, the surgical brain biopsy is unlikely to produce any new insight—not, as Carla says, real hopeful: "I don't know what they hope to gain by cutting open her head and taking a piece of her brain out . . . I can't help but think that maybe it's fifty-fifty, that yes, they want to help her, and yes, they want, for their own benefit, to know what's going on—just for the intellectual aspect of it."

To be fair to them, the consent form that Helen or Carla signed on admission to the hospital in effect cut a deal about this. They could have gone to a nonacademic hospital, where little or nothing would have been done "just for the intellectual aspect of it." They did not, because they hoped that these white-coated intellectuals would come up with something better than local doctors in a community hospital would. As for Dr. Basson and his fellow residents, learning is a major part of their job. Mrs. Supik gives them an opportunity to expand their understanding of how the human body works and breaks down; with her, they can push the envelope of what they, as doctors, are capable of doing.

Dr. Paul Oursler makes a most insightful statement: "Unfortunately, a lot of what we do here has to do with people who have had either a problem with alcoholism, drug use, smoking—and in fact that's another source of frustration to some extent. You realize that here we spend huge resources in order to take care of the acute problem, and yet we're pulling these resources away from preventative measures which would really work. We're spending 12 percent of the GNP here on problems which are not, in the end, medical problems. The underlying problem is the problem of poverty, leading to drug abuse, alcohol abuse, smoking, and lack of exercise and obesity, probably from poor diet. And I think all of those problems are going to be effectively addressed by people who are not doctors."

Mrs. Supik's biopsy yields no information—yet she begins to get better, for reasons none of her very numerous doctors can explain. Her sister, Lynn Simpson, expresses an understandable frustration: "It's just so overwhelming that in this day and age, with all the technology that they have, that something like this can happen that they don't know what it is. I mean, every day I sit and think, I just cannot believe it; I just cannot believe it." Carla, the daughter who is a nurse, is more frankly disgusted: "I'm glad she's getting better. But certainly, after all she's been through, you kind of expect a little bit more—like for them to tell you why she's getting better or how much better she's going to get, or what caused it." Even Dr. Basson speaks of her case as "humbling."

Unfortunately, Carla and her aunt's expectations are naive. There is real danger in the common opinion that doctors can now do everything, and that illness holds no more mystery. It inevitably leads to a tendency to blame doctors for not having been able to, as it were, read God's mind, to understand and conquer every blow, every threat that illness offers. Dr. Sulmasy, the young attending physician, says with an impatient, charming smile, "The function of medicine is not to relieve the human condition of the human condition. We can't do that! We're not about making people immortal, and we can't."

Sadly, Rev. Campbell—seemingly stabilized and awaiting further tests—dies in the hospital of a massive, unpredicted heart attack. No one has done anything wrong; when he came in he was eighty-six, frail, beset by multiple illnesses, and for years not even in contact with a physician. He knew that each day was a gift, and would probably not have been amazed to learn that his life was about to end. The gentle, sensitive, effective Dr. Alicia Fry does not in any sense blame herself—and she is right; but summarizing her experience as an intern, she thinks that she will probably return to the lab to do basic science research. She seems to feel frustrated by the wildness of the frontier of clinical knowledge—by what might be called the incompleteness of medicine. It's a pity to see her withdrawing from clinical work, but her problem is an almost universal one among patients and their families. Carla, for example, despite the fact that she is a nurse, cannot quite grasp how basically primitive medical science remains, and how much uncertainty there is even at best. It is often because of such exaggerated expectations that patients experience so much disappointment.

Isabel Humbles has the fluid drained from her abdomen—a quite painful procedure, but one that gives her dramatic and immediate relief. Advised about the deadly threat of drugs and alcohol, she packs a bag, along with a get-well balloon, and leaves the hospital apparently improved; certainly in much less pain. Yet no long-term stabilization is likely. As Dr. Townes says of her, "You can't help somebody unless they want to be helped." But she will not get even the limited benefit of a drug rehabilitation program, because there will be no openings in such programs in her area for the next six months.

Only a few blocks from Johns Hopkins, the Reverend Melvin B. Tuggle, a traditional black preacher at the Garden of Prayer Baptist Church, may be saving more lives than most African-American doctors in the temple. "Is there a doctor in the house?" he intones from his pulpit, and the congregation resonates in a classic answering style—but not loudly enough for him. "Y'all don't hear me," he says. "Is there a *doctor* in the house?" enunciating carefully and calling his flock to witness. Their voices rise again and the resonance enlarges. Later he will go on to say that Jesus is the cure, but with a new twist on this age-old message. Rather, he preaches a God-helps-those-that-help-themselves sort of medical revivalism: "Cigarettes!" sings this minister in a tobacco-growing state. "They are an evil and we will give any one of you the strength and support you need to put them out of your life."

Driving a visitor down what he calls "the Hopkins corridor," the stretch of slum between his church and the hospital complex, he compares it convincingly to a third-world country. It may sound like mere rhetoric, but his claim is statistically accurate, not only for the Hopkins corridor but for neighborhoods like it throughout the land. For example, Drs. Colin McCord and Harold Freeman, both of New York's Harlem Hospital, studied mortality in their hospital's neighborhood, using records for 1979 and 1980. While mortality fell in the United States as a whole between 1960 and 1980—even more for nonwhites than for whites nationwide—it stayed the same or rose slightly in Harlem. As McCord and Freeman stated baldly in their conclusion, "black men in Harlem were less likely to reach the age of 65 than men in Bangladesh."

This is strong language, but the article appeared in no less than *The New England Journal of Medicine*, arguably the most prestigious medical journal in the world. Physicians and scientists at the Centers for Disease Control were not surprised, since they have documented similar statistics for inner-city neighborhoods around the United States. And the figures are worse than they seem at first. If you remove infant mortality, and look at the life expectancy of a pre–school-age child, you find life expectancies for both boys and girls are *worse* in Harlem than in Bangladesh.

Our first reaction, which is to attribute the difference to violence and drug abuse, is less than half right. This was *before* the epidemics of AIDS and crack. More than half of the excess deaths were caused by the same diseases that claim lives in better neighborhoods: above all, heart attack, stroke, and cancer. According to World Bank statistics, the probability of death between ages fifteen and forty-five for black males nationally—slightly over 30 percent—is higher than the same statistic for underdeveloped nations such as The Gambia, India, and El Salvador.

Life and death in the "Hopkins corridor" have almost certainly followed a pattern similar to that in Harlem; and today, *with* crack and AIDS, the statistics must be worse. The irony of such human desperation, such relentless physical suffering, right in the shadow of a great modern hospital is not in any sense lost on Rev. Tuggle. "The closer you get to Johns Hopkins, as you'll notice, the more the health problems become viewable. You see people on the steps early in the morning with beer bottles, wine bottles. This is dope city." Rev. Tuggle's empathy for these people is palpable, yet his is no message of passive dependency. He says after a pause, "Hopkins needs to do more, and also the community needs to do more."

Under his leadership, the community does. In the basement of his own church, volunteer physicians and other health workers come down from the temple, where they feel that they can do more than hold back a relentless tide of overwhelming illness and dying. One bespectacled parishioner of about sixty, wearing a three-piece blue suit with a watch chain draped across his vest, makes a steady progress from station to station in different corners of the basement: diabetes check, blood pressure, cholesterol. Now he banters with Dr. Louis Becker, a prominent Hopkins cardiologist: "Do you drink?" "Only when there's a good game on." "How about cigarettes?" "No." "When's the last time you saw a doctor?" "That would have to be ten years ago." "What do you like to eat?" "I've eaten eggs every morning for thirty years."

This man's cholesterol is 315. Becker interprets this to him gently, and says, unfolding a pamphlet, "I'd like to show you a few things about cholesterol." Since the man's blood pressure is also high, he gets an appointment at a special hypertension clinic the following week. "That makes two today, about the average," Becker says afterward. "Walking time bombs waiting to go off. It's great when we can catch it before it happens." If this man gets his cholesterol and blood pressure under control—whether with diet or drugs— he will greatly postpone or perhaps avoid a heart attack or stroke— the sort of event on which Hopkins residents spend hundreds of thousands of dollars without feeling that they have accomplished very much.

Becker, a high-powered researcher, was an unlikely prospect for this sort of preventive care. But one day his wife, Diane—a Hopkins health expert who runs the program with Rev. Tuttle— dragged him along to a screening. He brought along a scientific medical journal to kill time, but never had a chance to look at it.

He was hooked. He feels that preventive screening has made him a better hospital doctor, and he now requires all cardiology fellows—subspecialty trainees who have completed medical residencies—to serve in church screenings.

One might ask why this wasn't required of them in the first place. The answer is that the Osler tradition is an almost entirely hospital-based pattern of training. The feeling has been for generations that young doctors must train by caring for the extremely, acutely ill. But what this means in the modern teaching hospital is third-tier, or tertiary, care, patients referred by specialists to whom they had already been referred by primary-care physicians—internists, pediatricians, or general practitioners, for example. In this specialized third level of care, patients have been passed on by doctors in the two other layers; those doctors either could not figure out what the patient had or figured it out but could do nothing more about it. Frequently Hopkins physicians cannot do anything about it either, even after spending a small fortune on tests and procedures. Yet sometimes they can, and it is in this hope that patients have always crossed their threshold.

If the patients are rich, they usually get the close and personal attention of top specialists, as well as visits from their personal primary-care doctor; if they are poor, they get the residents who are training under the specialists—supervised, of course, but not as closely. And they usually have no one doctor corresponding to the British general practitioner, responsible for coordinating the efforts of the specialists and for mediating between them and the patient. This crucial, comforting, sometimes lifesaving effort is often lost entirely in the United States. As a patient said in an excellent teaching hospital where I was a medical student—she had already been cared for by at least a dozen specialists—"I have no doctor here." It is easy to see how a person can lose hope even when, in a technical sense, she is in the best of hands. This is all the more true if the system has taken no interest in her before the point when it may be too late.

Rev. Tuggle's program, which is called "Heart, Body and Soul," attempts to touch those patients when they have more reason to hope. At his church desk he ceases to preach and becomes quietly thoughtful. "We're concerned with the natural state of man, the man's physical body, his physical heart, and his physical soul. Just as our Savior Jesus Christ was concerned with the common man, so should the church be.

"People have lost their faith in doctors. The old family doctor that maybe covered the whole neighborhood, people trusted him or her. Now with high-tech 'modernology'—computers, et cetera—coming into the hospital, people have become a number. It's machines that work on them, doctors do not work on them. The personal emphasis is gone now.

"We need hands-on, walk-the-street doctors, neighborhood doctors. At one time we had a lot of practices in East Baltimore. It's gone now . . . Doctors are scared."

Rev. Tuggle also notes that since doctors can't make enough money as general practitioners, most want to specialize. Physicians have traditionally justified specialization as a healthy trend that supplies the most expert care in the most specific way to the patient in the most dire need. Clearly in the post–World War II period, when many medical-specialty certification boards were just forming, this was true. Science was delivering on its turn-of-the-century promise, and miracle drugs like penicillin and streptomycin were controlling infectious scourges and making surgery unprecedentedly safe. Imaging of bodily organs, and other diagnostic technologies, became steadily better.

But somewhere a point of diminishing returns was reached. More and more money was being spent for an ever smaller return, whether measured in terms of deaths prevented or suffering relieved. An unbalanced system of payments made it unrewarding to practice any but the most specialized, high-tech medicine. Things were still improving steadily, but in smaller and smaller increments, and at length many concluded that the price had simply gotten too high. Of course, costs are always relative. Whether health-care expenditures as a proportion of gross domestic product are too high, especially in the United States, is a legitimate question, and one to which we will return. But *given* a finite health-care budget, the question whether too much is spent on hospital-based treatments that are expensive and often futile, relative to neighborhood-based primary care and prevention—the sort of thing we saw going on in the basement of the Garden of Prayer Baptist Church—is an easier one to answer, and the answer is a pretty simple yes.

The paradox is not new. In *The Care of Strangers: The Rise of America's Hospital System,* Charles Rosenberg shows that "hospitals have never been ideal places in which to receive care." As in medieval times, throughout the Renaissance and the early modern period hospitals functioned more or less like almshouses. They were refuges for the poor, the homeless, the hungry, and incidentally also the ill. In 1690, for example, the Hôpital Général in Paris had taken in six thousand people—1 percent of the population of the city at the time—including young men who refused to work and young women "in danger of debauchery"—debasement of their morals. But a century later, after the French and American revolutions, hospitals in the United States and Britain as well as on the continent began to be more focused on treatment and cure.

Still, few but the very poor would go to one in any event; the sick among the middle and upper classes would be cared for by private physicians and family members at home. There still was not much that could be done for most patients other than to offer comfort, some relief from pain, and, for better or worse, some prediction of the outcome. None of these could be done any better in a hospital than at home—unless of course you didn't have a home. Although sanitoriums for well-to-do people with tuberculosis were introduced in the 1850s—something like the Roman convalescent home for the wealthy of Pompeii—hospitals and poverty remained almost synonymous.

The next fifty years changed all that. At mid-century ether, the first effective anesthesia for surgery, was discovered and spread rapidly. Astoundingly, such surgery as was done before that time had been done with only alcoholic beverages to blunt the searing pain. Procedures often had to be completed in minutes. With ether much more could be done, and surgeons wasted little time in expanding their horizons to take advantage of it. In the years that followed, another enormous advance took hold: the germ theory of disease. Looking at a famous painting showing the first use of ether anesthesia, we are shocked to see the surgeons gloveless and garbed in Victorian dress suits, as if for a bank board meeting. But only after the role of germs was proved did sterile technique become relevant. Then, near the turn of the century, the X-ray machine was introduced, giving doctors the awesome ability to look through the body in their search for the causes of illness. And at around the same time, biochemistry was being born, with its potential for diagnosing disease through measurement of components of the blood. Hospitals were becoming, in important ways, scientific laboratories.

Now there were reasons to go to a hospital even if you were not poor. Few if any private physicians could afford to assemble all these services in their clinics. Nursing became a hospital-based profession, and helped to establish the scientific basis of sterile technique. Since nurses, not doctors, determine the quality of day-to-day hospital care, this professionalization of nursing was a prerequisite for the rise of the modern hospital. Centralization became increasingly advantageous for doctors, nurses, and patients, and hospitals became recognized as the right place to *learn* medicine— first in Europe, and later, with Osler's imitation of the European example, in America as well.

Even a generation before Osler's, ambitious young American doctors often went to Germany to study. Clarence Blake, a Harvard-educated physician who had served as one of the first house staff at Boston City Hospital, and then volunteered as a surgical assistant in the last year of the Civil War, wrote home in 1866 describing the Vienna General Hospital as "a small town of 3200 inhabitants" with nine thousand births a year, where "living specimens" could be pushed and poked more or less at will, and then in the end dissected. "A year here," he concluded, "is worth more than many years of private practice at home." Dr. Blake was planning to become a specialist, explaining that the pace of accumulation of clinical knowledge was too rapid to allow for competent general practice, so he would pursue the deep, narrow knowledge gained from concentrating on one field—in his case, ear surgery. Thus the pressure to specialize, 1866.

The German-speaking countries pioneered not only "specialism" but a rigorous scientific approach based on facts about a series of cases, and ultimately even on autopsies; these were the gold standard, since they were the ultimate test of hypotheses about the causes of illness and death. Rudolph Virchow, founder of the science of pathology, can be credited with a role comparable to that of Louis Pasteur, discoverer of the germ theory, in the establishment of scientific medicine. As we have seen in the prologue, Virchow doubled as a public health advocate, but his great contribution to laboratory science was to show that each true disease is an inherent, autonomous process with an identifiable course and a provable and specific derangement that could be located microscopically in the cells of the body. This delineation of one disease after another created a climate of unprecedented excitement in medical science.

One result was that patients as well as physicians, other health-care workers, and governments increasingly saw the hospital as the most promising, safest, and best place to care for the seriously ill, and later, by the mid twentieth century, as the best place to give birth. This would have seemed most improbable in the mid nineteenth century, when it had recently been proved that doctors caused deaths of hospitalized child-bearing women by carrying germs from one to another on their hands. The total number of hospital admissions in the United States rose from an estimated 146,500 in 1873—when the population of the country was about 40 million—to more than 29 million in the late 1960s, when the population was about 200 million. That is, while the country grew fivefold, the use of hospitals rose almost two-hundred-fold. "Specialism" grew so strong that the skepticism about general practice expressed by Dr. Blake in 1866 had become an article of faith, and the ever dwindling number of general practitioners were viewed by specialists with increasing disdain. Some specialists, including surgeons, anesthesiologists, radiologists, and clinical pathologists, became largely inseparable from hospitals.

Yet despite its successes, Rosenberg notes that "by 1920 almost all those criticisms of the hospital so familiar to us in the past two decades were already being articulated":

> Concerned observers . . . pointed toward a growing coldness and impersonality; they deprecated an increasing concern with acute ailments and a parallel neglect of the aged, of chronic illness, of the convalescent, of the simply routine. They warned of socially insensitive and economically dysfunctional obsession with inpatient at the expense of outpatient and community-oriented care . . . Medicine had to be brought out of the hospital and into the community—insofar as possible into the home. But such views were not to prevail.

The effectiveness of specialized hospital medicine grew ever greater. George Rosen highlights a striking 1938 comparison, by physician Alphonse Dochez, of the previous thirty years:

> He contrasted the histories of two patients with similar types of heart disease; one was recorded in 1908, the other at the same hospital in 1938. The total written record of the first patient occupied 2½ pages, and the observations represented the combined efforts of two physicians—the attending and the house officer—and of one specialist, the pathologist-bacteriologist. The record of the second patient . . . comprised 29 pages and represented the combined observations of three visiting physicians, two residents, three house officers, ten specialists, and fourteen technicians.

Only the naive would suppose that the rise of such intensive efforts of diagnosis and care is not a good thing. Yet increasingly in our era, critics within and outside of medicine are citing evidence of a point of diminishing returns, of costs that are no longer matched to benefits. Although generalists have remained numerous and effective in Britain—thus proving that they need not become historical relics—there too the rise of specialties, and of hospital admissions, has been very great. To a large extent increasing specialization can be justified in terms very similar to those used by Blake—you just can't become good enough at all the different things doctors do.

Although medical training is dominated by specialists in Britain as in the United States, general practice continues to be not only respectable but essential there. About half of all physicians are general practitioners. But the United States has had a grave geographic and social maldistribution of physicians, with a large unserved population—not only in places like Harlem in New York and the Hopkins corridor in Baltimore, but in rural farm areas that have no primary-care physicians. It is as if the corps of American physicians were an army without infantry, only pilots, tank commanders, and other commissioned officers. Measures have begun to be taken to rectify this situation, including the establishment of "specialty" boards for primary care and even "family practice"— an updated, better-trained form of general practitioner. But such programs are not popular among medical students, the problem of distribution of care is nowhere near resolution, and the situation of the ill poor remains very grave.

In these discussions it is sometimes hard to be sure whether we are talking about the problem of acute, high-tech medicine, the problem of lopsided medical training, or the problems of inadequate health-care delivery for the poor. That is because these are inextricably entwined. Among doctors, only residents can work cheaply enough to be cost-effective in care for the poor. Because of their need, the poor will tolerate being the focus of training, and consider the exchange a fair bargain. Meanwhile, those entrusted with the training of medical residents feel very keenly the imperative of training those young people *on the frontier*, not just the one between health and illness, and the one between what we can do and what we cannot—the frontier of current medical science.

So does this mean, in the words of Mrs. Supik's daughter after the biopsy, that half the reason these high-tech procedures are done is that they are useful in training? This is a great oversimplification, but there is a sideways piece of the truth here. Everything that was done in Mrs. Supik's half-million-dollar workup was done for her benefit in an honest attempt to find out what was wrong with her and to open some avenue, or at least a path, of treatment. But while her intern, Dr. Basson, was being exposed to the remarkable array of state-of-the-art procedures invoked for her—exposure he was obviously enthusiastic about—he was *not* being exposed to primary care in an outpatient clinic, or to preventive care in Rev. Tuggle's health fair. As his teacher, Dr. Stobo, says, if we don't train young doctors in primary care and preventive medicine, we abdicate our responsibility to patients. Dr. Heyssel, the hospital's recent president, agrees.

In a 1983 issue of *Time* magazine, the dean of the Harvard Medical School opined that "medical education is not in optimum health"; the dean of the Johns Hopkins School of Medicine concurred, adding that "we would like to reverse the trend toward early specialization and overemphasis on science as preparation for medicine"; and the dean of the Columbia College of Physicians and Surgeons stated that medical students must learn "how to deal with the patient, the patient's family, and his whole life, rather than 'the third bed on the left with a coronary.' " Listening to Dr. Stobo and Dr. Heyssel gave me the same stunned feeling I had had back then: If the people who run the system don't like it, why don't they change it?

There is a profound answer, and it is an anthropological one: they can't. No one at any place in the hierarchy, however high up, can willfully counteract the forces that make it work—or fail to work—the way it does. These forces include the steady advance of science; the cultural traditions of medical training (*I did it, so you have to do it*); the nation's need to use trainees to care for the poor; the insurance companies' misplaced sense of responsibility—greater toward their stockholders than toward patients; the bizarre patterns of reimbursement insurers maintain; the consequent disproportionate income and influence of procedure-oriented specialities; colossal administrative waste; greed and fraud; and the enormous impact of soaring malpractice litigation on medical decision making.

But perhaps a greater force than any of these is what I call the

"What-If-It's-Your-Mother Principle." What if Mrs. Supik were your mother? Would you want to hear arguments about how many lives could be saved through immunization using the half million dollars spent on her hospitalization? Or would you prefer that no expense be spared in the attempt to find out how to control and reverse the dreadful deterioration of a vigorous, vital woman full of life and hope? What if Isabel Humbles were your mother? Would you want to hear lectures about the need for her and others to stop drinking, and about the impossibility of getting her into a drug rehab program? Or would you want the doctor to stop preaching and lecturing and just draw off the fluid that was choking her to death?

Every congressional representative and county official asks these same questions when considering how to allocate health care. Most malpractice suits are driven by these questions, causing doctors to practice high-tech defensive medicine costing a fortune. And the officials and lawyers attend to these questions because they are on the minds of the average man and woman on the street. Not, *Why is my child—or even less, someone else's child—not immunized?* but *What will happen if my child has leukemia;* not *I wonder what my cholesterol level is,* but *What will happen when I have a heart attack?* Even doctors are not immune to the compelling drama of the illness that has become a matter of life and death.

No one has a right to ask doctors to think about drug rehab slots or prenatal-care programs or unimmunized children when they are standing over someone who is desperately ill and in pain. Indeed, at that moment it is wrong to have such thoughts; as Osler advised, you should confine your thinking to a twenty-four-hour cycle, putting everything else out of your mind. But somebody, somewhere must think those other thoughts. As long as there is a finite limit to health-care expenditures, some people who stare at the columns of black and red ink must think about where to put the money. As dreadful and coldhearted as it seems, someone must weigh Ms. Humbles's perhaps penultimate medical stabilization against the fate of other addicts who are not so sick but cannot get into drug programs. Someone must weigh some of Mrs. Supik's CAT scans against the fate of the unimmunized children.

It has been said that a civilized person is one who can look at a page of numbers and weep. Such people must be found and appointed to make the choice.

Recently I was talking with an extremely bright young doctor who had just completed a three-year residency in internal medicine. She spoke with great enthusiasm about the same state-of-the-art three-dimensional imaging that excited Dr. Basson as it guided Mrs. Supik's biopsy. But she also spoke with great enthusiasm about the satellite clinics set up by Atlanta's Grady Hospital to serve the poor of the city in their own neighborhoods. I said, "You cannot be equally enthusiastic about everything. Sooner or later we will come to a point where someone will say to you, 'Should we buy another six-million-dollar magnetic resonance imager, or should we build another satellite clinic? We can't do both.' Which will you choose?" Articulate and experienced as she was, she did not have an answer—not exactly an indictment of her, since neither, as yet, does anyone else.

THREE

THE MAGIC
BULLET

At around the same time that William Osler in Baltimore was inventing the modern teaching hospital, Paul Ehrlich in Frankfurt was laying the foundations of what we now call chemotherapy—the specific treatment of diseases with deliberately crafted drugs. His observations of diphtheria, a then-dreaded bacterial killer of children, had taught him that the body itself can produce chemical agents to damage an invading microbe *specifically*—what we now call specific immunity. And his studies of lead poisoning had shown him that some chemicals brought into the body—in this case a toxic one—home in on certain organs. His hope was for new drugs that would go directly to a diseased organ or to a microbe, destroying the germ and defeating the disease with few other effects on the body.

He used the phrase "silver bullet" to describe the dream chemical that would target a given disease. At the time he was working on syphilis, a then-devastating chronic disease caused by bacteria called spirochetes. These he watched under his microscope while continually making and trying new compounds that might have a chance of specifically killing them. The 606th compound he tried worked dramatically, and was marketed in 1910 under the name Salvarsan. In the age of AIDS it is worth noting in passing that Salvarsan, the model for most twentieth-century drug treatments, came out of the search for a cure for another sexually transmitted, chronically degenerative, deadly disease.

But unfortunately Salvarsan was not quite the silver bullet after all. It had major side effects that imposed a heavy burden on those who were helped by it. There was no doubt that on balance the treatment with Salvarsan was a very good thing—it marked the end of an era when many medicines were little more than generalized poisons, containing lead, mercury, and arsenic. Yet there was equally little doubt that the search for a better treatment than Salvarsan should continue.

"Magic bullet" is the phrase by which Ehrlich's concept has come down to us, and in the strict sense there is not one yet—for syphilis or any other disease. Every drug that has been of use against disease has imposed a cost on those who took it, in the form of unwanted effects on the body. Aspirin and acetaminophen (the active ingredient in Tylenol and Excedrin) seem at first like magic bullets for fever, but aspirin may burn a hole in your stomach— or if you are a child, may in rare cases give you the very dangerous Reye's syndrome—while acetaminophen may do permanent harm to your kidneys. Insulin seems at first a magic bullet for diabetes. But by doing what it's supposed to do—reduce blood sugar—too well, it can produce a potentially deadly insulin shock. Penicillin a magic bullet for, say, pneumonia? If you're not unlucky enough to be allergic, yes; but even so, it may still kill the normal bacteria in your gut, causing you some off-key digestion. And more important, over time and many treatments in a community, it will relentlessly breed bacteria that are immune to its effects—taking you right back to the start of the search for a magic bullet again.

In the end, we begin to realize that what we have been searching for is a contradiction: a chemical agent that acts powerfully on an illness—a living thing, whether microbe, tumor, or failing organ— but is completely without unwanted actions in the body. The trouble is that an agent that has powerful biological effects . . . has powerful biological effects. Evolution has not designed living things with absolute precision and specificity; rather, it has been a clumsy process, utilizing random changes and building on what it has at any point in time—something like a small child building a complex structure out of small, differently colored lumps of clay. If another child comes along determined to pull out all the (say) green lumps, the structure will be vulnerable in many places, not just one.

In the sense of absolute specificity, the magic bullet is in part a vain hope, the existence of effective drug treatments notwithstanding. But there is another, more important "side effect" of dream drugs: they lull us, even in anticipation, into a false sense of safety, an illusory world where anything that is broken can be simply fixed—where anything that is wrong with us has its own private molecular magic wand that, when waved over us, will make it go away. We can smoke ourselves into lung cancer and heart attack, drink ourselves into liver disease, and eat ourselves into diabetes and stroke.

We are fearless about these things because of a new version of the age-old denial of death. First, we inherit from our evolutionary past the basic animal feeling that says, *What is happening now will surely go on forever.* We add to that the ancient human tendency to ignore the future, especially if that future may be in some way worse than the present. If a thought is in any way painful, we decline to think it. But we compound these kinds of denial with an unrealistic vision of the power of modern science in the battle against disease and death. Deep down we think we have the system beat; we will make it all right again at the other end of the story. After all, aren't we approaching the twenty-first century? Drug company scientists can do practically anything with those molecules and test tubes—can't they?

In fact there are millions of people for whom newly invented drugs *have* been virtual miracle cures. James Nelson is one of them. In the late 1980s he had begun to suffer from Cushing's syndrome—

an array of unsettling symptoms caused by an excess of the hormone cortisol, which in normal amounts is one of the body's main aids in coping with stress. This disorder can affect virtually any organ. One common feature is a deforming type of weight gain in the abdomen, which may develop stripes due to stretching of the skin. Bloating of the face, muscle weakness, fragile bones, thinning of the skin with a lot of bruising, lowered resistance to infection, high blood pressure, depression, and impotence are all frequent components. In Mr. Nelson's case—by his own testimony and that of his wife—his life had become practically unlivable, their marriage little more than shared anguish.

The syndrome is often caused by a tumor in the gland that produces cortisol—a small, soft pyramidal structure atop each kidney called the adrenal gland. What the tumor does in these cases can be described as the gland's normal function run amok; the tumor works overtime to make unneeded and dangerous excess cortisol. This turned out to be what had happened to Mr. Nelson, and the tumor would be removed by surgery. But while they were searching for the tiny disease-producing lump—in this case a full year—he would have continued to go downhill in the functioning of several body systems. Some of this deterioration would have been irreversible, and even if he had survived, his life would have been truly dreadful while he was waiting for the surgery.

But Mr. Nelson was lucky enough to have access to the National Institutes of Health in Maryland, where Dr. Lynnette Nieman and her colleagues were conducting a study of a promising new drug called mifepristone. This agent, they had reason to believe, would block the effects of the excess cortisol on a number of body systems—essentially by tricking each organ into absorbing the harmless mifepristone while blocking out the dangerous cortisol. It turned out to be one of those happy situations in which a theory about the body's chemistry was in the event both true and powerful. A molecule that had been dreamed up by a drug company scientist, at the blackboard and in the laboratory, was administered by a doctor thousands of miles away, and it reversed Mr. Nelson's deterioration.

Since people with Cushing's syndrome have lives that are unpredictable and short, it is quite possible that, as he believes, mifepristone made all the difference: "I can honestly say that it played an important part in maybe even saving my life." His wife is more definite: "His life was like a complete turnaround—it was like a miracle. To go from one side of life and then to see the other, it was actually beautiful."

This kind of "miracle cure" is not rare in modern medicine, but it is not exactly common either. As we saw in the last chapter, most people who come into hospitals today have no quickly fixable ailments curable by miraculous drugs. They have instead chronic, degenerative conditions that can often be slowed by drugs, or even stopped, but not easily reversed. And even when drugs do work, they carry a cost in side effects that is often very high, sometimes unacceptably high. Have we reached a plateau at last after a century of uphill climbing? Has the advancement of drug treatment, seemingly at greater and greater heights in every decade, finally reached a point at which future gains will be small? Will we continue to invent new drugs like mifepristone, or will our drugs of the future be more like AZT—another new agent, helpful to AIDS patients for a while, but only a while, and really only postponing the inevitable?

In a sense, ether was the first great modern drug. Introduced in the 1840s, it caused a state of painless and safe unconsciousness that transformed the possibilities of surgical cure—functions that from ancient times were partly served by natural substances like alcohol and opium. But ether was an adjunct to treatment, not really a treatment itself. Quinine, a very effective antimalarial extract from the Peruvian cinchona tree, may have been the first commercially marketed treatment. But probably aspirin, first marketed by the Bayer pharmaceutical firm in Germany, has the honor of being the first truly mass-produced drug treatment. Felix Hoffmann, a chemist at the company, developed the method while searching for a treatment for his father's painful arthritis. Aspirin was marketed for the control of pain, inflammation, and fever. But it was certainly not an invented molecule. It had been known from ancient times—by Native Americans among others—that willow bark had medicinal properties. A Rev. Edmund Stone in the mid-1700s had reported to the British Royal Society that because it tasted to him like quinine, he had tried it on fifty patients with painful and debilitating rheumatoid arthritis; all, he claimed, had benefited. It was used increasingly in the nineteenth century until the means developed to isolate aspirin (salicylic acid), manufacture it in large quantities, and market it commercially.

Meanwhile, techniques of drug production were emerging. A way to mass-produce sugar-coated pills was developed in France, and a tablet-compression machine was introduced in England; pharmaceutical companies like Squibb, Eli Lilly, and Parke-Davis were founded in the United States and became influential. The Civil War provided a sad stimulus to the manufacture and marketing of drugs. Purified forms of ether and chloroform made anesthesia safer, and plant products were analyzed to isolate morphine for systemic pain control and cocaine for local pain. Indeed, one might think of the late nineteenth century as the first phase of modern pharmacology, the phase of pain control.

If so, the first half of the twentieth century would have to be the phase of infection control. Unlike the agents of pain control, medicines for infectious disease could fairly be seen as allies in a battle; the hordes of microbes assaulting the body seemed a tangible enemy. Ehrlich fired the first shot with his not-quite silver bullet Salvarsan, and quinine derivatives were extensively used in malaria. Arsenic and other toxic elements continued to be used against tropical parasitic diseases. But it was not until the 1930s that Gerhard Domagk, a research director for the Bayer company, discovered that a new fabric dye contained the first true chemotherapy agent: sulfanilamide. As in Ehrlich's dream it targeted bacteria and prevented them from multiplying, giving the body a needed chance to mount its own defenses. Yet it worked faster and with far fewer side effects than older treatments had. Among the infectious scourges treatable with it and related "sulfa" drugs were childbed fever, meningitis, and most pneumonias—all of which had often been deadly since ancient times.

Penicillin was even more powerful. Identified in 1928 by Alexander Fleming and developed in the 1930s by Howard Florey and Ernst Chain, it came into widespread use during the Second World War. It dramatically improved survival from battle wound infections, as well as curing many cases of syphilis among soldiers—a magic bullet apparently as penetrating and accurate as any Paul Ehrlich had dreamed of. In 1944 Selman Waxman, a microbiologist who was an expert on funguses in soil, discovered streptomycin, a component of one such fungus, which appeared to be effective against the tubercle bacillus—the killer of countless TB sufferers with wrecked, bleeding lungs for centuries. The British Medical Research Council, after several years of clinical trials (formal studies of patients) announced in 1948 that they had "the clearest possible proof" that acute, progressive tuberculosis, the most devastating kind, "could be halted by streptomycin."

The rising prestige of medicine during the half-century since has been built on this enthusiasm for "miracle cures." Not only drug treatment but surgery too received an immense boost from antibiotics, just as it had from ether. All too frequently until then, skillful surgery was doomed by infection. Dramatic books and movies recounted the stories of the "microbe hunters"—heroes, at mid-century, almost as luminous as the victorious Allied commanders. Although these heroes were laboratory types, the men in white coats (there were few women doctors then) in the clinics and hospital wards found that the luster rubbed off on them. Knowing how and when to fire the magic bullets against bacteria transformed them from dark presences, able to do little more than assuage pain and predict the downhill course of the patient's life, into virtual guardian angels.

But chinks had already appeared in their armor. The first dose of penicillin injected into a patient had been given in January 1941. By about a year later, in early 1942, physicians found strains of bacteria that resisted penicillin. It *should* have targeted them. They were staphylococci—the same wound-infecting species that had been dramatically susceptible a year before. Yet not only were they resistant, but they appeared regularly in hospitals by the early 1950s, spreading through patients and hospital staff alike.

By 1946 strains of gonorrhea resistant to penicillin had emerged and began to spread. By 1960 doctors in Britain had to use doses fifty times the original ones to combat these new microbes, and by 1980 the doses required with some strains were simply intolerable. Syphilis, Paul Ehrlich's old nemesis, also arose in resistant strains. By the 1970s sexually transmitted diseases thought by many to have been conquered rode the wave of sexual permissiveness to new epidemic heights. And in the 1980s minor or obscure viruses, not susceptible to antibiotics in the first place— hepatitis, herpes, and the dreaded AIDS—overtook a chastened and saddened human consciousness.

The "restless tide" was a phrase used by Dr. Richard Krause, who at that time, the early 1980s, was director of the American National Institute of Allergy and Infectious Diseases and since winner of the coveted Koch prize for research on microbes, to describe the way these tiny organisms keep coming back at us: the sense is one of an ocean shore continually disturbed by waves. They recede for a while, and may lull the unsuspecting into a long, secure reverie. But they always return in one form or another to beat again against the poorly protected shores of our health and safety. Only a crafty vigilance proves responsive enough to their vagaries, and even such vigilance is often not enough, so that we find ourselves surprised, repairing damage already done but not really anticipated.

Consider the change of metaphors for the microbes that cause disease: for Paul Ehrlich, a tangible enemy that could be named and targeted with our hoped-for magic bullets, a war that could eventually be once and for all won; for Richard Krause, a restless, nameless, formless tide surging endlessly at our boundaries, licking away at the sodden sand, predictable only in its eternal recurrences. Ehrlich might have guessed it if he had studied his Darwin—*The Origin of Species* had been published when he was a child. Like all forms of life, microbes are constantly evolving, adapting to new conditions that the environment presents to them. Penicillin did not spell doom for the streptococcus and gonococcus; it merely presented them with an unusual evolutionary challenge. In the end the microbes could almost be seen to be thumbing their noses at us: the more we fired our pharmacological bullets, the more the bacteria adapted—a classic case of what has been called an "evolutionary arms race" between a predator and its prey. As for the virus that causes AIDS, it appears to be an evolutionary novelty—a former monkey virus that evolved the ability to colonize humans—and one that takes full advantage of our many human frailties, not least of which is the absence of any effective antiviral drug.

Roussel-Uclaf—now part of the international giant Hoechst-Roussel—is one of the leading pharmaceutical houses in France, and the one that makes the drug that probably saved James Nelson's life—mifepristone. It was the product of what is known as *rational drug development*. At its best, this process uses basic theory in chemistry—an understanding of the molecular structures of the targeted disease—to arrive at the sort of molecule that is needed: one that will break through a bacterial wall, say; or in Mr. Nelson's case one that will fit the receptors for cortisol like a hand fitting a glove, but that will also get stuck there. Then the tremendous excess of cortisol produced by his tumor would become impotent, and the destruction it wreaked would heal and pass away. Now, this was far from a definitive cure for Mr. Nelson; a cure could only be offered by the surgery that ultimately removed the tumor. But in the interim it worked like a "designer drug" on the receptors—just as it should, according to the abstract diagrams of chemical theory.

Finding a new and powerful agent against disease was not a new experience for Roussel. The company's history is a good case study for the development of modern pharmaceutical firms. In the early decades of the century—and the company's life—it was extensively involved in the production of horse serum, and scores of horses were stabled at the company to be injected with microbes and later bled. This effort, bizarre as it seems, was based in part on a scientific concept: horses or other animals would raise their own antibodies to the microbes, and their serum, carrying these antibodies, could help fight off the microbes in the bloodstream of a critically ill person. This strange system is still in use in one situation today: a snakebite that carries venom toxic to nerves can kill a person quickly, but injection with antivenin—serum from horses exposed to the venom—is often lifesaving.

However, this approach does have major drawbacks. Horse serum, including the relatively purer form used against snakebites today, will occasionally cause an overwhelming systemic collapse called anaphylactic shock—a total-body reaction as deadly as any microbe or venom. In addition, Roussel marketed a *non*specific form of horse serum as a tonic—an example of overmarketing of a type that has often been repeated in various ways by many drug companies since. Even in the case of specific microbes, the early-twentieth-century serum produced by Roussel and others simply did not work well even when shock was avoided.

The advent of antibiotics changed all that. According to Edouard Sakiz, a chemist who heads the company, the modern era at Roussel-Uclaf began when it purchased a company called Sofrapen—for Société Française de Penicilline. Demand for its product grew rapidly during the Second World War and thereafter, establishing the company as a major presence in the pharmaceutical industry's increasingly international market.

But this energetic production and distribution of penicillin, which was engaged in by a number of firms and a great many doctors, almost immediately began to generate resistant strains of microbes—the adaptive rising of the "restless tide." Patients were being hospitalized and were dying once more of pneumonias and other infections that had seemed completely curable a few years earlier. Understanding of the evolutionary realities of bacterial growth dawned on doctors and scientists, and the search for new and different antibiotics intensified. Bacteria were adapting to penicillin's action; this made it essential to understand what that action was, and to develop new kinds of antibiotics that did not just mimic penicillin's mode of attack, but rather utilized a different chemical tactic or strategy.

In retrospect, it seemed to chemist Sakiz as if he and his colleagues at Roussel were engaged in an endless war. This war eventually produced a new weapon: cefotaxime, a molecule that the company named Claforan. It had turned out that the way penicillin fought bacteria was to throw a chemical wrench into their machinery for making the walls around them—crucial to the microbes' survival. Resistance to penicillin was eventually understood to come from bacteria that could manufacture their own weapon against the drug. This was an enzyme called penicillinase, because it broke down and destroyed penicillin. Streptomycin, the first new antibiotic after penicillin, used a new strategy: it interfered with the bacteria's protein-making machinery. But this action made it dangerously toxic to patients in the long run.

Claforan was one of a general category of new drugs that used the same strategy as penicillin—preventing bacteria from making their own protective walls—but added a new tactic: a molecular shield against penicillinase. Thus many bacteria that could destroy penicillin were helpless against Claforan. Roussel had invented a decisive new weapon, one still in use today. And there have been many other new agents in our response to the adaptive challenges constantly offered by microbes. Roussel itself will soon market a new antibiotic more powerful than Claforan. In the best medical centers, the newer, more potent agents are guarded closely and kept for situations where all else has been tried and has failed. Such restricted use can greatly lengthen the time it takes for bacteria to adapt and to resist a new agent.

But resistance will still develop eventually. Ironically, the most intractable infections are acquired by patients in hospitals. These "nosocomial" diseases—*nosocomium* being a Greek word for hospital—develop most readily in settings that are dense with antibiotics. In effect the modern hospital is a focal point of bacterial evolution. Here, the microbes face the most secret weapons of the medical-care army, the newest, most penetrating "magic bullets"—and in time "learn" to deal with them.

But ordinary people such as you and I walking into the doctor's office are as much to blame as anyone for the rise of resistant microbes. It is we who, throughout the 1950s and 1960s, and to a lesser extent thereafter, have pressured doctors to give us antibiotics for ordinary colds, stomach viruses, and flu—viral conditions for which antibiotics are useless. Since all of us are constantly colonized by bacteria, including some that in larger numbers cause illness, every time we take a course of penicillin or erythromycin we don't need, we turn our own bodies into little laboratories for the breeding of resistant germs. Widespread feeding of antibiotics to livestock exacerbates the problem.

Because restrictions on the sale of antibiotics are much looser in the developing world, where the drugs are often sold over the counter, the development of resistance has been a greater problem there. American men and women serving in the Gulf War, for example, contracted bacterial forms of diarrhea that proved resistant to a distressingly wide range of antibiotics. And the more resistance there is, the more money pharmaceutical companies have to invest in new antibiotic research, money that they then feel they have to recoup—as well as gaining substantial profit—by charging very high prices for the very newest drugs. Centoxin, a new agent for resistant septic shock—a dire, life-threatening cardiovascular collapse caused by bacteria spread in hospitals—is made through the latest techniques of biotechnology. It works very well, and it clearly saves lives. But it costs $3,800 a dose.

Jarrow, in Newcastle in the northeast of England, is a community of working people that has experienced in microcosm the cycle of success and failure of antibiotics throughout the developed world. George Grant and David Gregory have been in the general practice of medicine there for more than four decades—most of that time together—and Dr. Grant can in addition draw on his physician father's experience before him. During the 1930s severe unemployment—with no unemployment benefits—produced a type of poverty that repeated nineteenth-century conditions and so invited infectious disease, with inadequate medical care that few of the poor could afford anyway. Grant recalls that in the immediate postwar period, Jarrow had the highest rate of tuberculosis in Britain, and he vividly remembers the impact of the first use of streptomycin.

One of his patients, Mary Harding, was a young woman married a year, with a new baby, when she was hospitalized with "a particularly virulent, bad form of tuberculosis," as Grant reminded her forty years later. "You were very ill, and practically everybody who had that condition died—until 1950, when this wonder drug, streptomycin, was invented. And you had streptomycin." Mary Harding had an injection of streptomycin every day for 150 days. "After four injections, I felt really . . . well, alive. Once I started on that streptomycin, I could've come home if they would've let me." Dr. Grant had been taught as a medical student that nobody recovered from such a virulent case of tuberculosis. But he and her other physicians had been alert enough to give Mary Harding this brand-new agent, streptomycin, and four decades later he was chatting with her about her grandchildren.

To Grant, it was "even more dramatic to me than the invention of penicillin, which had preceded it, because this was a chronic condition . . . and it was marvelous." But by 1955 tuberculosis had become resistant to streptomycin, so that doses had to be increased to levels that could cause deafness. Combination drug regimens began to be used, and soon streptomycin was replaced by a new, two-drug treatment program. Drug-company scientists were already caught up in their race against bacterial evolution, and by the 1960s antibiotics had created a multibillion-dollar market worldwide.

Marjorie Jobling, a patient of Dr. Gregory's, faced in 1989, when in her forties, a situation not very different from what Mary Harding had faced when Jobling was only a baby. She had suffered from asthma for many years when she developed a severe chest ailment, not in itself life-threatening. "Asthmatics do tend to develop chest infections. We went to see her on a call, and she was pretty ill, but she clearly had an infection. So I put her on amoxycillin, which is a standard broad-spectrum penicillin, and that didn't seem to work. So I changed it to erythromycin, which is the usual treatment for less typical infections causing pneumonia, and it's almost guaranteed to clear them up. But in fact that didn't work either."

Jobling continued to decline for three weeks, and eventually was sleepless and hallucinating for eight days. She was hospitalized, where the same two drugs were tried again without success. "They put her on a very old antibiotic that's been around a long time—

chloramphenicol—which is considered rather dangerous. It can produce some blood side effects." These can be devastating, but fortunately they did not occur, and the drug cured Marjorie Jobling's pneumonia.

Dr. Grant and Dr. Gregory struggle constantly, in general practice, to keep abreast of the restless bacterial tide. At the same time they must negotiate the shoals of drug-company marketing, with its confusing array of "me too" drugs—drugs with the same effects but different names—and with high-pressure sales techniques that sometimes verge on bribery. Drug companies in the United States, for example, spend thousands of dollars per doctor per year to bring their message to practitioners. Yet Spanish physicians prescribe twice as many antibiotics as Americans, and Germany has been called "the last Garden of Eden" for the drug companies. Concerns about this illogical variation have led Drs. Grant and Gregory to serve on an international panel trying to rationalize prescribing. Given the many pressures from patients, drug-company representatives, and even scientists enthusiastic about their latest discoveries, a doctor in practice must have not only good judgment but great strength of character to adjust the prescribing regimen in a way that is truly and exclusively best for the patient—especially in the many cases where no one is really sure what the best regimen is.

Antibiotics, important as they have been, are only one category of drugs. Others are painkillers, anticancer drugs, heart drugs, and blood pressure drugs, to name just a few. Each without exception raises the red flag of risk to one degree or another, because none has a perfectly focused range of effects. That is why every prescription is in fact a balancing of risks. In the case of cancer drugs, a process almost analogous to bacterial evolution goes on in the body as susceptible tumor cells fall by the wayside and resistant ones come to the fore. Even when they are successful they have a wide range of unwanted effects. Cancer is essentially runaway cell growth. Drugs that work interfere with the production of new cells, which means they prevent new cells from forming in normal organs too. Thus the devastating effects they have on blood cells, on hair growth, and on the lining of the gut. In a sad irony, many of them—for example, cyclophosphamide and nitrogen mustard—are to some degree cancer-causing agents themselves.

But this classification by purpose—heart drugs, tumor drugs— is too crude for physicians and scientists, who must know in addition the kind of chemical structure a drug has. Analysis of this structure will eventually lead to an understanding of how the drug works, and then to the rational crafting of new and even more useful molecules. One such category is the steroids, a group of molecules with tremendous biological importance.

Among the naturally occurring steroids are the main sex hormones of women and men, estrogen and testosterone; the pregnancy hormone progesterone; and the "fight or flight" stress hormone cortisol. All are more or less flat molecules made up of four rings and consisting mostly of carbon. They vary in function as atoms of carbon, oxygen, and hydrogen are added to or removed from the four-ring lattice. In size these molecules are middling, far larger than a molecule of table salt but tiny compared to proteins like insulin. The body's own steroids are all made from cholesterol—in excess a dangerous substance, but at lower levels essential for body functioning.

Artificial steroids now number in the thousands, but in the late 1940s techniques of making them were just being worked out. Understanding of their structure came mainly from study of the adrenal glands, which produce the stress hormone cortisol. Physicians and scientists at the Mayo Clinic in Rochester, Minnesota, managed to synthesize cortisone, a modified form of the adrenal glands' own hormone. This manufactured agent proved to combat inflammation, just as the natural hormone does. When they gave it to patients with rheumatoid arthritis, a crippling, excruciatingly painful condition, some who had been confined to their beds in contorted positions for years were able to flex their limbs again. A Nobel Prize for some of the scientists in 1950 recognized this series of accomplishments.

Here, apparently, was a miracle drug that worked not against an infectious microbe but against a derangement of the body's own processes. Unfortunately the effects of cortisone on arthritis were not permanent, but a bridge had been crossed into a scientific region full of new possibilities. The lesson was not lost on the pharmaceutical industry, where many companies geared up for turning out new steroid molecules. Powerful new ones were effective in inflammation, head injury, and treatment of disorders of the adrenal glands, such as the illness of James Nelson.

But chemical mastery of this family of molecules had enormous implications for other body systems—the ones in each sex that control reproduction. Drugs with potential for the treatment of infertility, lack of sexual desire, menstrual disorders, and problems of pregnancy were being developed. One of the earliest of these was actually synthesized in Britain in 1938 by Charles Dodds, and slowly gained currency as a treatment for women who had trouble maintaining a pregnancy. There was a plausible theory behind it: the drug, diethylstilbestrol, or DES, was a synthetic estrogen, and estrogen was one of the main hormones of pregnancy. There were also some very poor, uncontrolled studies at the time—standards of medical research were then much lower—that seemed to show that it worked.

In time, controlled studies showed that DES did not work, but by then millions of normal women had been given the drug during pregnancy just on the thought that it might be helpful. Tragically, a very small proportion of the girls those women gave birth to—between one in ten thousand and one in a thousand of those exposed to the drug—grew up to develop a previously rare and often deadly cancer of the vagina. At best these women were forced, when in their teens or twenties, to choose between their reproductive organs and their lives, since only radical surgery had a chance of saving them. Fortunately they have so far only numbered in the hundreds, and the drug is no longer in use. Early reports of disorders, including testicular cancer, afflicting the *sons* of women given DES in pregnancy, have not been confirmed. Candice Tedeschi, a nurse-practitioner at the Long Island Jewish Hospital in New York, runs a clinic devoted to DES victims. She has tried to survey all known DES exposure and its consequences, and she knows the dangers as well as anyone. Yet she speaks in a surprisingly balanced way about them:

> We don't call it the practice of medicine for nothing. It *is* practice. We are human, we are not perfect, we make mistakes. And this mistake of DES was a combination mistake, between the drug companies and the medical profession, so blindly accepting this drug and giving it so widely. Here on the East Coast they gave this drug to almost everybody. I have doctors here who gave it to almost every single pregnant woman who walked in—not because they had any particular problem, but to make normal pregnancies more normal.

Few people would suggest that we wait twenty or more years to see the ultimate results of a new drug before using it. But this drug was a needless and useless one. Together with thalidomide—a nonstereoid tranquilizer that in the 1960s caused severe birth defects when given to pregnant women to help with morning sickness—the artificial estrogen DES had the effect of changing drastically the way physicians and scientists prescribe drugs for pregnant women.

But by far the most important reproductive steroids—indeed, the most momentous pharmacological discoveries of the 1950s—were the agents that had the power to prevent unwanted births. These oral contraceptives, mostly steroids or molecules resembling steroids, began to provide women and their partners with decisive choice about when to conceive. Although like all drugs they had a down side—increasing the risk of stroke, for example—there is no doubt that the formulations used today are remarkably safe and effective when properly prescribed and used.

However, these drugs had another dimension: a broad and strained interface with society. Vigorous opposition from the Catholic church and some other religious groups threatened the whole concept of artificial birth control. As current director Edouard Sakiz recalls it, Roussel-Uclaf had been well positioned scientifically and organizationally to make a major contribution to this "classical" period of birth control drugs, partly because of its experience with steroids. But the then-director, Sakiz's boss at the

time, frustrated his efforts completely because of religious opposition to birth control. For perhaps the first time, new drug development was being influenced not just by medical and scientific
considerations but by powerful currents of culture (although even
Salvarsan had had its opponents, who thought treating syphilis
would encourage sexual license). Sakiz always remembered—and
regretted—this lost opportunity, and when he took over as head
of the company he promised himself that future chances like it
would not be passed up.

By the 1970s an intensely creative physician-scientist, Etienne-
Emile Baulieu, was involved in steroid hormone studies at the
French national medical research institute, and had worked out
some very fundamental facts of how steroids affect cells. Georges
Teutsch and other scientists at Roussel, like Ehrlich in an earlier
èra, were generating thousands upon thousands of compounds in
the hope of finding active and safe new agents. Baulieu collabo-
rated with them in an attempt to make a safe and effective analogue
of progesterone, the hormone that promotes fertility and helps
maintain pregnancy. The result of this work was a new molecule
that blocked progesterone powerfully. Compounds at the company
labs were given the RU tag, for Roussel-Uclaf, and a number; this
one, the 38,486th compound tested, was designated RU 38,486—
for short, RU 486.

RU 486 was soon shown safe in monkey studies, and then was
shown effective in bringing an early end to pregnancy in nine of
eleven women who requested a first-trimester abortion. By 1991,
a little over a decade after research had created the new molecule,
somewhere around a hundred thousand women in France alone
had received the drug, in combination with a well-known agent
called a prostaglandin, given two days later. This treatment had
proved very safe, with only 3 per 100 experiencing unsuccessful
or incomplete abortion (easily completed with surgery) and less
than 1 percent excessive bleeding. All were easily treated with
other methods. This rate of success compares very favorably with
that of the far more onerous procedure of surgical abortion.

By 1988 gynecologists, family planners, and women generally
were hailing RU 486 as an enormous medical advance, in effect a

magic bullet for early unwanted pregnancy. But the company received hundreds of letters from antiabortion groups and individuals who considered the drug a "death pill." Some would later compare Etienne-Emile Baulieu—by then a member of the extremely prestigious National Academy of Sciences of the United States and an obvious candidate for a Nobel Prize—to Adolf Hitler. Threats of boycott of all the company's drugs, some vastly more important commercially than RU 486, led Roussel to withdraw the drug from the French market in late 1988.

But as luck would have it, the World Congress of Obstetrics and Gynecology was meeting in Rio de Janeiro at the time, and Baulieu was speaking there. The company soon received a petition bearing the signatures of hundreds of these experts and practitioners in reproductive medicine threatening a boycott of their own, and demanding that the drug be released again. Those who signed included many who stood to lose income if surgical abortion were to be replaced by a drug. On account of the French government's financial interest in the company, Claude Evin, the health minister of France, became involved. He soon put an end to Roussel's indecision, and ordered the drug back on the market, threatening among other things to give the patent away. He justified his decision by saying he "could not permit the abortion debate to deprive women of a product that represents medical progress. From the moment government approval for the drug was granted, RU 486 became the moral property of women, not just the property of the drug company."

Baulieu, who often says, "I am a medical doctor who does science," fully agreed, and he has interrupted much of his science to be an advocate for the drug. He recalls his early, impressionable days in medicine when—at the age of eighteen or nineteen—the suffering of patients affected him permanently. He describes the desperate situation he saw in India, where population explosion produced widespread disease and death in childhood. And he rarely fails to mention the two hundred thousand deaths a year worldwide—"one every three minutes"—of women who have suffered botched abortions. The father of three and grandfather of seven, he would like to see unwanted birth stopped not in spite of his love for children but in part because of it. Largely due to his leadership, France, a Catholic country with a potentially vigorous opposition and a long medical tradition strongly favoring motherhood, has become the undisputed world leader in the medical termination of unwanted pregnancy. Britain lags behind but is moving, while the United States has not yet awakened from its slumber.

The French do not consider abortion a great idea; like pro-choice people throughout the world, they consider it the lesser of two evils. Mme. Aubeny, an experienced nurse who directs a clinic in Paris, has given RU 486 to hundreds of women. She too has had her early impressions. "I remember one of the first times I ever came in the hospital. I saw a twenty-year-old woman die from a failed abortion. And a little later there was a thirty-five-year-old who also died, very painfully, from septicemia, leaving five children. These are things you never forget, and never want to see again."

She reflects too on a harsh and inescapable historical reality. "Women have always wanted, since earliest times, to use medicine to produce an abortion. What pills and potions they've taken in this hope! And now at last their wish has come true. We have a drug that can trigger an abortion. But there is another aspect to it that I believe is moral. It's giving back to women some control over their own bodies. In effect, they decide to have an abortion, and *they* supervise it. It's no longer the doctor, the technician, or the surgeon who takes this step. Morally, that's important. It's not a miracle pill; on the contrary, it's a pill that gives great responsibility." As Claude Evin had put it, it is "la propriété morale des femmes françaises"—the moral property of French women.

We could scarcely have a better demonstration of the fact that medical science does not exist in a social vacuum, but on the contrary is stimulated, buffeted, and sometimes blocked by what anthropologists call the "social construction" of scientific advances—a fancy way of referring to what people in a culture collectively think the advance means. RU 486 is now licensed and being used in Scandinavia, Britain, China, and elsewhere, but it is not even permitted to be *tested* for pregnancy termination in the

United States, because of the well-organized and vocal antiabortion minority in this country. This minority could destroy the market of any pharmaceutical firm in America that even begins to test it. Although states such as New York and California have been trying to circumvent these obstacles, the present government in Washington is highly unlikely to be of any help.

Tragically, this has implications far beyond the abortion issue. As Baulieu points out, the ideal fate of a new drug is to take advantage of multiple targets and uses of same molecule. The very problem of unwanted effects of a powerful agent—the fact that it goes to various cells and combines with different receptors—also provides an enormous opportunity. The steroid hormone system that Baulieu has spent his life studying makes it possible for RU 486 to be used in a number of different medical settings. Not only does it have other obstetric uses—promoting expulsion of an already dead fetus that is endangering the mother, for example, and stimulating labor so that a woman who is past term can give birth to a normal baby. It is being tested in Montpellier, in the south of France, as a treatment for breast cancer, and it shows great promise. Physicians in Holland and elsewhere are testing it against certain brain tumors that are promoted by progesterone. And in Finland, researchers are experimenting with it as a conventional contraceptive.

Even in the United States, some research teams have gotten quietly into the act, testing the drug in glaucoma and advanced breast cancer. But the most successful American test so far has been for the illness that James Nelson had—Cushing's syndrome. That is because RU 486 blocks not only progesterone receptors but, in higher doses, receptors for cortisol, the body hormone that Mr. Nelson had in devastating excess. RU 486 *is*, by another name, mifepristone, the drug that Mr. Nelson got from Dr. Nieman in an experimental program at the National Institutes of Health in Washington, and the drug that in all likelihood saved his life.

Although the "magic bullet" concept originated with Ehrlich, the focus on microbes as a singular cause of infectious disease preceded him by several decades. At that time, it was a new notion. One of the most dominant ideas in nineteenth-century medicine had been that *social* conditions foster disease. Hygienists, as they were called—today we would call them public health workers— repeatedly showed that people living in bad social and economic conditions were much more vulnerable to the great infectious scourges that still assaulted the modern world. And "bad" in the nineteenth century meant really *bad*. Millions in Europe (including Britain) and the United States lived in overcrowded conditions without effective toilets, running water, or fresh air, and ate food from unsupervised markets that were frequently contaminated. In the United States dreadful conditions were continually renewed by vast waves of immigration from a dismally overcrowded Europe. Although the notion of microscopic creatures causing disease had been discussed for a long time, it was still considered fanciful, and many thoughtful people who looked at the statistics saw strong evidence that most disease was caused by poverty and the social life tied to it.

Their work was known as the sanitary movement in Britain and the social hygiene movement on the Continent, and they believed that disease would never be effectively combated without great changes in society. Rudolph Virchow of Vienna is known to physicians as the "father of pathology" and one of the greatest of all medical scientists. But as we saw in the last chapter, he was also an extremely active social hygienist throughout his life, and even supported the revolutions of 1848 because he believed it his duty as a doctor to change the social conditions that cause disease. "Don't we see," he wrote, "that epidemics everywhere point to deficiencies of society?"

Half a century later, even after the dawn of modern drug research, the great Russian playwright Anton Chekhov—who was also a physician, calling medicine his wife and literature his mistress—did a health survey of the island of Sakhalin off Siberia, where convicts and their families lived under dismal conditions. By then surveys like it were fairly common, although usually closer to home. Chekhov saw the Sakhalin survey as discharging his "debt to medicine," in other words, as part of the responsibility of a doctor. In three months he interviewed almost everyone on the island, and drew a conclusion: servitude, whippings, alcohol abuse, prostitution, and poverty combined to produce inevitable disease. The viewpoint of Virchow still seemed valid to Chekhov at the dawn of the twentieth century.

But between Virchow's youthful activism and Chekhov's principled voyage there intervened half a century of changing medical thought. Pasteur established the germ theory—ancient but not accepted—on a firm scientific foundation. Claude Bernard, also in France, founded the field of experimental physiology as a testing ground for medical theory. And Virchow himself, in his role as a clinical and portmortem pathologist, promoted the concept of disease entities—systematically known processes that could be clearly identified from their paths of destruction in the body. These three currents of thought flowed together in the ideas of Robert Koch, a younger German contemporary of Virchow, who devised a paradigm for the interpretation of disease. In this method, a microscopic organism had to be identified, then located in the diseased organs, and finally shown to be capable of causing the disease in an experimental animal. What had been seen a few decades earlier as a complex result of social, economic, and cultural conditions was now seen as an attack by a singular microbe—one type for each disease, strong but not invincible.

The stage was set for Paul Ehrlich, working on syphilis, to imagine his silver bullet. No longer was it necessary to moralize about prostitution and promiscuity, as the religious branch of the sanitary movement eagerly did, or to point out how poverty and middle-class marital customs, such as men using prostitutes as a sexual outlet, contributed to the disease's spread. Now there was a new approach: magic bullet against nefarious microbe. It was fine as far as it went—and we have already seen something of both its success and its limitations. But more important than side effects, more important even than the evolution of resistance is an indirect result of the magic-bullet viewpoint: the neglect of all the conditions that make life easy for the microbe, and that weaken the body's stance against invasion.

These are the same social and economic conditions Virchow had

understood during the revolutions of 1848. While Ehrlich was inch-
ing his way toward Salvarsan at the turn of the century, Chekhov
was dying of tuberculosis. He knew quite well that among his
fellow sufferers were a disproportionate number of the poor, and
he established a sanatorium for their care before he died. But what
he could not have foreseen was that effective treatment would
elude physicians for another half-century, and that during that
time—between 1900 and 1950—tuberculosis would decline enormously because of improving social conditions. When George
Grant talks about his physician father in Jarrow, Scotland, battling
this same disease in the depths of the 1930s depression, he does
not mention that social conditions had been much worse in earlier
decades; that TB had already been enormously reduced; and that
vast numbers of lives had been saved and would continue to be
saved, by social, not medical, intervention. Today TB is rising again
fast, for many of the same reasons, especially among our poorest
communities.

What had always been true of infectious disease was also increasingly true of other, newer diseases—like the ones we saw the
young doctors at Johns Hopkins struggling against. Heart attack,
stroke, chronic lung disease, and several major cancers rose dramatically in our century, and they have proved to be more common
in the poor. Poverty today brings with it lack of access to timely
medical care, as well as abuse of alcohol, cigarettes, street drugs,
and food, not to mention prostitution and violence—all currently
major routes to death among the poor. Yet ironically the Hopkins
doctors, and their patients as well, are still burdened by the "one
disease, one microbe" magic-bullet approach to treatment. The
quick fix that was insufficient for infectious disease does not even
begin to be appropriate for chronic disease of the sort we have
today. The social conditions that helped cause the nineteenth-
century scourges are at least equally implicated in our own twentieth-century ones. The Harlam study showed this, while attrib-
uting half the excess mortality to conventional causes like heart
disease. As for East Baltimore, a 1991 study showed that blacks
there have twice the rate of blindness that whites have—much of
it preventable with timely care. And that is why Rev. Tuggle may

be making more headway against them from his pulpit or in the basement of his church than the Hopkins doctors do in their high-tech hospital.

Baulieu himself, for whom Ehrlich is a hero, says in his charmingly accented English, "I don't like very much the word 'magic bullet,' in fact. Number one, I don't like 'bullet,' because I'm rather pacifist. And number two, 'magic'—I don't like 'magic.' Because what we are doing in fact is, in humanistic terms, a rational approach of nature. And there is no space for magic." When he thinks about RU 486, he does not imagine a quick fix, not least because pregnancy is not a disease. Instead, his mind is on women who bleed to death in botched abortions—one every three minutes—and on the unwanted, starving children he saw in India. He knows that the culture of poverty is partly responsible for these things, but he sees no point in sermonizing to women about sex, especially ones who are already pregnant. So he invented not a magic bullet, but a tool for women to use right now—a stopgap measure in the war against botched abortions, until all people are prudent, until the world becomes a substantially better place.

Few anywhere in the world today doubt the power of the profit motive in unleashing human energies, and that applies to drug development as much as to anything else. It is very unlikely that a government sponsored steroid hormone research program could produce and screen 38,486 molecules—the number screened by Roussel—in search of a few effective ones. The billions that drug companies glean from the world market buy some expensive lunches, to be sure. But they also pay the salaries of thousands of scientists and the upkeep of their laboratories. Many of these scientists have discovered extremely valuable drugs, and some, like Gertrude Elion, have won the Nobel Prize for truly exceptional contributions—in her case, for work on anticancer drugs. Government cannot support all the needed research on drugs, and the annual budget of the private sector is several times that of the entire National Institutes of Health and other public research-funding agencies. We cannot move forward in this kind of research without the profit motive—the greed, if you like—of investors in pharmaceutical firms around the world.

But as we accept this necessity, we must also realize that it carries risks. Candice Tedeschi, who has spent many years identifying and caring for the tragic victims of DES, says poignantly, "I don't want to come across negative against drugs . . . Drugs are wonderful things that we need desperately in our world, to help us have long, healthy, productive lives. But somewhere we have to have some sort of control over, *Is the drug doing more good than it's doing harm?*" A large proportion of the most frequently prescribed drugs for the elderly, prime consumers of drugs, are misprescribed; either they should not be given for the condition in question or there are better drugs or other treatments for the same problem. According to Dr. Sidney Wolfe, who represents a Washington public interest group that evaluates drugs for consumers, a large proportion are dangerous; 104 of the 287 most frequently prescribed drugs for people over sixty-five are deemed by his assessment to be too dangerous for them to use. Many more are of questionable value, or duplicate at greater expense the effects of older drugs.

The avidity of drug-company salespeople, the aggressiveness of their advertising, and the non-public-spirited nature of their activities exacerbate misprescribing, and in some countries with over-the-counter sales they bypass physicians altogether. The thousands of dollars, pounds, francs, or yen spent by the firms every year to bring their at best biased message to each physician make objective medical decision-making difficult. In a fascinating study published in the *Annals of Internal Medicine* in June 1992, Dr. Michael Wilkes and his colleagues at UCLA examined 109 full-page pharmaceutical advertisements in the leading U.S. medical journals. The ads were sent to more than one hundred medical scientists and more than fifty pharmacists, all highly experienced in evaluating research in the specialty of the ad. Pharmaceutical advertising in general is far more accurate than nonmedical advertising, yet more than half the ads were judged by at least two out of three reviewers to be misleading enough so that they should have been rejected outright by the journal or accepted only after major revision. Although the FDA has published standards for such advertising, they are very difficult to enforce, and more than 90 percent of the ads were judged by reviewers to violate those standards in at least one minor or major way. Misprescribing—including unnecessary prescribing and the failure to use generic substitutes—is a major factor in the widely recognized waste of health-care funds. And today in the United States a network of illegal pharmacies has grown up around AIDS victims, creating a black market in useless and dangerous illegal drugs. In Spain and elsewhere some pharmacists, dismayed by bloated drug-company claims, have turned in frustration to completely untested and potentially harmful herbal remedies. While some useful drugs may yet arise from ancient nostrums (as they have in the past), others will no doubt prove harmful. Just as with commercial drugs, only scientific research can determine which is which. Any rational plan for health care at the national level has to include attempts to reduce all this uncertainty and waste.

Some of our expectations as consumers are exaggerated and irrational as well. People demand more stringent control on manufactured drugs; yet they also go to herbalists seeking substances subject to no standards of purity and never properly tested at all. (One such seemingly harmless "natural" substance, tryptophan, which caused a small epidemic of serious muscle disease because of impurities in the preparation, was sold over-the-counter in health-food stores.) People demand that no new drugs be marketed unless proven conclusively to be both useful and safe; yet the AIDS patients' movement in the United States—where new drug evaluation has long been more stringent than in Europe—requested and then essentially forced the FDA to release several major new drugs without leaving time for legally mandated testing. Ironically and sadly, the search for an AIDS vaccine is being held back by drug manufacturers' valid fears of lawsuits that may follow testing—placing the AIDS vaccine in a growing category of new or proposed drugs that are "orphaned" because public demands for drug safety have reached such an exaggerated and threatening pitch. Medicine cannot be all things to all people; we must decide for ourselves what risks we are willing to take in order to reap the potential benefits of drug development.

More important, perhaps, is the lulling effect of dream drugs. In the minds of many people, there are or soon will be magic bullets for every disease or complaint. This tragically mistaken belief produces a half-conscious state of mind in which we cease to think about our own responsibility. So we blithely go on with the behaviors and habits that bring disease on or make it worse. In East Africa there is a myth that AIDS can now be cured—a myth apparently centered on an experimental and untested drug called Kemron, developed in Kenya. Millions of people will contract the virus and die because they are soothed by this belief. But before we relegate this kind of effect to places like Africa, consider the almost identical process we in the West go through ourselves.

We have heard that in the last few years new drugs have appeared that can reverse the atherosclerosis—fatty thickening—that clogs the arteries and leads to heart attacks or stroke. So we reach for the extra cream puff or the "juicy" steak with subconscious confidence that whatever harm it may do to us can be fixed later on. We have heard, too, that the new gene technology methods will revolutionize cancer treatment, so millions of us go on smoking with the quaint tacit assumption that lung cancer will be curable by the time we get it. These mental processes are as primitive as any in Africa, and far less excusable, since we have access to good information that most Africans do not have.

In a sense we may need to reverse in part the process we went through in the second half of the nineteenth century, when the hygiene movement was replaced by the aggressive modern focus on microbes. This was before the rise of heart disease, stroke, and cancer as the greatest killers. Back then, it seemed so simple: each major deadly disease had its very own microbe-cause; identify it, find its weak point, destroy it—end of disease. But of the most dangerous ailments in the industrial world today, only AIDS has a good chance of one day being preventable by vaccine (and not soon); none of these illnesses has a good chance of a pharmacological cure. The drugs that work are messy, dangerous, and only partly effective.

Yet we can do things now that would reduce mortality from these major killers by millions of deaths a year—or at a minimum postpone those deaths until very old ages. And most of our options have to do with social conditions and cultural habits. In chapter 2 we saw how the social conditions of East Baltimore, including lack of access to timely medical care, foster advanced and incurable chronic illnesses. But is this really like the fostering of infectious scourges by nineteenth-century poverty through malnutrition and lack of sanitation?

In a word, yes. Self-abusive habits target human vulnerability, just as surely as microbes do. The vulnerability of the poor has three separate components. The first is lack of information. But doesn't everyone know that cigarettes are coffin nails? Yes, but as advertisers are well aware, information must sink in; it must be repeated again and again in different contexts, and be supported by expert advice and word of mouth. That is why more-educated people are less likely to be smokers and why doctors and nurses have very low rates of the habit. Poor people are exposed to far more disinformation about cigarettes, through advertising and word of mouth, than to information. And the truth is not reinforced by the milieu. Similar arguments can be made about alcohol, cocaine, heroin, dangerous foods with high levels of animal fat, even high-risk sex.

The second component of vulnerability is the tremendous incentive that draws people toward these habits and addictions. Consider how well-meaning advice must strike impoverished people: *You mean, in the midst of all this misery, you want me to give up the one thing I really enjoy? You must be kidding.* Healthy pleasures, like gym workouts and health food, and creature comforts like an upscale car and a house in a safe neighborhood, cost money that these people do not have. So they turn to the pleasures they *can* afford, and for a time at least they really do enjoy them.

Finally, all this is compounded by the lack of disincentives, the most tragic vulnerability of all. The concept that you may be sick ten or twenty years from now if you don't stop your X-Y-Z is fine for those who can envision a decent future. But for people who know that they have no future—whose future is bound to be filled with the same misery as the present—there is no very good reason to make a serious effort to get to it. It is this lack of hope that may be the most damaging social condition of all. Add to this the exuberant heedlessness of youth, and the damage is clearly going to be greatest for the young.

So the solutions of the social hygienists of the mid-1800s are still valid today. As Leon Eisenberg, head of the department of social medicine and health policy at the Harvard Medical School, has asked, "Rudolf Virchow, where are you now that we really need you?" And although dangerous habits are more common among the poor, the rich too indulge in them, and the culture as a whole encourages many of them. As was true in the nineteenth century, and as Virchow said then, disease points to "deficiencies of society." Behavioral scientists, epidemiologists, teachers, and a few enlightened politicians, journalists, and clergy are the social hygienists of the future. And as we attack the diseases of the present and future, our slogan could well be "No magic bullet."

FOUR

CONCEIVING THE FUTURE

IN ALDOUS HUXLEY'S novel *Brave New World*, readers of the 1930s were treated to an unsettling vision of the future. The story opens with a tour of the Central London Hatchery and Conditioning Centre, its entrance graced with the motto of the World State: "Community, Identity, Stability." We visit the Fertilizing Room, the Bottling Room, the Social Predestination Room. We hear the director of the Centre discourse a bit on the difficulty of making a large enough number of genetically identical human beings. This difficulty stands in the way of adequate production of lower orders of individuals—Gammas, Deltas, and Epsilons—destined for various kinds of menial labor. Only Alphas are permitted to remain unique. In the Hatchery the entire nine months of human gestation takes place in test tubes, and along the way the fetuses are treated with chemicals that will help match them to their destiny in society. After birth, Pavlovian methods of conditioning will continue the shaping process. The human products that emerge at the end not only will be suited to their fated roles in life; they will be positively terrified of departing from those roles. Most amazing of all, they will be happy. Scientific control of human destiny will be total.

It is a chilling vision of a grotesquely overorganized future, yet if Huxley were alive today he might feel we are well on our way to it. At this writing the first "test-tube babies" are thirteen years old. Although only the very first steps of development can take place outside the womb, and although no one so far has tampered with their destiny by altering those steps, thousands of human beings have begun life "in glass." Some eggs, whether in test tubes or in wombs, have been fertilized by sperm taken from Nobel laureates and other genetic fathers picked with exquisite care. Wombs can be rented, for a price, by those with cash on hand; and frequently their genes travel down the social scale to a womb whose much poorer owner needs the same cash. In addition, at least the last third of gestation can now take place outside the womb, in incubators brimming with up-to-the-moment life-support technology.

We do surgery on other fetuses to correct some of their defects, leaving them to finish gestation inside the womb. Still others we deem unsuitable for survival, and these we remove and dispose of. If a woman is carrying too many fetuses—quintuplets, say— we selectively kill some of them to save the others. Inadvertently at least we use alcohol and cocaine to damage some fetuses' brains, limiting their destiny, while others get carefully chosen vitamins and minerals, destining them in turn for better things. We are still far from bringing an egg along until it becomes a baby, injecting it with this or that to shape it to our visions, but the idea no longer seems like mere science fiction. Later in the growth process, years after birth, we use amphetamines to correct certain forms of behavior, in an effort to create a child who will do better in school. And some people use growth hormone, now manufactured in DNA factories with unprecedented ease, to stimulate growth in shorter children who are not at all deficient in the hormone. The idea is just to make them grow up taller.

Of all our budding accomplishments, the most remarkable is gene control. We are already deeply engaged in a technological revolution that matches the industrial revolution in importance.

The roughly 100,000 genes every human being has, each one a string of thousands of life-determining molecules, are being systematically mapped. Some of them have already been manufactured and stored in test tubes. Others have been experimentally altered in blood cells withdrawn, transformed, and returned to their owners. In animals, genes have been transformed within fertilized eggs, to be passed on from generation to generation, a permanent change in the biological heritage of the organism.

Medically, these methods will be far more important than the magic bullets used by past generations against microbes. Gene control will be our superweapon in the war against cancers, the most feared diseases of our time. Genetic disorders like sickle-cell anemia and cystic fibrosis—biochemical derangements that start at the outset of life with defective genes and proceed to destroy children and young adults slowly and painfully—will become truly manageable for the first time in history. Even diseases caused by microbes may be solved by gene control. The AIDS virus, to take an example, works its effects by invading the genetic machinery of human cells; so an important part of research on AIDS is attempting to understand and control that process. Even some drugs that have nothing directly to do with genes—the insulin needed by some diabetics, for instance—are already being manufactured in a purer form than ever through the same technology of gene control. Those who would stand in the way of this technology must be told: You are asking us to pay an enormous price in human suffering.

Yet such opponents exist, and their arguments have a certain degree of ethical and political legitimacy. Today we identify certain genetic errors in a man and a woman proposing to marry, and we advise them of their chances of having a child with the same or a worse defect. Tomorrow perhaps we will forbid them to marry, or even sterilize them. Today we detect certain abnormalities in the fetus partway through gestation, and we offer parents the option of an abortion. Could it be that tomorrow we will require one?

To those who find such scenarios implausible, consider: they are already done by law in China. Early fears about genetic mutants escaping from gene-control laboratories and wreaking havoc in the

biological balance of the world—soberly debated in the seventies
and eighties—have in the nineties become antiquated concerns.
But that is far from saying that serious abuses are unlikely, when
we are able to peer into and tinker with the basic machinery that
makes us what we are. So we cannot brush the fears aside. Yet
they must be balanced against the enormous good that is coming,
and will certainly continue to come, from gene-control technology.

Thalassemia, or Mediterranean anemia, is a serious disorder of
the blood. Hemolytic—blood-dissolving—is the appropriate medical adjective, since the essence of blood, the red cells, is relentlessly destroyed. As a result, the oxygen-carrying capacity of the
blood is severely compromised. Enervating fatigue, physical weakness, and lowered resistance to microbes are common. The child's
bone marrow—the blood-forming organ—works overtime to try
to resupply red cells, but it is a futile effort that further weakens
the child and compromises growth. Bones thin out and change
shape, so the look of the child's face becomes abnormal.

The liver and spleen swell massively; heart failure is common.
Doctors try to catch up with continual blood transfusions, but
these have the side effect of overloading the body with iron. Death
due to lowered resistance, heart failure, or iron overload occurs in
the teens, or at best in the twenties. I remember a young thalassemia patient in Boston whose constant hospital visits failed to
relieve his pain. He turned to street drugs, almost in self-defense;
it was the first time it occurred to me that drug abuse could be
logical. He died of organ damage from iron overload, at twenty.

The disease begins with a genetic error, so it runs in families,
and is much more likely in certain populations than in others.
Relatives of the victims, known as carriers, are partly resistant to
malaria; parasites, it turns out, need oxygen too, and the compromised red cells don't give them enough. So the worldwide
distribution of thalassemia follows the distribution of malaria. For
example, carriers make up 15 to 20 percent of the people of Vietnam
and Cambodia. But even places where malaria has been eradicated
continue to have high rates of thalassemia; it is easier—and inci-

dentally, less controversial—to outfox even a clever parasite than to alter the transmission of the genes.

But Dr. Antonio Cao is planning to outfox the genes too. He lives and practices medicine in Sardinia, a beautiful Mediterranean island burdened with thalassemia—one in seven people is a carrier, and until 1974 around a hundred babies were born with the disease each year. For a population of one and a half million, that was a burden. For the victims, it was a life taken away. Since malaria was no longer present on the island, having been eliminated by the early 1950s, there was no longer any advantage to being a carrier. Hence Dr. Cao's vision, "to overcome the problem of thalassemia in Sardinia":

> As treatment became more effective we faced a huge health problem. The cost for each child was enormous. We didn't have enough blood donors and we didn't have enough money. If I hadn't established an effective prevention program we would now have to treat an additional two thousand patients. This would be an impossible burden for this community.

Ironically, as doctors learned to chase red blood cell destruction with well-timed, frequent transfusions, prolonging children's lives, their very survival would have presented an insoluble problem. Even today Sardinia must import blood to care for the patients it has; yet there are only four or five new patients born a year now, and these well-cared-for children live well beyond the limit of age ten that was typical two decades ago. In other words, Cao has come close to his original goal of eliminating thalassemia from Sardinia, while greatly enhancing the lives of its remaining victims.

He did this not with a medical instrument or a drug but with a public health program and an institute of medical genetics, "the largest and best organized in Italy." As the architect of the program and a leader of the institute, the Ospedale Regionale delle Microcitemie, he has been able to combat the illness effectively. Television commercials urge Sardinians to donate blood—and while they are at it, to take a simple blood test that identifies carriers of thalassemia. Carriers married to other carriers—around one in fifty couples—are urged to come in for a test at the institute at nine or ten weeks of pregnancy. One in four pregnancies of such couples will be a fetus destined not to be a carrier but to have the full-blown disorder. Couples notified of this sad fact usually choose abortion.

From a hundred down to five cases a year: an impressive achievement. But it raises certain questions. For one, to those who think abortion is murder, Dr. Cao's solution is no more acceptable than killing a thalassemia-stricken child would be. For another, it would seem to be difficult to draw the line. Dr. Cao's *opesdale* tries to control not only thalassemia but cystic fibrosis, a genetically caused lung disease, and muscular dystrophy in similar ways. He modeled his program on efforts by Ashkenazic Jews in the United States to eliminate their particular genetic burden: Tay-Sachs disease, a devastating form of mental retardation that usually leads to death by age two.

But where do we stop? Do we also consider aborting carriers of these defects? In the case of thalassemia, that would eliminate those most resistant to a possible reintroduction of malaria in the future. How about a disorder like Huntington's disease, a dreadful assault on the nervous system but one that rarely starts before age thirty? How about the genetic form of Alzheimer's dementia— also dreadful, but emerging even later in life? How about susceptibilities, say, to heart disease or breast cancer, that may or may not lead to diseases? And how about minor problems like a tendency to obesity or a need to wear glasses? How far will we carry our ability to eliminate defects, our zeal for human perfection?

Some believe we have already carried it far enough. American critics within biology, such as Richard Lewontin and Jonathan Beckwith, both of Harvard University, have repeatedly sounded alarms about the dangers inherent in trying to improve human genetics. They point to the tragic history of this effort, called eugenics, especially in Germany under the Nazis. Forced sterilization of alleged mental defectives was only the mildest variety of their attempt to better the species. Legally sanctioned killing, not of fetuses but of adults, was another step, and then the concept of defectives was extended to embrace all Jews and Gypsies; killing these "biologically inferior" elements, together with their children, would supposedly purify the European race.

This is a well-known story. What is less well known is that eugenic laws preceded the Nazis in Germany, and that those laws in turn were modeled on American examples. Indiana became the first state to allow sterilization of the mentally ill as early as 1907. Two decades later, twenty-eight other states had followed suit. Fifteen thousand individuals had been sterilized—"unsexing" was another term—involuntarily by 1930. The attorney general of California, upholding its law in 1910, wrote:

Degeneracy means that certain areas of brain cells or nerve centers of the individual are more highly or imperfectly developed than the other brain cells, and this causes an unstable state of the nerve system, which may manifest itself in insanity, criminality, idiocy, sexual perversion, or inebriety . . .

He went on to say that "many of the confirmed inebriates, prostitutes, tramps, and criminals, as well as habitual paupers" belonged in this group eligible for legal castration.

Eugenic ideas became very prominent in the popular mind both in the United States and in Britain, where eugenics began. In this country waiting periods between the application for a marriage license and the wedding were imposed by law to give people time to reconsider genetically dubious matches. Fitter Families contests were held at state fairs in Kansas and elsewhere—a strange amalgam of medical assessment and sideshow, where people were tested, measured, and compared like livestock. IQ testing, developed during the First World War, began to be used mandatorily on prospective American immigrants, without such subtleties as ascertaining whether the subject spoke English, the language of the test. Leading American psychologists such as Lewis Terman and Robert Yerkes helped shape congressional legislation that kept out Jews, Italians, and other eugenic undesirables with "low" IQs. The resulting immigration quotas prevented hundreds of thousands, or possibly millions, of Jews in Nazi Europe from taking refuge in the United States.

In the Weimar Republic—pre-Nazi, democratic Germany—the spread of eugenic notions was also rapid. Two "scientific" journals on "racial hygiene" and "social biology" had begun publication shortly after the turn of the century, and books on the subject were read and discussed widely by the end of World War I. In 1920 a jurist and a psychiatrist, both well respected in Germany, published a book called *The Release and Destruction of Lives Devoid of Value*; it advocated not just sterilization but large-scale euthanasia for the improvement of the race. In 1923 a director of health in Zwickau tried to persuade the minister of the interior that the time was right for eugenic sterilization. "What we racial hygienists promote," he wrote in a letter, "is not at all new or unheard of. In a cultured nation of the first order, the United States of America, that which we strive toward was introduced and tested long ago."

The skeptical minister ordered a study, and was convinced by the resulting report on American sterilization laws; if America could do it, so could Germany. A decade later, after Hitler came to power, the "lives devoid of value" began to number in the millions. A decade after that, those millions were actually being destroyed.

What is important to grasp here is that every step in this process was viewed as stemming from and consistent with advances in medical science—"racial hygiene." Sober scientific institutes, weighty treatises, and technical journals all promoted race purification as a public health measure. It was not a coincidence that at the Auschwitz death camp a physician selected the small number of people in each trainload whom he considered fit enough to live and engage in slave labor for a time. The remaining majority had to be officially, medically certified as suitable for the gas chambers; each consignment of victims required a document that carried the signature of a physician.

So in addition to the universal human soul-searching inspired by these facts, medicine must undergo its own particular search. We must ask not just, *How could these things have happened?* but also, *How could medicine have become so perverted as to play such a central role?* And of course, we must ask whether medicine could be so perverted again.

For Baptist fundamentalists, Jehovah's Witnesses, and some others, the answer is that it is happening right now in all countries where abortion is routine. These are the kinds of people who compare Etienne-Emile Baulieu to Hitler, and who see routine abortion as mass murder. These people are in a small minority, much smaller than the "pro-life" contingent, and even they are not consistent in their beliefs; for example, they don't baptize or mourn when they have a late menstrual period, although these are often very early spontaneous abortions.

Still, one does not need to be an extremist to sense some analogy with Nazi "eugenics" when abortion is specifically used to eliminate "defectives"—lives, one might say, devoid of value. Not surprisingly perhaps, some of the most sensitive monitoring of this unsettling possibility is occurring today in Germany, where the experience of carrying and bearing a child has become intensively medicalized. In a number of countries, obstetricians have been sued for "wrongful life" by women who have borne abnormal babies and have felt that the doctor should have warned them so that they could have chosen abortion. One British obstetrician whose patient had a child with Down's syndrome, a form of mental retardation easily detected at ten weeks of pregnancy, was ordered by a court to pay £70,000 in damages for failing to recommend testing.

With precedents like this one, obstetricians everywhere understandably are growing edgy about allowing an abnormal pregnancy to continue. They monitor pregnancies closely and strongly urge their patients to undergo prenatal testing. Yet not all women respond well to so much technology. Just as in the 1970s women in many countries began to insist on increasingly natural childbirth, and got it, today in Germany a similar resistance is emerging in response to prenatal testing. In Bremen, an organization called CARA provides pregnant women with an alternative to the usual modern medicalized experience. Begun by women who are all health professionals, CARA is a shop-front counseling center where women are urged to view disability as a part of the normal variety of life.

Anne Waldschmidt, disabled from birth by a rare genetic disease, deeply fears the tyranny of perfect health:

> Medicine reflects our culture, and in a high technology society we have become concerned with perfection. As we strive for this perfection we seem to be less and less tolerant of imperfection. We are never going to wipe out birth defects, and technology is changing the experience of pregnancy.

Since she has been an adviser to the influential Green Party on genetic engineering and reproductive technologies, her words can perhaps someday alter policy. She says unequivocally: "Society should accept such things as thalassemia—otherwise where do you stop?" She sees prenatal selection as a more subtle continuation of the eugenic tradition of Germany's recent Nazi past. Health, as Waldschmidt puts it, can become "a totalitarian concept."

It is both moving and persuasive to see Germans, of all people, trying to draw a clear line in the shifting eugenic sand. And those who view their fears as greatly overblown would do well to review recent events in China. Two provinces, Gansu in the northwest and Liaoning in the northeast, promulgated compulsory sterilization laws. Three other provinces followed, and a national eugenics law has been under discussion for several years. Trends in China today are eerily similar to the popular spread and legal sanctioning of eugenics in the United States, Britain, and Europe during the early to mid twentieth century. In Gansu, Liaoning, and Sichuan, certain categories of individuals must undergo examinations before they are given permission to marry. If viewed as unfit, they are barred from marrying pending sterilization, and if they elude sterilization and begin a pregnancy, they can be required to have an abortion.

People subject to these laws include those with mental illnesses, mental retardation, and hereditary diseases. Sterilization is invoked if both potential spouses are retarded "at middle degree" or if one is retarded "at severe degree." If these laws are emulated at the national level—a step supported by many health officials and by the Chinese Association for the Handicapped—approximately 50 million physically or mentally handicapped people throughout China could be affected. Although an estimated 20 million of these people may actually have hereditary diseases, the majority acquired their handicaps through environmental insult, and therefore sterilization will be pointless for them.

Western scientists are agreed that the Chinese program is an extremely crude one, in addition to being unjust, but Chinese intellectuals who defend the program cite the ancient Confucian tradition that subordinates the individual to the good of society. They as well as health officials readily resort to language such as that used by Zhang Zhongjian, chief of the women-and-children's office in Liaoning province's health department: "The purpose of making the law and regulations is to raise the population quality and reduce the state's burden and family misfortunes"; or that of the national health minister, Chen Minzhang, who told a 1990 conference that the low quality of the population has become a "heavy millstone around our neck in the journey to catch up with international competition and modernize."

Clearly what is intended here is not very far from "racial hygiene." Thousands of compulsory sterilizations and an unknown number of mandatory abortions had already taken place within a year of the first law's enactment in Gansu province in November 1988. In time, if the national law is enacted, millions will be affected. As if to close the circle of similarity to the Nazi past, foreign critics have warned that these laws may be invoked especially against China's ethnic minorities in impoverished rural areas. Such minorities, who have received at best questionable treatment from the Chinese in the past, include Tibetans, Mongols, and Turkic minorities in Gansu province, as well as Koreans in Liaoning.

And another oppressed group that is not a minority—females— is also the target of selective abortion. This has happened not only in China, where the push for the one-child family has made having a son the first time all the more urgent, but even more so in some northern provinces of India, where prenatal diagnosis has been used surreptitiously for the sole purpose of determining sex, and vitually all girls are aborted in some samples of tested fetuses. These are parts of India that have traditions of extreme preference for males deeply embedded in the culture. But even in the United States and Britain, physicians providing prenatal diagnosis get the uneasy feeling at times that they are serving the goals of some parents who absolutely insist on having boys.

Meanwhile, in those same Western countries, the most costly and the most broadly organized initiative in the history of biomedical research has captured—captivated, really—many of the most talented minds who ever applied science to human welfare. James Watson, Water Gilbert, and Leroy Hood are only a few of the stellar scientists who have made leadership in this new program their top research priority. Their enthusiasm has caught fire with thousands of younger scientists, and with science funding administrators, who have made this program the closest thing in biology to "Big Science"—the blue-chip physics of massive particle accelerators and space stations.

The program in question is the Human Genome Project, and its goal is to identify and determine the chemical sequences of all the 100,000 or so genes that make each of us what we are. Many of those genes are being pursued individually—personally, one might almost say—by scientists who realize that they hold the keys to some of the tightest locks in the whole realm of human disease. An example is the gene for sickle-cell anemia, a more severe cousin of thalassemia, but one that overwhelmingly affects blacks, with pain that can make some youngsters wish for death; or the one for cystic fibrosis, the most widespread genetic syndrome affecting whites, with deadly, sticky lung secretions that gradually choke the life out of the young victim; or the at least equally critical genes that switch on or stifle the runaway cell growth that creates cancer.

But in parallel with this sort of specific gene-hunting, which quite understandably grabs headlines, the unsung common soldiers of the Human Genome Project slog away month after month decoding the whole, seemingly endless string of highly structured DNA that is triply coiled upon itself in the nucleus of every human cell. (Gilbert invites us to think of it as the information contained in a thousand thousand-page telephone books.) Along the way, in this tedious but necessary task, they will pick up on thousands of genes whose existence we now do not even suspect, suggesting new and possibly easy paths in biomedical science. A few such discoveries will no doubt produce a table-slapping "Aha!" reaction that matches a new, unexpected gene to an old and baffling disease. But for the most part the effort will just slowly but surely unravel the code, molecule by molecule and ultimately gene by gene.

The project is meant to be completed within two decades, but its reverberations will echo in medicine for many decades more. And their impact will certainly not be limited to such crude tactics as prenatal diagnosis followed by abortion. Through an elegant process called reverse genetics, sequenced genes are being followed through to the proteins they generate; where these are deficient or abnormal they will be augmented or replaced if possible. Protein functions that become apparent through this process will lead to new paths in rational drug design—and many new, effective drugs will then be found through old-fashioned methods. We will unlock such secrets as how to make replacement skin for people with severe burns and how to orchestrate reconnections in the severed spinal cord of a paraplegic—secrets that will start with genetic research but that in the application will have nothing directly to do with genes. Yet genes themselves will be delivered into patients—they already have been in limited ways, using carefully modified viruses as vehicles—and these genes will correct or replace defective ones in the owner's original collection.

And for those for whom abortion is not an option, but who want to abolish, say, muscular dystrophy from their families—from their children and grandchildren and further descendants forever—it will one day be possible to subject their fertilized eggs to "gene surgery." Such correction of a sequence in a gene, right in the fertilized egg, will decisively negate the harsh reality of the defect, which had stood as truth for perhaps hundreds of generations. What was a burden and an anguish through century after century will become a mere memory, and eventually not even the memory will remain.

But we will still have to sort out just what is being eliminated. Those who believe we need genetically caused physical handicaps to maintain the richness and variety of human life will probably always be a small minority. Even if we accept the main thrust of their argument, there will always and everywhere be environmental damage; acquired illnesses, chemical exposures, accidents, and violence will produce enough handicapped people—they, not patients with genetic flaws, make up most of the disabled today—to satisfy any philsopher's need for human variety. And looking back on the history of the conquest of disease, we find some observers of a philosophical bent decrying the effort to cure syphilis, on the grounds that such a cure would foster immorality; or obliquely admiring tuberculosis, because it appeared to be associated with aesthetic sensitivity. Perhaps we should not cure leprosy, because what sort of world would it be without lepers? There is no reason to privilege genetic disorders when assessing the philosophic value of imperfection; and conversely, if it is well to abolish acquired disability, it should also be well to abolish the genetic kind.

But the questions about where to draw the line will remain, and nowhere more strikingly than in the realm of behavior and intelligence, where passions run high in response to human variety, and where the greatest difficulties are encountered in defining disability. To take an example, the elimination of Down's syndrome fetuses following prenatal chromosomal diagnosis has become routine for women in their late thirties or older in a number of Western countries. Yet even though Down's syndrome produces mental retardation, some affected children function at quite a high level. There has even been a television series focusing on a teenage boy with Down's, and every episode teaches another touching lesson about this boy's human value to his family, friends, and schoolmates—not to mention himself. The issue is partly moot, since many babies with the syndrome will continue to be born to younger women who aren't routinely tested; but the philosophical questions remain, and are not trivial.

A different sort of question is raised by Huntington's disease, a devastating form of brain degeneration, but one that begins only in mid-life—in the thirties or forties. It destroyed the popular folksinger Woody Guthrie, but not before allowing him a rich and full creative life. In some cases the first symptoms to appear are psychiatric ones, so the syndrome proves the power of a simple genetic defect decisively to alter the human mind. It was also the first human gene of any kind to be linked to a part of a chromosome—a smallish region of the short arm of chromosome 4—using the new methods of molecular genetics. Within a few years of the gene's being located, scientists offered a diagnostic test. People who lost a parent to the disease had long known that they had a 50-50 chance of coming down with it. Now they could find out, yes or no—could plan for shorter lives, or for their deaths. Theoretically, it could even be done prenatally; and many people in these families will no doubt exercise their right to abort an affected fetus. But would we really have wanted Woody Guthrie, whose songs include "This Land Is Your Land" and "Daddy's Takin' Us to the Zoo Tomorrow"—not to have been born?

For Alzheimer's disease, the most widespread form of senility coming late in life, the parallel questions are even more nagging. There are genetic forms of the Alzheimer's type of senility, running in families, and some of these families appear to have an abnormal gene on chromosome 21. As with Huntington's disease, we can imagine wanting to know in advance if we are headed for Alzheimer's. Few things are feared more by older people today than having a wise old age turned into a mewling, doddering, tantrum-filled second infancy; than being robbed of memory itself, one of the things that most makes life—especially later life—worth living. But are we going to abort a fetus because it may become a demented old man after seventy years of perfectly normal life? Are we going to abort the *majority* of fetuses from all sorts of families, since the majority are likely to get the disease eventually, one way or another? Surely that would be carrying the quest for perfection too far.

But in contrast to Huntington's disease, much more is known about how Alzheimer's works. The affected brain has certain distinctive features under the microscope—plaques and tangles, they are called—and brain chemists have begun to figure out what those tiny but decisive abnormalities are made of. One defective protein found in the tangles, beta-amyloid, is also apparently made from a gene on chromosome 21. There are more details emerging, but the point is that year by year, experiment by experiment, scientists are slowly moving toward the goal of a complete understanding of this tragic illness—from the biochemical defect in the gene (not yet known), through the abnormal protein or proteins, to the changes in brain structure, to the loss of memory and self-control. Every step of this path will offer opportunities for thwarting the process of Alzheimer's—using as yet undiscovered drugs—once the path is properly traced and the process understood. Genetics will be perhaps the most crucial research tool, but the treatment may be conventional and far removed from the actual genes.

Still another genetic brain disorder, PKU, or phenylketonuria, begins its assault on the human mind within hours of birth. It is clearly controlled by the genes, yet it has been solved for a long time, long before any details of the location or structure of the gene were known. How this was done is an object lesson in the surprising solutions we can expect for genetic disorders. The disease got its name because of phenylketones, chemical products found in the victim's urine. Old-fashioned biochemistry had shown, long before the era of modern genetics, that these ketones came from excessive amounts of phenylalanine, an ordinary amino acid not only present in most proteins—in milk and many nuts, for example—but essential in human diet.

Elementary chemical reasoning led to the conclusion that victims of this genetic disease lacked a crucial enzyme—one of the large helper molecules that speed up the body's normal reactions. The normal enzyme missing here was one that helps convert the phenylalanine into certain neurotransmitters, hormones, and other products. Without it, some of those products can be made in other ways, but the phenylalanine eaten normally every day piles up in the brain until it begins to poison brain cells. Severe mental retardation seemed inevitable.

But the physicians of the 1950s did not decide to wait for the genetic revolution to repair or exclude the defective gene. They attacked the disease on a completely different front: they changed the diet. And the result was successful prevention of the disease—merely by giving the child a specially prepared diet with very little phenylalanine. What needs to be noticed here is that a genetic disease was basically cured by a method that had not only nothing to do with genes, but also nothing to do with eugenics. The genes were simply being left in the population, and instead of trying to change them the environment was changed. There is probably no better demonstration of the interaction between genes and environment, of the simple fact that defective genes are only defective in relation to some environment. If you change that environment it may become meaningless to think of the gene as defective.

Consider: By supplying corrective lenses we render the genetic "defect" causing myopia powerless; with countless work-saving machines we abolish the ancient evolutionary superiority of muscular force majeure. Thus the genes for nearsightedness and relative muscular weakness must inevitably become more common in the human population. So why don't we worry about these common genetic "defects" and about the eugenic consequences of their spread for the human species? Because we know that they have ceased to matter in the environments that we humans create for ourselves; that, in a real sense, they are no longer defects at all.

Philosophical doubts have been raised about the goal of eliminating even severe genetic defects, and cautious policy questions must be raised about any attempt to eliminate mild ones—characteristics which some doctors see as defects, but which most others see as part of normal human variation. But few enthusiasts of molecular genetics have confronted an even more distressing possibility: that in their zeal to eliminate variations that look like defects, they may inadvertently destroy variations that are advantageous. This possibility clearly exists in the case of manic-depressive illness.

Also known as bipolar mood disorder, this serious psychiatric problem carries patients through enormous mood swings. They go from manias characterized by a fast-talking flight of half-baked ideas and dangerously risky behavior to depressions marked by inactivity, helplessness, hopelessness, and a seemingly inescapable sadness. "My mind's not right," wrote the great modern American poet Robert Lowell, who suffered from the illness. "I hear / My spirit sob in each blood cell, / As if my hand were at its throat . . . / I myself am hell." Before the advent of lithium and other treatments discovered by modern psychiatry, the illness often did end in suicide.

It clearly is a disease, if any psychiatric entity is. And it clearly has an inherited component. Studies of twins, at least one of whom has manic-depressive illness, have shown that if the other twin is genetically identical, he or she has a likelihood of between 67 and 80 percent of also suffering with it. But the corresponding percentages for nonidentical twins are far lower. Similarly, people who were adopted in infancy and who later commit suicide have *biological* relatives with a suicide rate far higher—six to twelve times higher—than their *adoptive* relatives, or than either the biological or adoptive relatives of *non*suicidal adoptees. According to Dr. Elliot Gershon, a leading authority on psychiatric genetics, the chance that a person with manic-depressive illness will have a child who will grow up to have either the same disease or very serious depressions is roughly one in four.

One attempt to use molecular genetics to locate the gene for manic-depressive illness on a particular chromosome proved to be a false start. Data on a large extended family among the Amish of Pennsylvania, where there were a number of cases of the disorder, seemed to link the defect to a genetic marker on chromosome 11. But this link dissolved when two family members who lacked the marker later developed the illness. Another series of studies linking it to the X chromosome—near the gene for color blindness— is probably more robust, but also probably only accounts for a subset of manic-depressiveness. Yet even in this preliminary state of research, patients come to Dr. Gershon requesting definitive prenatal tests that will enable them to abort fetuses destined to have these illnesses. These he routinely discourages, not only because of the vague state of present knowledge, but because these diseases are now largely treatable.

Some doctors, and certainly some patients, will undoubtedly be tempted to use prenatal testing and selective abortion to stave off the disease in future children. But they will have to come to grips with another set of facts, now at least equally scientific: we may not know what genetic markers manic-depressive illness is linked to, but we know for sure it is often linked to creativity.

This is scarcely a new idea; Aristotle no doubt exaggerated when he wrote that "all those who have become eminent in philosophy or politics or poetry or the arts" are of the melancholic temperament. But the personal histories of Beethoven, Dickens, van Gogh, and Newton, among many other creative geniuses, bear him out. But it was only in the late 1980s and early 1990s that the connection between mood disorders and creativity was scientifically established. We can now say unequivocally that although most creative people are not mentally ill, and although most people with mood disorders are not especially creative, these two forms of human experience occur together too often for their connection to be explained by chance alone.

Kay Jamison, a psychologist at the John Hopkins Hospitals who is an authority on manic-depressive illness, studied forty-seven eminent British writers and artists. All had been awarded one or more of the top British prizes in their fields, or received comparable other recognition. Thirty-eight percent of these accomplished Britons had been treated for mood disorders, three-fourths with medication or even hospitalization. In addition, 30 percent more had experienced what they described as severe mood swings. The first figure compares with an estimated 5 or 6 percent for the population at large.

Psychiatrist Nancy Andreasen was a literary scholar before entering medicine, and she later decided to study writers. Thirty faculty members at the reknowned University of Iowa Writer's Workshop were compared with thirty other professionals matched for age, sex, and education. Twenty-four of the writers (80 percent) had experienced some sort of mood disorder, as opposed to nine (30 percent) of the control group. Thirteen of the writers had had manic-depressive illness in some measure, which was true of only three of the controls. During the fifteen years of the study, two of the thirty writers took their own lives.

Dr. Hagop Akiskal, a psychiatrist at the University of Tennessee, and his associate Kareen Akiskal, a Parisian gallery owner, studied painters, sculptors, and writers in France and blues musicians in the American Southeast. While they found no evidence of the more severe forms of manic-depressive illness in these groups, they did find definite evidence of marked mood swings—more moderate mood disorders. And in a separate study they did of 750 American psychiatric patients, this link was strongly confirmed in the other direction: people with moderate mood disorders are more likely to have a significant, recognized creative ability.

Finally, Ruth Richards, a psychologist at the Harvard Medical School, has found creativity to be overrepresented not only among patients with severe or moderate manic-depressive cycles, but also among their relatives, as compared to the relatives of "normal" controls. Richards and her colleagues proposed that the genes for manic-depressive illness are like the genes for thalassemia and sickle-cell anemia in one important respect: the people who have high doses of them may be maladapted, but those who are only "carriers" may have a distinct advantage. In the case of the genetic anemias, carrier relatives are more resistant to malaria—no advantage in the absence of malarial parasites. In the case of manic-depressive illness, relatives are apparently more creative.

It is difficult to conceive of a human environment in which superior creativity is not an advantage, and the roster of people with serious mood disorders includes some of the most revered creators in human history—among them William Blake, Samuel Taylor Coleridge, Honoré de Balzac, Johann Wolfgang von Goethe, George Frideric Handel, and Pyotr Ilich Tchaikovsky; not to mention leaders such as Winston Churchill and Abraham Lincoln, both of whom suffered from quite serious mood swings. Clearly, if we set out to eliminate genes responsible for the manic-depressive type of psychiatric illness, we will in all likelihood also eliminate some genes that have produced abilities that no sensible person would want to consider losing.

Armed with this caution, we are ready to take up the strange case of Tourette's syndrome, currently the focus of a wave of intense enthusiasm in the small but growing circle of scientists and physicians who study it. Named for the French physician who first described it in 1885, Tourette's even now is known to very few people. Until a few years ago most doctors who recognized the name would have told you a fascinating tale of rare patients with uncontrollable tics—not only muscular but verbal ones, often embarrassingly vulgar words shouted repeatedly in public settings where they were the last thing that should have been said. One effective treatment for Tourette's has been haloperidol, a drug that blocks the receptors for dopamine, one of the brain's internal transmitter chemicals—much the way RU 486 blocks the receptors for progesterone.

In the last five or six years a dramatic change in the thinking about Tourette's syndrome has occurred. What was once seen as a rare disorder now seems, in varied and subtle forms, a relatively common one. What was once a mystery in terms of cause and effect has been replaced by a partial explanation: genes play an important role. And what was once a little backwater in the byways of specialized neurology has become almost a thoroughfare, not only for sober medical study but for questionable philosophical speculation.

Groups of researchers at Yale, at the University of Rochester, and at the City of Hope Hospital in Los Angeles have become fascinated by Tourette's, and in following patients with the problem have made some important discoveries. Under the leadership of Dr. Roger Kurlan, investigators at Rochester and Yale followed a lead presented in 1983 by a Tourette's patient, David Janzen, who was very worried by a misdiagnosis—he'd been told he had Huntington's disease—and very eager to help when he found out it was Tourette's. Fortunately for science, he came from a large family of Mennonites relatively isolated in a tiny town in rural Alberta, Canada. His many relatives in the pacifist Christian sect were local, easy to trace, and for the most part cooperative; 159 were personally interviewed.

The result was much new information about the disorder. For one thing, most of the 54 family members diagnosed with some form of the syndrome—over 80 percent—never were bothered enough by their symptoms to seek medical help; contrary to received wisdom, their Tourette's was usually very mild. David Janzen himself had disturbing repetitive outbursts of movements and words, but his affected cousins tended to have only a tic or two— say, a noticeable but untroublesome facial twitch.

Dr. David Pauls, a Yale colleague of Kurlan's, explored a more diverse set of smaller families related to Tourette's syndrome patients in Connecticut. In addition to tics, which mostly affected male relatives, 10 percent of the family members suffered from out-of-the-ordinary obsessive thoughts or compulsive acts—for example, having to get dressed over and over for hours each morning. These people were mostly women. Pauls began to think that perhaps the same genetic background could be expressed in some relatives (mainly boys and men) as tics or full-blown Tourette's syndrome, while in others (mainly girls and women) the same gene or genes produced more complex obsessions or compulsions, less tied to bursts of muscle activity. Pauls and his colleague James Leckman found it hard to interpret the pattern of heredity of Tourette's just sticking to the core symptoms, but if the relatives with obsessive-compulsive disorder were included, a clear inheritance pattern emerged.

Meanwhile Dr. David Comings, a Los Angeles geneticist at the City of Hope Hospital also interested in Tourette's, became convinced of a quite different genetic pattern, showing the large degree of uncertainty on this small frontier of medicine. Yet Comings was willing to go much further, not only in his scientific interpretations but in his approach to patients and their families:

It's often been felt that there are separate genes for alcoholism, for schizophrenia, for depression, for Tourette's Syn-

drome, for attention deficit disorder. One of the things we
seem to be finding is that there is a similar set of genes that
are at the basis of a lot of these different disorders . . .

I mean, one could argue that up to 10 to 20 percent of the
population has some type of genetic behavioral problem . . . All you have to do is look at the problems with alcoholism, the problems with depression, the problem with
manic-depressive disorder, to see that they have an extraordi-
narily severe impingement on the functioning of society, and
if we can begin to make some dent in this and understand it
and treat these conditions, especially identify them early in
life and get these children treated before they have these
breakdowns or problems, I think it would be an enormous
benefit to society.

In this speech all the worst fears of those who cite the abuses of
eugenics are realized and converge. Dr. Comings, who is not a
psychiatrist, deems up to 20 percent of the human population to
be abnormal in some way in their behavior. He would use genetic
medicine to lop off 20 percent of the variety in human action,
personality, mood—in effect, 20 percent of the human spirit. Excessive activity, drinking, oppositional behavior, sadness—all
these and more would be subject to correction in his vision of
future medicine. For his present patients, he uses clonidine, primarily a blood pressure medication, to treat not just tics or Tourette's syndrome but any of these other problems. If any of these
behaviors change, he considers the drug a success.

More sober minds bristle at this confident, all-inclusive approach. Dr. Kenneth Kidd, a leading psychiatric geneticist who
works with Pauls at Yale, says, "I think that the case is definitely
not proven for this very broad involvement of a single gene that
causes Tourette's and many other disorders. Our own data collected here at Yale very strongly argue the other way." He also
says, in a tone of concern, that "people with Tourette's syndrome
are starting to call up and say, 'I want my children tested for this
gene.' There is a lot of misunderstanding out there."

Of course, unlike the case for thalassemia, Huntington's disease,
or PKU, there is no test for Tourette's syndrome, genetic or oth-

erwise. Yet incautious statements to the media continue to raise false hopes and fears. Sue Levi-Pearl, head of the Tourette Syndrome Association, is worried that "folks with Tourette's syndrome are getting information—for instance, that their disorder is distinctly related to alcoholism, their disorder is distinctly related to addiction, sexual aberration, and so they become very, very frightened . . . A woman called, and said that her daughter has a brother with Tourette and that she was pregnant and now she was not only concerned about having a baby perhaps with Tourette's syndrome but would this baby also be an alcoholic. Now that's utterly absurd. There are too many questions that have yet to be answered."

All this for a syndrome that only bothers one in five people who have it enough so that they complain to a doctor. As for treatment, Dr. Comings places his confidence in clonidine, delivered through a patch on the skin. But other authorities on the disorder, such as Arthur and Elaine Shapiro, believe that "clonidine is only rarely effective," and point to the large number of patients who get better spontaneously and to the lack of proper drug studies. Even haloperidol, a more standard and probably better treatment for Tourette's, has yet to be proven effective in a well-planned controlled trial. Both these drugs can have serious side effects; although each is approved for other purposes, the balance of risks and benefits for Tourette's is far from clear.

Dr. Donald Cohen, a psychiatrist at Yale, also uses clonidine, but only in the context of a much more complex and subtle treatment. He believes that "the best people to be involved are people who can see the child as a whole person, see what he's experiencing and have a view of where he's going to be developing. And that wouldn't be someone who's just interested in the tics and getting rid of the tics." Tommy is a young man who has been one of his patients since childhood. He is self-possessed, articulate, and sensitive as he describes his difficult childhood, fraught with ostracism because of his tics. Yet he feels less angry at his thoughtless childhood friends than his mother does on his behalf. "His philosophy," she says, "is 'Well mother, what can you expect? . . . they're not taught to be understanding . . . and so it's not their fault.' I remember him going out and saying, 'Look, I have a problem but I'm not a problem. I do things that seem crazy but I'm not crazy.' "

Anne Waldschmidt, the disabled woman in Bremen who fears intolerance of imperfection, is right when she says we will never eliminate birth defects. But if we can take Dr. Cao's success in Sardinia, reducing thalassemia births by 95 percent, and repeat the success with sickle-cell anemia and cystic fibrosis, with muscular dystrophy and Tay-Sachs disease, and with other unequivocally tragic genetic syndromes—with these efforts alone we will have gotten our money's worth from the genetics revolution, even if it were not expected to help cure AIDS and cancer. Yet Waldschmidt's fears are being realized in China, even as Western doctors decry those fears as implausible. When the line is crossed between birth control and forced sterilization, from a woman's right to choose to compulsory abortion, then we may indeed be on the slippery slope that runs down to Auschwitz.

But as for voluntary choice of genetic counseling, selective fertilization, prenatal testing, and abortion, who has the right to stand between a family and those options? Since the family will bear the brunt of the impact of disability, it would seem that the family has the right to take any available medical measures to avoid that impact. These measures will be ever more varied and powerful. But surely a vigilant society with full respect for civil rights can continue to tell the difference between the removal of a fetus destined for a short, painful life, and the kind of "eugenic" nightmare finally realized by the Nazis. And eventually selective fertilization, or even "gene surgery," may make such programs as Dr. Cao's workable *without* abortion.

But we must recognize how large a set of questions we are facing. Of the hundred thousand genes that are strung together to make up the human DNA, probably thousands are polymorphic—normally differing from one individual to the next. Each of us carries five or six mutations—genes that are clearly defective in one of the two copies we carry; genes that, if paired with another matched defective one in the complex dance of mating, would produce a devastating illness. We cannot go after all these defects, and we would never want, I hope, to go after the normal variation.

Lewis Thomas, the famed physician-essayist, has written, "The capacity to blunder slightly is the real marvel of DNA. Without this special attribute, we would still be anaerobic bacteria and there would be no music . . . it is no accident at all that mutations occur; the molecule of DNA was ordained from the beginning to make small mistakes." What he means is that without damage to genes there would be no variation, and without variation not only would there be no evolution, there would be no unpredictable variety in the world of the sort that makes life worth living. The problem is to find some way of defining a "slight" blunder that makes it possible to differentiate it from a colossal one. This, it turns out, will not be easy.

It is not a brave new world of total control that genetic medicine seeks. Rather, it is the goal that has inspired physicians since ages before Hippocrates: the rational conquest of illness, and the reduction—rational or otherwise—of human suffering.

FIVE

RANDOM CUTS

Aт a recent physicians' dinner I attended, a joke was told by one surgeon on another, in the course of honoring him near the end of a long career. "I was talking with Dr. Randall the other day," the speaker said, "and chanced to ask him how he would change his life if he should win the Florida lottery. He looked thoughtful for a while. Since the lottery was then going to pay about $40 million, he had a lot to think about. 'Well,' he finally said, 'I suppose I would continue to operate. But I would only do indicated procedures.'"

Indicated is doctor talk for justified, purposeful, needed. Every physician in the room who had ever performed an operation, ordered a CAT scan, or hospitalized a patient without feeling sure that the step was really necessary and in the patient's best interest, rather than in the interest, say, of defensive medicine, scientific curiosity, or profit—and that meant almost everyone present— must have felt the bite of that jibe. All the doctors present laughed at the speaker's joke.

They were of course also laughing at their patients. In the American system, where tens of millions of uninsured or underinsured people are denied needed procedures, it is no small irony that many millions of others *able* to pay are subjected to needless ones. Needless procedures, alas, have a long medical tradition on both sides of the Atlantic. In some places in the ancient world, the sick had holes drilled in their skulls to let out damaging spirits, and for most of European history bloodletting was a standard medical response to a wide variety of illnesses.

These procedures were done in good faith, of course, not just with the goal of collecting a fee. The doctors and patients involved believed that they worked, and felt that *something* had to be done. Because the beliefs were strong, the psychological impact of the procedures was strong as well; and through the placebo effect they may have produced improvement. But there was never any evidence that they worked for the reasons doctors did them, or achieved the goals they were done for, beyond the placebo effect. Yet few doctors or patients had the slightest doubt that they were the right thing to do.

The question is, has anything comparable gone on in recent times—even today—under the same broad umbrella of medical self-assurance? Consider the American experience with tonsillectomies. In 1934 a study was done in New York City. Of 1,000 eleven-year-olds in the public schools, 611 had had their tonsils removed. The other 389 were evaluated by a panel of physicians for possible tonsillectomies, and the operation was recommended for 174 more. (Fortunately, these children were not actually sent to surgery!) Different physicians looked at the remaining 215 and chose to "operate" on 99 more, leaving only 116 from the original thousand "surgery-free." Now *these* were evaluated by a third panel of doctors, who recommended 51 *more* of them for surgery.

Today second opinions are thought of as a way to *reduce* the likelihood of surgery. From that group of 1,000 school children, 93 percent would have been sent to surgery if up to three opinions were given. Today tonsillectomies are done on only a small fraction of children, but a decades-long surgical fad swept up millions of American children in its overenthusiasm. As one of those millions,

I remember waking from anesthesia crying and spitting blood, surrounded by other kids in the consulting-room assembly line, all doing likewise. I was five, so the year would have been 1951— right in the midst of the enormous American enthusiasm for tonsillectomies.

In 1977, John Wennberg and his colleagues at the Harvard School of Public Health studied the rates of tonsil removal in thirteen Vermont Hospital Service Areas beginning in 1969. In that year the rate for the United States as a whole was comparable to the Vermont rate. Yet there was a *thirteenfold* difference between the highest- and lowest-rate hospital districts in the state. These facts were reported back to Vermont doctors through the state medical society. The number of tonsillectomies began to decline in Vermont; by 1973 the rate was 46 percent below what it had been in 1969, and was also far lower than the corresponding national rate, which had also declined markedly.

This pattern of decline was greatest by far in the hospital district that had had the highest rate at the outset. Here, your chance of keeping your tonsils until age twenty-five was 63 percent in 1969. The district went from more than triple the national rate in that year to less than half the national rate in 1973—despite a 46 percent national decline in the same period. Overall, the district had an 89 percent decline in five years. Careful analysis led Wennberg and his colleagues to credit the district's sharp drop mainly to feedback—simply letting the doctors know where they stood in relation to other doctors.

Writing in 1977, the authors said that "at least for a decade there has been a decline in the popularity of tonsillectomies in the United States," and they attributed a good part of it to review of the procedures done and feedback of the information to practicing doctors. This was good news. Still, their phrasing makes the "popularity" of operations seem eerily like the ups and downs of television sitcoms and heavy-metal rock groups.

The problem is hardly limited to tonsillectomies. One of the most curious, inexplicable, and—well, unsettling—facts about modern medicine is variation in how often many procedures are done. Consider the figures for all surgical operations. By 1976 there were about half again as many operations in Canada (per million people) as there were in England and Wales, and there were nearly half again as many in the United States as in Canada. These differences have persisted. Age and sex differences among the three countries come to mind as a possible explanation; a country could have more old men who could need more prostate surgery, or more women who might need more hysterectomies. But the comparisons are already corrected for such problems—the rates are adjusted so that it is as if the countries had identical age and sex makeup.

Of course, different countries have different lifestyles, different diets, even to some extent different genes, so why wouldn't they have different rates of illness? More gallbladder problems, more gallbladder surgery. The three countries also have three different ways of paying for health care, so there are different incentives for surgeons to perform operations. These facts may well help explain the international differences. But the question leads to an even more puzzling phenomenon. Differences *among* Canadian provinces are as great as or greater than the international differences; so are the gaps among states within the United States. Nine of the ten provinces were studied from 1968 to 1977, and the variation was as large as for the three different countries.

As for gaps within the United States, a Rand Corporation study completed in 1986 counted surgical procedures in Medicare patients in thirteen geographic areas spread over eight states. The most consistent operation was hernia repair, which was only one and a half times more common in the place with the most than in the place with the fewest. The operations with the largest place-to-place variation were total knee replacement (up to *six*fold differences between the highest and lowest surgery rates), destruction of benign skin growths (up to eightfold differences), and repair of an ailing hip (up to elevenfold).

All of these comparisons are corrected for age and sex. So we think next of regional differences in the rates of illnesses, but also of the fact that, despite relatively uniform payment systems, some parts of Canada or the United States are more advanced in standards of medical care than others. This would seem a good bet for explaining the widely differing rates of surgery. But there is more to the puzzle yet. *Local* variations *within* provinces and states are also very large. A study of forty-four counties in Ontario showed from two- to fourfold differences between the highest- and lowest-ranking counties for various kinds of surgery—except for removal of part of the colon, which showed a *nine*fold difference.

Similar local variation exists in the United States and the United Kingdom. For twenty-one districts in the West Midlands alone, variation for seven different operations (hernia repair, appendectomy, and removal of the gallbladder, prostate, uterus, tonsils, or hemorrhoids) ranged from one-and-a-half- to more than fourfold for each type of operation. Local variation within the region of New England shows a similar range of values for the seven operations, despite the fact that absolute rates of surgery are much higher in New England than in Britain. Hysterectomy, for instance, is about two and a half times more common in New England, yet the ratios of highest to lowest local rates—about 2 to 1—are almost identical. Even Norway, studied by the same investigators, with rates of most surgery also far below those of New England, has similar within-country variation.

What are we to make of these strange numbers? Although some have assumed that the high rates are usually the right ones—that the communities with lower rates are more backward medically and need to catch up—there is little evidence that this is generally true. On the contrary, the evidence is growing that for many types of surgery too many operations are done in some places; that is, in many instances the surgery not only was ineffective or harmful, but could have been predicted in advance to be so, on the basis of the patient's status and record.

Cesarean section makes a good case study. Its frequency has risen over the last few decades in the United Kingdom, Canada, and the United States, but it is much the highest in the United States, where—again, with lots of local variation—it hovers around one fourth of all births. American physicians defending their practice cite the steady decline in infant mortality that accompanied the rise in C-sections. However, since the United Kingdom and

Canada have had similar declines in mortality with lower rates of C-section, and have lower absolute mortality rates than the United States, the association can be questioned. More compelling is the fact that Ireland, with an approach of carefully managed vaginal delivery, has experienced quite comparable declines of infant mortality in recent decades while keeping the section rate down at around 6 percent of births.

Every culture has its folklore about health and illness, and for Germans the tradition has more or less been that if your heart is fine the rest of you will follow. Concrete signs that this folklore is still influential are a tendency among doctors to prescribe many different drugs for low blood pressure, a condition less likely to be thought of as an illness in other countries, and a very high frequency of prescribing digitalis, a medicine that strengthens the heartbeat—elsewhere reserved for seriously weakened hearts. The Germans also have a tradition of sending patients to spas to convalesce in peaceful surroundings for a full six weeks after a heart attack, an approach that would strike American doctors as counterproductive—putting a vigorous person who could be back in the stream of life out to pasture instead.

With this emphasis on caring for the heart, Jürgen Müller, an East Berlin radiologist specializing in heart and blood vessel imaging, viewed the 1989 collapse of the Berlin Wall with a unique kind of excitement. For Dr. Müller it meant a first-time ticket to the frontier of cardiology. The East had no-frills medicine, the West had every conceivable new technological advance, fresh from the laboratory and factory. For the first time in his thirty years of practice, Dr. Müller began to look at his Western colleagues' equipment with something other than anguished, distant envy.

Siemens, a West German firm, is one of the leading producers of medical technology in the world. Siemens would like to supply the state-of-the-art cardiac catheterization lab—equipment for making images of the insides of the arteries supplying the heart, and for repairing some kinds of disease found there—that Müller would love to have, to replace the broken-down, ancient system he has used for seventeen years. According to Siemens executives, the modern increase in life expectancy is due mainly to drugs and equipment. This is far from true; as shown by Thomas McKeown, a leading authority on the history of health, among others, it is mainly due to economic, social, and lifestyle changes, and to a lesser extent to specific preventive measures such as vaccines. Drugs and equipment compete for last place in importance. But in an almost-twenty-first-century industrial society, it is understandable that some avid fans of technology would be hard put to see how change could come from anything else. Nevertheless, it does. And increasingly, hardheaded physicians and medical economists are proving that expensive advances on the frontier of technology—magnetic resonance imaging, for example (an elegant advance in making pictures of the inside of the body that reveals great detail without the risks inherent in X-rays or CAT scanning) or the Siemens company's latest in cardiac catheterization—are greatly overused in a way that far exceeds their effectiveness and that relentlessly saps and wastes resources which used in more modest ways would make a much greater positive impact on health.

For Professor Lothar Heinemann, an East German epidemiologist who specializes in heart disease, the medical floodgates opened by the recent collapse of the Wall are not an unalloyed blessing. "I worry about the big-pocket medicine we are now implementing," he says.

> Before the Wall came down, we talked about preventing this development. Now it's here and we can't prevent it any more—we have to cope with the new procedures. Prevention needs to be more emphasized. But I am pretty sure both patients and doctors are mainly looking for big technology, what's new, fascinating, which is increasing the faith of the population in medicine. Doctors are great believers when new technology is being implemented. They believe there are only advantages for the patient, [but] the advantages are exaggerated.

Preventing the spread of lifesaving technology? Professor Heinemann speaks wistfully, even regretfully, about East Germany's technologically backward past. Is he some sort of antimedicine Luddite, ready to smash the catheterization imagers turned out by Siemens—a simpleminded fundamentalist trying to hold back the future?

Hardly. In fact he is on the crest of a wave currently breaking worldwide that includes many of the most sophisticated thinkers in medicine. While the supposedly practical men and women in white coats in the operating theaters and catheterization labs scrub up and *do*, without hesitation, *whatever needs to be done*, professorial types like Heinemann—shifting their numbers around, making their calculations, scribbling their summaries—turn out to be the practical ones, while the "doers" are often shown to be dreamers and bumblers. And since these dreamy doers often have our lives in their hands, we must face the fact that frequently they do not really know what they are doing.

Consider, for example, the artificial heart. The problem seemed a simple one. The heart is a pump; engineers make innumerable excellent working pumps; therefore we should be able to make a pump to replace the heart. In the United States, Utah was the focus of activity, and the Jarvik artificial heart was developed in Salt Lake City. There and elsewhere, heart transplants had been gaining credibility through increasingly evident effectiveness. But the dream of the manufactured heart remained: no donors, no thorny ethical questions, no supply snags, no tissue compatibility problems, just lovely machines gliding off the assembly line into the hands of the surgeon—and from there only a short way to the patient's waiting chest.

But the machines once implanted were not so lovely. They were rejected by the patients' immune systems as vigorously as foreign tissue ever was, and more; and, lacking living tissue's ability to repair itself, they could not withstand the brutal burden of endless pumping that any live, healthy heart finds routine. They accumulated the gook of clots and immune-system cellular buildup, while pounding themselves to the breaking point trying to keep up the normal activities of life. Barney Clark, the middle-aged man who became the Jarvik's first patient, developed complications, was reoperated, developed more complications, and finally succumbed. He was followed by one patient after another; they lived for a few months, or a year, or occasionally most of a second year.

Each case cost hundreds of thousands of dollars. Even physicians used to spending that kind of money and more were questioning whether the Jarvik heart was worth it. Finally, in 1985 and again in 1988, special U.S. government committees were convened to evaluate the procedure. Their conclusion was that public funds should no longer be used to support the program. Despite strong advocacy by patients and their families, as well as by congressional representatives from the state of Utah, government funding for the program was withdrawn—tantamount to abandoning the program. But this turned out to be temporary. Pressure from Congress, instigated by representatives of the state of Utah with no knowledge of the scientific and medical issues, led to resumption of the program.

West German heart doctors, as we might have guessed, continue to strive toward the goal of a completely implantable artificial heart. For Professor Heinemann, the skeptical East German epidemiologist, a success with it would be "very important for a few persons at very high risk—it's a last hope for them. But for the majority, it is a loss of money and by the end I am sure a loss of health."

Interestingly, the parallel progress of natural heart transplantation during the early 1980s had what seems at first glance to be exactly the opposite outcome. Rejection was largely subject to control, reoperation rates were satisfactorily low, and five-year survival rates climbed steadily to the point where the majority of patients— at least 65 percent—were alive after five years. Today such statistics are still improving, and heart transplantation is a widely used and thoroughly accepted method of treatment, limited mainly by the number of hearts available. But at second glance, it still costs a fortune.

Dr. Thomas Preston, a University of Washington (Seattle) cardiologist and a historian of the field, views the artificial heart program as an expensive, unsupervised experiment that was properly suspended and should have been left at that. But he warns that it is only the tip of an iceberg of similiar follies, some just as costly, that health care could founder on. In fact, the modern history of surgery on the heart and the blood vessels shows one procedure after another being widely adopted before it was proven effective, and used in the end on many patients for whom it was not appropriate. Some of these operations should not have been used on anyone at all.

Take, for instance, surgery on the carotid artery and its branches, which are among the most important vessels supplying blood to the brain. (The carotid is the one that gives you a pulse next to your windpipe.) A lifetime of bad habits, especially excessive intake of saturated fats, will cause ugly plaques to develop in the artery, especially at its branching point high in the throat. These blockages reduce blood flow to the brain, and may cause dizziness, blackouts, or perhaps only a noise heard by a doctor holding a stethoscope to the throat—referred to by the French word *bruit*, it's a little whooshing sound that blood makes when squeezed through a narrow space. As with the artificial heart, the simple facts of the plumbing made the solution seem obvious: go around the clogged stretch of artery.

A logical way of doing this was devised, using a less important artery from outside the skull—the one that gives you the pulse in your temple—and inserting it where it could supply the brain inside the skull, or "cranium," directly. Logically, the procedure was named the extracranial-intracranial, or EC-IC, bypass operation. In fact it was so logical that reports of its success with individual patients led more and more surgeons to do the procedure on more and more patients, until it was being done thousands of times a year in the United States alone. The only drawback seemed to be that there was no real proof that it worked. So Canadian neurologist Dr. Henry Barnett conducted a large international study of almost fourteen hundred patients randomly assigned, including hundreds in Europe and Japan, as well as in the United States and Canada, to be treated either with drugs or with the EC-IC bypass operation. The result was very hard for many doctors to believe: there was no advantage to surgery.

Barnett and his colleagues' study had to weather a storm of controversy lasting for years, but in the end the EC-IC bypass suffered a fate similar to that suffered temporarily by the artificial heart: the U.S. government stopped paying for it. An $8 million study had called a halt to a procedure that would otherwise waste $250 million a year on thousands of unwarranted operations. As Dr. Barnett put it,

> This stunning reversal of what everybody thought made a lot of people think that a lot of surgical procedures had to be evaluated with controlled studies. I think it was in that way, for those of us involved with the nervous system, a bit of a landmark study. It taught us that we simply couldn't go on believing that what we were doing was right without proving it.

But the question remains: How could hundreds of surgeons throughout the world have been permitted to do an operation thousands of times a year if it had not been properly tested first?

The answer is distressingly simple: There is no procedure for formally scrutinizing operations or diagnostic tests unless they involve new substances. The U.S. Food and Drug Administration has a mandate to, among other things, run studies of new drugs to determine that they are one, safe; and two, more effective for the stated purpose than placebos. Such legal standards *do not exist* for new operations or new diagnostic tests, except to the extent that they involve new substances; their adoption or rejection is left to the judgment of experienced practitioners.

Now, because of the threat of malpractice litigation, practitioners do not want to be out on a limb alone, doing an operation or test few others have adopted. There is an old saying in medicine that you should not be the first or the last to start using a new drug or procedure. But being part of the medical crowd is no assurance against doing harm if the crowd's collective judgment is based more on enthusiasm than on evidence. In fact, after a certain critical mass of doctors in your area have adopted the practice in question, you can be more legally vulnerable by shunning it—this is in fact the case with cesarean section, for example—since the "standard of practice" you will be measured against in a court of law is precisely what your colleagues are currently doing. The result is that there can be a sea change in practice, a widespread adoption of a new procedure, without clear evidence that it works.

The infamous frontal lobotomy was a case in point, perhaps the worst episode of its kind, though not the only one. Egas Moniz, a Portuguese neurologist already known for discovering the technique for imaging brain blood vessels, developed in 1936 a way of severing the connections between the frontal lobes and the brain's emotional centers. This was a startlingly simple procedure that seemed to have an almost magical calming effect on psychotic and other mentally disturbed patients. Moniz emphasized that it should not be used except where all other methods had failed, but its use spread rapidly in this country despite this warning. In one version it could be done as an office procedure, by introducing a slender blade through the bony case of the eye deep within the skull and rotating it back and forth to slice through the brain's wiring. The procedure's popularity grew steadily, and many thousands of such operations were done. Thirteen years after its invention, in 1949, its prestige was such that Moniz shared the Nobel Prize in medicine for inventing it.

But it was about to be almost completely discredited. During the 1950s many studies of patients who had been subjected to the procedure revealed that their mental and emotional lives had been severely damaged—so much so that no amount of calming down could justify the losses in most cases. Indeed, the word "lobotomized" became synonymous with a devastating loss of ability and identity. The number of lobotomies performed in the United States went from thousands a year to none in less than a decade. And the doctors who had done them quietly retired or turned their talents to other methods.

How could such an anomalous history have unfolded? Essentially, the same way that the tonsillectomy fad came and went during those decades, and the hysterectomy fad a little later: credulous doctors sent their patients to overconfident surgeons, whose standards of practice were shaped by colleagues' anecdotes and by their own experience rather than by rigorous scientific research. The Office of Technology Assessment of the U.S. Congress and the Institute of Medicine of the U.S. National Academy of Sciences have been attempting for years to design mechanisms for the systematic evaluation of medical technology, just as drugs are evaluated by the Food and Drug Administration. These efforts have been systematically hampered by recent Presidents on the advice of some physicians and other members of the health-care "industry." Yet in Britain, where the profit motive is not an issue, it has been similarly difficult to institute such controls. This fact underscores how intrinsic to modern medicine is the technological imperative and the concept of the easy surgical fix. It also points up our reluctance to participate in randomized trial; rather than frankly recognize that the choice is a toss-up, and participate in an experiment for the advancement of medical knowledge, we encourage our doctors to exaggerate their confidence in a given procedure, so we can choose it wholeheartedly for ourselves.

And what fads might we be in the midst of today? Cesarean section and cardiac pacemaker implantation are clearly excessive, but what other operations? Prostate gland removal? Surgery for low-back pain? The fact is we just don't know. For these procedures and a dismaying number of others no rigorously controlled scientific studies exist to serve as the foundation for the practice. Doctors believe in these procedures because people have a good chance of coming through them successfully. But there are no studies to answer the obvious next question: How much worse off would the patient have been without the operation? And the next: Is that enough to justify the risk, the discomfort, and the cost of the surgery?

Although most cardiac operations have fared better than the implantable artificial heart program, and although some have been almost miraculous—the correction of deadly congenital defects, for example, which has given countless children their lives through deft, quick snipping and sewing—the field has certainly had its share of fiascos. The Beck operation, for instance, was designed to relieve angina, heart pain usually caused by reduced blood supply in an artery blocked by plaques. Claude Beck was a chest surgeon who reasoned that if the thirsty heart muscle were deliberately injured, new blood vessels would grow into it and resupply it with blood. The procedure was to strip off the top layer of heart muscle and then scrape it with asbestos, irritating it until it was bloody. In a 1958 article in the *Journal of the American Medical As-*

sociation, Beck claimed an amazingly high success rate in relieving heart pain.

Actually, there was no more real scientific evidence for the procedure than there is now, when it has been long abandoned for lack of such evidence. But the way it developed remains instructive. First, it is crucial to understand how painful angina can be. Patients often describe it as a crushing pain whose onset almost seems timed to stand in the way of a normal life—climbing a flight of stairs, say, or walking to the grocer's. Then, too, angina is often the harbinger of a heart attack, that final destruction of cardiac muscle which has been starved for blood for too long. Unlike angina, heart attack damage is irreversible, and all too often results in death. Putting ourselves in the place of surgeons in the early to mid twentieth century—a time when the number of heart attacks rose enormously—we might imagine ourselves searching for something, anything, that might stem this plague among our patients. And as an old medical saying goes, desperate maladies require—or at least suggest—desperate remedies.

The Beck operation was not the most desperate. In France in 1922 a surgeon tried the expedient of cutting the nerve that carried anginal pain from the heart to the brain. This seems a bizarre tactic, since it would destroy the early-warning system which, by telling the brain to slow the body down, could often prevent a heart attack. But we have to appreciate how severe the pain can be, and how hopeless advanced cases were in 1922. Today a surgeon may cut nerves in a dying cancer patient to relieve pain; everyone is aware that the treatment is destructive, but as a last resort we may turn to it to mitigate horrible suffering. It was in that spirit that angina was treated by severing a vital nerve. Another procedure involved removal of the thyroid gland in an effort to reduce heart stimulation by hormones. This operation, by causing all the symptoms of thyroid deficiency, also did more harm than good.

These procedures always made some kind of physiological sense. One might say that they suffered from too much convincing scientific theory and not enough practical scientific proof. Another operation that became popular in the late 1940s was called internal mammary ligation. This meant tying off some important arteries in the chest wall in the hope of shunting extra blood toward the heart. By the late 1950s articles in medical journals reported relief of angina by this procedure in one third to two thirds of the cases.

However, the surgeons reporting these results had forgotten an elementary rule of real science: Compare your experimental group with a control group. A group of cardiologists at the University of Washington in Seattle, led by Dr. Leonard Cobb, decided to do just that, in a study published in *The New England Journal of Medicine* in 1959. Seventeen patients agreed to undergo surgery considered experimental, and eight of them got internal mammary ligation. But the other nine got the whole procedure except the tying-off of the arteries. Remarkably, these sham-operated controls (no longer allowable under today's ethical standards) got as much benefit from the surgery as the ones who had their arteries tied off. They experienced reduction of pain, took fewer nitroglycerin tablets to control their angina, resumed normal activity, and even had improvements in their electrocardiogram tracings—all to the same extent as those who got the full operation.

Though very small, the Cobb study called attention to the basic flaw in uncontrolled studies that merely reported the results for patients operated on. A powerful placebo effect could result from real or fake operations, possibly due to an enormous reduction of anxiety in the days after waking up from surgery. This effect, along with the natural ups and downs of a disease like angina even without any treatment at all, should have made physicians and surgeons skeptical of subsequent reports—of the claimed success rate with the Beck asbestos procedure, for example.

But there was little such skepticism. Arthur Vineberg, a Canadian surgeon reporting in leading medical journals in the late fifties and sixties, claimed success for a procedure even more drastic than Beck's. He took one of the same internal mammary arteries that would have been tied off in the earlier ligation procedure and tried to divert it so that it would supply the heart muscle instead. An incision was made in the heart and a cut mammary artery was turned and sewed into the wound. The hope was that it would actually generate some normal branching and a new blood supply.

Subsequent studies of dogs and pigs showed that this rarely

happened, but the Vineberg operation continued to spread throughout the 1960s based on journal articles about uncontrolled trials—series of patients who were reported improved after the operation, but who were not compared to randomly assigned controls. By the early seventies a group of medical scientists was poised to do a proper controlled trial of the Vineberg and Beck procedures. But—once again on the basis of weak evidence—both were being replaced by a new procedure that was sweeping cardiology: coronary artery bypass surgery. This operation was supremely logical, involving as it did the replacement of clogged arteries with segments taken from unclogged arteries and veins elsewhere in the body. It awaited two important developments of the 1960s: the heart-lung machine, to do the work of the heart while it was under the knife; and truly effective imaging of the coronary arteries.

By 1975, about 60,000 bypass operations were done each year in the United States; by 1987, about 230,000. For most of this period the results of randomized controlled trials of "cabbage"—the surgeons' slang pronunciation of CABG, for coronary artery bypass graft—were not yet available. Two large American trials, the Veterans Administration Cooperative Study and the Coronary Artery Surgery Study, whose results appeared during the mid-1980s, showed no difference in survival between angina patients randomly assigned to get the operation and those randomly assigned to drug and other nonsurgical treatments only. A large multicenter trial in Europe, the European Coronary Surgery Study, did find about a 10 percent greater five-year survival in the CABG group than in the group that had no surgery. But even this was disappointing for such a highly touted operation, and the advantage had declined further by the twelve-year follow-up.

Heart surgeons responded by saying that the quality of the surgery in the trials was not high enough, that the patients were not sick enough, and that pain reduction, which was successful in the trials, is a legitimate goal distinct from that of lengthening life. Their first point, if true, was partly moot; the average patient is not likely to be operated on by the very best surgeons in the world.

So we need to know how well things work when done by less exalted hands.

Their second point was accurate, and has led to practical consequences: today only the sickest patients—those with blockage of the largest coronary artery, the left main, or of three other arteries to the heart—go directly to bypass surgery, since these patients clearly benefit in terms of survival. Their third point was also well taken, and still is, because randomly controlled trials have proved the benefit of surgery over drug treatment in most categories of patients when the key measure is not mortality but pain. Critics of bypass surgery tend to discount the impact on pain in the absence of an impact on survival, an approach that is unfair to many suffering patients.

But while we were getting around to figuring out these rules for when bypass grafting should really be done, the operation was done tens of thousands of times unnecessarily, at least by today's standards. If CABG had been a new medication, the Food and Drug Administration in the United States would have put it through three phases of testing, including large randomized controlled trials, before it could be brought into widespread use. (As we have seen in chapter 3, even this does not necessarily prevent widespread abuse.) But since it was a surgical operation, widespread use could occur before such testing, and proper controlled trials had to play catch-up with practice. The same is true for all procedures as *procedures*. It is interesting that the great 1992 debate over breast-augmentation surgery hinged on damage done by silicone, a foreign chemical brought into the body, and not on the surgery itself. Substances are regulated; operations are not. Although this may be on the verge of change, it has not really changed yet.

During the 1980s another procedure, PTCA, or "pizza"—percutaneous transluminal coronary angioplasty—joined the ranks of heart treatments that spread widely before they were properly tested. PTCA has revolutionized the treatment of angina because it is in effect an operation that is not an operation. It is an extension of the technique for imaging arteries in the heart: a long thin tube is introduced through the body's blood vessels into the coronary arteries, but instead of a dye being released to show up on an X-ray film, a tiny balloon is inflated within the clogged artery, and the compromised channel is widened.

The patient may be awake, and may even be sent home shortly after the angioplasty. Best of all from the viewpoint of the cardiologist, angioplasty can be learned and done by that same doctor, with no need for referral to a surgeon. As the trials of CABG began to show that patients with one- or two-vessel obstruction were not living longer after bypass, it became routine to send many of these less sick patients for PTCA (one of the rare situations in which pizza seems healthier than cabbage). Yet the scientific evidence even for this decision needs to be much improved before we can feel confident that it is the right one routinely. Recent research suggests that there is an excess of angioplasties that may equal the excess of bypass grafts. It is clear that some patients' arteries close up again within months or years of the procedure, and the long-term effects remain uncertain. Accordingly, research trials are under way in Germany, Britain, the United States, and the European community. But the accelerating frequency with which angioplasty is done shows no signs of slowing pending the results.

Still another technique, rotoblation, has been catching on in both the United States and Britain. A tiny, diamond-studded brass burr attached to a flexible wire is introduced into the blocked artery in much the same way as an angioplasty balloon. However, it can be used in curved sections of arteries and other tight spots where the balloon really can't be properly positioned to do the job. The burr is rotated on the wire at high speed, like a dentist's drill. Early evidence suggested that it causes no damage to flexible tissues like the normal blood vessel wall; yet when it engages the hardened, calcium-filled plaque of atherosclerosis, it wears it down stunningly, widening the channel. Unlike the balloon, it can supposedly even be used to reopen a channel in an artery *completely* blocked by calcified, fatty plaque.

Cardiologists on both sides of the Atlantic showed great immediate enthusiasm for the rotoblator. But once again, randomized trials lagged far behind practice; no trials compared rotoblation to angioplasty, coronary bypass, or, certainly, medical management. And in the summer of 1992, existing rotoblators were recalled due to serious technical flaws. Still, laser angioplasty and other new techniques are under active study.

The meaning of medical management is also a moving target. In the 1980s several new drugs were introduced for the lowering of cholesterol, and they have recently been shown to actually widen the channels of arteries clogged by fatty plaques. Not only that, but changes in diet and lifestyle alone—without drugs or surgery—have also been shown capable of reducing the clogging of arteries. Most interesting of all, these effects will be permanent if the lifestyle changes are continued, while the relief provided by the more dramatic procedures—bypass or angioplasty, cabbage or pizza—is temporary in most cases, lasting at most only five to ten years. Most ironically perhaps, none of the currently popular procedures has been proved to be superior to cholesterol-lowering drugs or mere lifestyle changes in increasing the blood supply to a thirsty heart.

When I was in medical school I was taught, tongue partly in cheek, the four laws of medicine; one of them was, When you don't know what to do, don't do anything. This, it seems, is the hardest rule of all for the modern physician. It was easier, perhaps, for nineteenth-century physicians, since there was not very much they *could* do; so they watched and waited and comforted and, when they could, relieved pain as the illness took its course.

But in the mid to late twentieth century physicians understandably came to feel a certain confidence of being able to change the course of illness, and often to turn illness into health. Antibiotics destroyed some diseases, surgery many others. Techniques of imaging made it possible to see right through the body, not in vague shadows but in stunning, precise detail. Increasingly complex chemistry laboratories offered scores, then hundreds of different measurements. Blood could be safely replaced, then the heart and the kidney could be bypassed by dazzling machines, and finally those same organs could be lifted out when disease struck and replaced with new and better ones. Every day, in every medical practice, people who should have been crippled or dead were sent home to go on with their normal lives. Is it any wonder that doctors became a little too sure of themselves?

Medical advances have continued, but not all of them are equally effective; and inevitably the "miraculous" cures that were there to be found—"jewels strewn on the landscape waiting for us to pick them up" was how one old heart surgeon described them to me in 1980—became fewer and farther between. Each generation of antibiotics reached the limits of its usefulness as microbes evolved and adapted, and new drugs were needed just to maintain past gains. Obviously needed and effective operations, like the removal of deadly cancers and the rebuilding of malformed infant hearts, were boldly instituted, and they worked; but many other operations came and went, and some remained in common practice whose value, if any, was not so easy to prove. New technologies of measurement and imaging were always and everywhere in great demand; they often provided advantages over older, cheaper methods, but few physicians or patients asked whether the added value was great enough to justify the cost.

Dr. David Eddy embarked on his present career—that of professor of health policy and management at Duke University—after dropping out of a prestigious training program in cardiovascular surgery. A man with an intellectual as well as a mathematical bent, he began reviewing the evidence in favor of the procedures he was learning in his apprenticeship. He wanted to understand the science that these operations were based on, and he discovered to his dismay that in many cases there wasn't any—at least not any convincing science. Randomized controlled trials, the gold standard of medical experimentation, had simply never been done to test the value of most procedures in his chosen field—procedures he was being taught and would have to do for the rest of his life. Dismayed by this lack of evidence, he decided to study the mathematical tools for making decisions and for assessing the outcomes of those decisions; he dropped out of the surgical residency, and eventually acquired a Ph.D. to go along with his M.D. Since then he has carried forward the work of John Wennberg and others, asking tough, relentless questions about why doctors do what they do.

In a series of carefully crafted, hard-hitting columns in the *Jour-*

nal of the American Medical Association over the past few years, Eddy
has expressed sympathy for the situation of practicing physicians—but not without letting them know that they are wasting
billions of dollars and subjecting millions of patients to unproven,
possibly harmful procedures. His assessment is uncompromising:

> In fact very little of medicine has been carefully evaluated in
> well designed, well controlled studies. It's really quite amaz-
> ing, but after hundreds of years, in fact, I would estimate that
> only about ten to twenty percent of medical practices have
> been evaluated properly. What that means for the patient—
> and not just the patient but for the physician—is that for a
> large proportion of practices we really don't know what the
> outcomes or what the effects are.

The momentum generated by truly great medical advances served
to keep the system moving and confident even when the advances
were small, or perhaps even nonexistent. Thus each new and costly
medication had to prove itself only against placebos, not against
tried-and-true less-expensive drugs. Procedures like tonsillectomy,
coronary bypass, and angioplasty worked and were needed sometimes, but in many advanced countries each was done thousands
of times a year more often than was warranted, at an unacceptable
level of cost and risk. Magnetic resonance scans slipped into common use; they were better for some purposes than the widely used
CAT scan. But they were not three times better, although they cost
three times more.

Under the what-if-it's-your-mother principle, these declining ratios of benefit to cost are not a problem; if it helps at all, or even
if it *might* help, you want it. You don't want the doctor to stand
there and do nothing. In fact, you want so badly to see something
work that you and the doctor may share in a bit of barely conscious
collusion: "no evidence that it works" is subtly transformed into
"well, it might work" and then into "sure, it's worth a try." *We
can't just do nothing* haunts you with its clear, convincing resonance.

According to David Eddy, very often you can, and should, and
must do nothing, painful as that may be. Every time you do some-

thing medically unjustified you not only expose a patient to need-less risk; in the real world of limited resources you take away something from some other patient—someone who could be get-ting a treatment that really will work, but is denied it because you have used the resource for something needless.

Eddy, who is Professor of Health Policy at Duke University, is devoting his life and his considerable talent to raising the con-sciousness of doctors about this simple set of facts. But his program faces formidable obstacles. Ignorance and greed are only the ob-vious and easy ones. The hard ones are the felt need to get out there and *do*; the what-if-it's-your-mother rule; the persistence of medical custom, sometimes idiosyncratic or even irrational; the lingering impact of outdated training; the medical equivalents of fads and fashions; pressure from patients to have the latest and the best; and the misplaced confidence of some doctors, too daz-zled by the history of their science and insufficiently skeptical of the power in their hands.

The remedy Eddy offers is a simple one. It is called *practice policies*. These are guidelines for physicians as to what they should do in various given clinical situations. They may be set by local or national physicians' organizations, by corporate employers of phy-sicians, by hospital boards, by insurance companies, or by gov-ernments. What they have in common is that they are based on outcome studies; ideally on randomized controlled trials, but at worst on careful statistics documenting what has actually been done for and to patients, and above all, what the outcomes were.

Outcomes can be defined in many different ways. Death is an out-come, but so is pain; the rate of blood flow through an artery, the strength of a stream of urine, the force of a breath, the dosage of ni-troglycerin pills needed, the number of return visits to the doctor, the continued enjoyment of sex—all these are outcomes. For a distress-ingly large number of common medical and surgical procedures—most, according to some serious studies—we do not know what the outcomes are; therefore we cannot design rational practice policies.

The willingness of ordinary people—patients, you, and I—to participate in such studies, including random assignment to dif-ferent treatments of uncertain value, is fundamental. As Dr. Julian

Tudor-Hart of Britain's Royal College of General Practitioners has put it, "If we want to benefit from real medical knowledge, we should also contribute to it." Yet if we face up to the uncertainties that really exist in medicine, we can see that allowing ourselves to be randomized is no great sacrifice because—and this is the whole point—*no one* knows which of the experimental groups we may land in by chance is really better—if either is. And indeed there are now sophisticated mathematical techniques for determining as early as possible in a study if and when one of the choices has in fact proved better. At that point the study can be cut short—as has been done in several recent experiments, including a study of low-dose aspirin in preventing heart attacks—and all the participants in the study can take advantage of the new treatment, whose value they themselves have helped to prove.

But what we do sacrifice is a sense of control, a full-force belief in the effectiveness of what is being done to avert the threat posed by the illness. That means, too, a sacrifice of the placebo effect—which, as we know, can be a perfectly real and important part of the treatment. Not everyone can be called on to make this sacrifice, especially not everyone facing a life-threatening illness. This, alas, is what is missing from Dr. Eddy's otherwise excellent formulation. One could say that it is *too* rational, but in fact a completely rational analysis must take into account the *ir*rational element in human affairs and in medicine. Perhaps it was because he was disturbed by this paradox that Dr. Eddy dropped out of clinical medicine. As every practicing clinician knows, the irrational is an inescapable part of any doctor-patient encounter, and not always an undesirable one. Without an intense, occasionally excessive, desire to help, we would have no doctors at all.

Still, every doctor, if not every patient, should be capable of a planned pause in the battle against illness, during which a fully rational analysis can be focused on what he or she is doing. As Dr. Tudor-Hart has written: "Good doctors are those who are prepared to measure, or let others measure, how bad they are; or, more constructively, are prepared to accept that their work can be convincingly improved only if they are prepared to start by measuring its outcomes, errors, and omissions."

Like Dr. Eddy, Dr. Caldwell Esselstyn of the Cleveland Clinic has begun to question some tried-and-true surgical wisdom. Although he continues to operate for many purposes, he too has found another activity that he considers more important, as he argued recently in "Beyond Surgery," his 1991 presidential address to the American Association of Endocrine Surgeons. Dr. Esselstyn's new mission is the development of a diet that will help not only to prevent but to reverse the atherosclerosis of the arteries that causes anginal pain, heart attack, and many strokes. Amazingly, we now know that all the operations invented over the years to treat this condition—including some recent ones that seem to work rather well—can be avoided if the patient goes on an anti-atherosclerotic diet.

That means a diet low in saturated fat and cholesterol, with adequate fiber and complex carbohydrate. Before Dr. Esselstyn presumed to put his patients onto the diet, he put himself on it, to find out if he could lower his blood cholesterol to below 150. This is considered by most physicians to be an almost unreachable goal, although throughout the world rural people living on traditional diets have had cholesterol levels in that neighborhood. So in effect, to do so, far from being impossible, really only means returning to a pattern once common everywhere. To say that it is difficult in a world in which we have become accustomed to devastatingly dangerous fast-food fare and desserts that add insult to injury may well be true; but to say that it is impossible may be simply to abdicate a part of one's responsibility as a physician.

Dr. Esselstyn succeeded in lowering his own cholesterol to less than 150. Having found that he could do it without ceasing to enjoy food, he proceeded to apply the same principles to patients—the sickest patients the cardiologists could send him. As a result of being under his care these patients have avoided surgery that they had been assured was essential. Some have had serious problems; one has died. But that makes them as a group no worse off, and probably better off, than they would have been if sent to surgery. Although there was no control group in Dr. Esselstyn's research, others are doing carefully controlled studies.

For example, Dr. Dean Ornish, along with colleagues at the

University of California at San Francisco and the University of Texas Medical School in Houston, is conducting a study known as the Lifestyle Heart Trial. Forty-one patients with serious coronary artery disease were randomly assigned to one of two groups. Twenty-two patients in the experimental group followed an extremely low-fat diet, walked half an hour a day, and attended two four-hour stress-reduction sessions a week. Nineteen in the control group followed their regular doctors' orders—which included some reduction of fat intake and some exercise. Patients were given angiograms—X-rays of their coronary arteries—and PET scans to document the clogging of their arteries, which was substantial before the study started, markedly increasing their risk of heart attack.

The study will follow patients for four years and is still in progress, but according to a report in the distinguished British medical journal *The Lancet*, the experimental group was doing much better than the control group after one year. Eighteen of the twenty-two patients showed significant reduction of the blockage in their arteries. Three more showed slight reduction and only one, who failed to comply with the experimental regimen, showed a worsening of blockage. As a group, they claimed a 91 percent reduction in the frequency of chest pains. But the control group reported a major increase in chest pains, and on the more objective measure of blockage in the arteries, ten of the nineteen had worsened. Dr. Claude L'Enfant, director of the U.S. Government's National Heart, Lung, and Blood Institute, a mainstream institution, said that the Ornish study "offers strong scientific evidence that lifestyle changes alone can actually reverse" clogging of the coronary arteries, "without the use of cholesterol-lowering drugs." Dr. Alexander Leaf, professor of medicine at Harvard Medical School, has said emphatically of Ornish's approach: "We can't go on merely buying a little time by doing bypasses and angioplasty, but having the disease continue to worsen, when you can reverse the disease with these methods."

The Lifestyle study has been criticized because of its small sample, and it has been pointed out that many patients would probably find it very hard to comply with the diet involved. But both Dr.

Ornish's patients and Dr. Esselstyn's have actually complied quite well, probably because considerable effort in each case went into creating a diet that was palatable as well as healthy. Although most physicians would sneer at these doctors' involvement with something as simple as diet, they have in fact cured some of their patients of coronary artery disease. This is something that has never been done with bypass surgery, angioplasty, rotoblation, or any other surgical technique known to science—all these being more or less clumsy repair jobs that figuratively as well as in some cases literally bypass the underlying disease process. Ornish and Esselstyn have made many of these patients essentially heart attack–proof, if not permanently at least long enough so that they may live to die of something else.

As Dr. Esselstyn points out, none of these impressive mechanical techniques address the fundamental molecular, biochemical disorder involved in this disease—while diet certainly does. Yet despite the great emphasis on molecular science in medical school, little is taught about diet, one of the most powerful ways of changing the molecular processes of the body. Cardiovascular diseases are the leading killers in industrialized nations, exceeding all cancers and thoroughly dwarfing a so-far comparatively minor problem such as AIDS. Yet they are almost completely preventable, and most are effectively treatable, with dietary measures. In the last few years carefully designed studies have begun to prove the effectiveness of diet and other lifestyle changes in shrinking the growths blocking arteries supplying the heart.

So why are there so few Esselstyns when there are thousands of bypass surgeons and angioplasters? Because neither medical science nor medical education nor health-care economics have caught up with the facts of life and death as they are affected by diseases of the arteries. Because the technological imperative and the profit motive have dazzled physicians, hospital corporations, and health insurers. And also, certainly, because patients—people in general—have relentlessly insisted on abdicating responsibility for their own health and their own treatment, choosing in almost every case the quick fix; and then, of course, being bitterly disappointed when it doesn't really work.

SIX

DISORDERED STATES

PSYCHIATRY HAS LONG been medicine's neglected stepchild. Throughout most of European history the mentally ill—certainly those with serious disorders—were looked upon as demonic, or at the least "possessed" by demons. An unsympathetic, intensely religious populace confronted them with a mixture of fear and contempt. At worst they were ritually tried and done away with as witches or heretics; at best they were permanently locked away, in places where their care was poor enough to ensure that they would not live very long. Beset by psychic pain—pain that all who have been close to it deem terrible and terrifying, worse perhaps than almost any form of physical suffering—their raw, open emotional wounds were relentlessly worsened by the responses of the ignorant world around them, and they were confined and condemned to physical illnesses that gave embodiment to their suffering.

In the late nineteenth century, scientific views of mental illness began to prevail over primitive religious ones, but there was still little scientists or physicians could do. The early twentieth century saw a distressing rise of eugenic ideas about the mentally ill; these led to laws that mandated sterilization of the mentally ill in the United States and extermination of them in Germany. This history should have taught us that science can be as inhumane as any religious zealotry. But in the late 1930s and 1940s science produced the frontal lobotomy, which calmed the mentally ill at the cost of grave damage to mind and personality. By the time, at midcentury, when we discovered its dismal failure, we were back to the strait-jacket and padded cell, to four-point restraint and lockup—anything to prevent a psychotic from harming someone, most likely himself. It is hard to think of a straitjacket as humane, but to do so one only has to spend a few minutes with a floridly psychotic person intent on self-harm. By then, too, psychoanalysis had spread throughout the Western world, but it had little to offer the most seriously ill, who dwelt in a delusional world of frankly psychotic thought.

In the 1950s these facts changed forever. Jean Delay and Pierre Deniker, two psychiatrists in France, discovered that chlorprom-azine, a drug used against nausea, had the effect of blocking the thought disorders of schizophrenics, even in the absence of general sedation. The consequences were stunning. Within a few years of the discovery, psychotic patients throughout the world who had known only incarceration and restraint began to function well enough and safely enough to be discharged. To be sure, they still needed supervision and care, especially to guarantee that they would continue to take their medicine. But they could be set free at last from the institutional settings to which their illnesses had consigned them and others like them since the dawn of civilization.

As it became clear that at least a partly independent life would now be possible for many schizophrenics, some observers began to believe that it should be mandatory. Mental institutions were widely seen as centers of confinement more than treatment, and in some quarters it was taken for granted that institutionalization was always and everywhere bad for patients—something that psy-chiatrists and hospital administrators did for their own benefit.

Independent life for these patients began to be seen as a civil liberties issue, not primarily a medical one.

This in fact was a tribute to the success of chlorpromazine and other related antipsychotic drugs. By 1975 almost two thirds of the resident patients in American mental hospitals—more than 400,000 people—had been discharged. For a time this was seen as an unreservedly positive development. But it turned out that the history of neglect of the mentally ill was not over. No longer were they mainly incarcerated and ignored; now they were mainly discharged and ignored. Antipsychotic drugs were a boon, but no cure. The thousands who were discharged needed many kinds of support: nursing homes, halfway houses, job training programs, day care, family therapy, and frequent contacts with well-trained nurses, social workers, psychologists, and psychiatrists. They needed to be medically monitored for the neurological disorders that 10 to 20 percent of them would develop as a side effect of the drugs they took—or in the case of lithium, for blood levels of the drug and for rare but catastrophic blood disorders. Although diagnosis and medication were improving steadily, most of these commonsense support services were not available, and did not become available as time went by. Some of those that did appear were so inferior that conditions for patients were worse there than in residential institutions—and sometimes much worse, not excepting physical cruelty and dangerous neglect.

But the taxpayers who had been willing to pay a small fortune to keep a schizophrenic incarcerated were apparently not willing to spend considerably less to maintain the same person in a decent and safe situation outside the hospital. The result was that many thousands of schizophrenics became homeless wanderers, hoboes, and bag ladies, street people vulnerable to involvement with toxic alcohol concoctions and illicit drugs guaranteed to worsen their illnesses, and generally living in a marginal status that was neither properly stabilized on antipsychotic drugs nor quite bad enough to be reinstitutionalized—at least not more than occasionally. Pathetically vulnerable to crime and abuse, neglected by definition, persistently dangerous to themselves if not to others, they are in a situation where the mental hospital may often be a boon, and may indeed be the closest thing they will ever have to a home. The ranks of the non-mentally-ill homeless have grown markedly, but still it is estimated that at least a quarter of all the homeless in America have a serious mental illness, and around half of those appear to be schizophrenic. Looking at it from the other side, one recent study in Kansas found that 40 percent of hospitalized mental patients had no home to go to if and when they were discharged.

Dr. Jack Gorman, director of a clinical research ward for psychiatric patients at New York's distinguished Columbia Presbyterian Hospital, regards deinstitutionalization as a failure.

> I take in very few homeless schizophrenics because I have nowhere for them to go at the end of their three-month stay. The mandate for my program is that they must have somewhere to go that can sustain them, before I can take them on. It must be remembered that there is no cure for schizophrenia . . . All [the drugs] have side effects. The big problem remains the lack of a support system.

For those lucky enough to fulfill Dr. Gorman's mandate, he provides state-of-the-art comprehensive care. That includes a carefully selected spectrum of the latest antipsychotic drugs, subtly monitored for side effects in individual patients; an accepting, supportive milieu on the ward, where patients get help and understanding from others with parallel illnesses, as well as structured activities and professional intervention; and perhaps above all, ultimate discharge to some kind of stable environment, either in a halfway house that continues needed professional care or in a family willing to make the sacrifices and learn the lessons that can postpone or even prevent a sorely troubled loved one's next breakdown. Not least, and perhaps even most important, it must be an environment that will somehow ensure that the person in question continues taking the medicine.

Maggie, a patient of Dr. Gorman's, resembles most psychotics the world over in denying that what she experiences can be anything other than real, and she accordingly resents the people taking care of her for refusing to believe in her reality. "I'm stuck here with voices that they will not tell me what to do about because they believe them to not be real. I believe them to be real people and it doesn't go away for me." She feels she would be better off with people who could see things her way.

> I really don't know if I can be helped merely with medication. I think my life situation is a struggle and a dangerous one, and I'm fighting for my life sometimes . . . If I even ask for help people say, 'I don't know where you're coming from . . . ' What I'm here for is supposedly the voices, you know quote they're coming from my head . . . I think it's a crock of shit I think they're witches. I think they're using supernatural powers from far away to hurt me.

She knows that the voices are bad for her and that she must rid herself of them, but she believes that will never happen unless she is helped by people who share her view of them.

> I'd like to relate to people. I mean I'd really like to relate to someone who can understand me, my interests and my problems. If I had someone to be with twenty-four hours a day that would probably cure me. I mean if I had somebody with me all the time without leaving me I'm sure the voices would go away completely.

Few psychiatrists would take this prediction at face value, yet elements of it are worthy of serious attention. For one thing, there is good evidence that supportive relationships have real therapeutic value for people like Maggie. For another, psychiatrists have long speculated that an illness like hers might have a different course if she were among people who to some extent saw things her way. She says, "I'm into sorcery . . . er . . . religion . . ." Undoubtedly she would still be suffering, and would still seem abnormal, even among others who were also "into" sorcery and other non-mainstream religious ideas. But they would not be flatly denying the reality of her witches, her voices. Perhaps she could be right in thinking that such people would have a different sort of access to her, and to her illness.

Still, most of the psychotics in New York would be lucky to be in Maggie's shoes. She is in a superb treatment facility, and she has the very sturdy support of her sister and brother-in-law—in fact, it is part of her ticket of admission to the facility. In Jack Gorman's harsh calculus of healing, he wisely refuses to spend tens of thousands of dollars' worth of medical resources on patients whose out-of-hospital situation is so hopeless that their hard-won stabilization will not last even a few months. Impoverished, homeless, threatened, abused, constantly tempted to go off their prescribed medicines and substitute street drugs, drifting in and out of touch with the people taking care of them—these are the forgotten ranks of the mentally ill, cut off from the stream of life almost as much as they were when institutionalized.

Scores, if not hundreds, of them can be found a short way from Gorman's state-of-the-science unit, using some of the thousand beds in the Armory. This is a vast single room where each inhabitant is allotted an eight-by-eight-foot space to unshoulder some physical burdens and sleep. All are men; 70 percent are black. In a sense they are the responsibility of the "Super," a sort of overseer who represents City Hall. But the schizophrenics and manic-depressives among them are the burden of the *medical* superintendent, Dr. Alan Felix, and he takes this burden seriously:

> I think that having an understanding of what the relationship consists of and what your reactions are to the patient is vital. Sometimes the whole treatment will hinge on that, because if you are angry, do something that's punitive, or withholding, then you can lose that patient. And then you know, all the Thorazine in the world won't help because you don't have a patient.

It is in the nature of schizophrenia that patients are cut off by the illness from normal social and emotional ties to others; for some, social stresses may figure in the breakdown. Therefore, social support *must* figure in any treatment, almost by definition. Expecting medicines to do the job alone would be like expecting aspirin alone to heal a broken leg, without ever setting it in a cast, and without ever using exercise or physical therapy.

Taking care of these poor, homeless, extremely ill people in the Armory, without even a fraction of the resources Dr. Gorman has just across the street, may not be a fool's errand but it is certainly an uphill fight. Consider Denis, a young schizophrenic who used to freebase cocaine, in his case a fairly sure way to bring on a psychotic break. By his own account he once defecated on himself and didn't care—about what he looked like or even what he smelled like. Where one eye was missing he had a closed, sunken eye socket, without an artificial eye or a patch. His account of his appearance speaks volumes about his social ties at the time—or rather, lack of them; there was simply no one who had enough of a relationship with him to make him want to care at all how he looked. It was all he could do to control himself in the terrifying presence of the voices that constantly broke into his consciousness, telling him to kill himself and others.

Even in the bleakness of the Armory, with Dr. Felix's oversight he has learned to care more. But the environment is dangerous:

> It is a frightening experience, because you don't know if they have any idea that you have money on you, and you get hurt seriously. They . . . they pick out the ones that they think is the weakest, and they will attack them. They will take their food and whatnot. I have one eye, and a lot of people would get over on me because I do have one eye and, and take my milk off my tray or take my food because I can't . . . they know which side to do it on because I was wearing a patch at that time.

During a stay at Manhattan's Bellevue Hospital, Denis was able to get a glass eye, regain some of his physical strength, and get the upper hand over the voices for a time. Then he was able to go out again to the Armory and, with the help of Dr. Felix, have a chance at some further stability.

Homeless mentally ill women in New York are even more vulnerable, but the shelters are smaller, and some of them at least appear to be safer. Florence, one of the residents at the shelter at 350 Lafayette Street, is grateful:

> I heard stories about shelters, that they beat up women,
> they . . . they rob you, they molest you and stuff like that,
> and basically I was petrified. But I had faith in God, so I went
> to the shelter and from, from 85 Lexington they transferred
> me here to 350, and I felt very comfortable here, it's like
> home. Nobody bothers you, it's like a family here, and
> it's . . . it helped my mentality. Helps me, keeps me strong—
> it makes me focus on what I gotta do with myself.

She also calls it "a place just to rest my head," doubtless meaning a lot more than what we mean when we say those words. She likens her medication to the insulin a diabetic must take—a compelling analogy that highlights the enormous, lifesaving importance of this kind of psychiatric drug maintenance. Clearly, Florence is getting some of the social support she needs so badly at this shelter.

Still, another woman at "350" reminds one that this is not even remotely a normal social network:

> You know, sometimes you feel, like, isolation. You know I got
> kids, and it's very hard because . . . there are times I . . . I
> got there on a Saturday, and my son says to me, "Mommy,
> when you gonna come home, when you gonna get an apart-
> ment for us?" So I'm like, I'm like playing a big hero to him,
> and it's like I can't break his heart. I can't just say to him,
> Well, I'm in a shelter now and I can't take you with me. But I
> do tell them that I am sick, I am trying to get myself together,
> they're giving me medicine to, so I go see a doctor and every-
> thing and it's, One day I'll get an apartment for all of us and,
> you know, have faith with me, you know, take care, you
> know, don't worry—I still love you . . . When I leave my son,
> I see, like, tears come out of his eyes, and he says "Mommy,
> you gotta go now," and I say yes I have to go, and I—it's

hard to say good-bye to them, you know, it's like, O gee I
wish I hadn't to go through this, you know, you be like O
God here I go again . . . it's very hard.

Both these women talk about faith, but no ministry beside the
psychiatric one seems to play a role in their care. This is ironic,
after centuries in which the interpretation and disposition of suf-
fers like them was almost entirely in religious hands. The absence
of people who can help turn their faith to healing advantage is
distressing, and I also found it so when working in psychiatric
hospitals in the Boston area during my medical education. Where
are the chaplains? One would think that theirs would potentially
be one of the most powerful ways to reach people who are, after
all, spiritually troubled by almost any definition. Yet among the
mentally ill poor one sees few examples of religious ministry,
whether explicit or indirect.

But this is not true everywhere, not even everywhere in New
York. Near the Church and Friary of Saint Francis of Assisi there
is a welfare hotel that, like all such places for the poor, includes
many who are mentally ill. Two members of the order chose to
step outside Saint Francis and to devote themselves to the medical,
social, and spiritual care of these lost, needy people. One, Father
John McVean, speaks of this ministry matter-of-factly, thinking
back to the dramatic changes of the 1970s, when he began it.

I stumbled into this privately owned [welfare] hotel near our
monastery—and it turned out that this building was *filled*
with people that had been what we now call deinstitutional-
ized. I don't know if the word even existed back then, but
these were people who had been stabilized on these new
medications, and it was felt that they could be released back
to the community. Unfortunately there was no community.
There was no family, no support system that would see that
they would take the medications. Consequently they would
get sick again, go back in the hospital, restabilize, back out,
go off the medications, go back in the hospital. So what I
stumbled upon back in the early seventies, as a social problem, was not homelessness, but it was something called *the re-*

volving door syndrome. In fact what we created was a surrogate family, a surrogate community for these folks that didn't have a community—to provide the services that would enable them to stay out of the hospital.

The extent to which this community really serves as a family is indicated by the fact that when one of the residents dies, it is often the Franciscan brothers who arrange for the burial; there is frequently no one else to do it. Unfortunately most of the mentally ill poor in New York do not have even a surrogate community much less a real one. People like Father McVane, or Dr. Felix for that matter, who are prepared to give a significant part of their lives to provide desperately needed continuity of care for people with no other hope, are always few and far between.

It is tempting to blame psychiatrists and other doctors for not solving the problem, but this is another sign of our immaturity; we insist on the pretense of omnipotence and exaggerated altruism in doctors just so we can lay the blame elsewhere than on ourselves. But the doctors have been telling us clearly: their resources are gone, done, finished, long before their patients' needs have even begun to be met. They have told us clearly, too, that no magic bullet exists for schizophrenia or any other psychosis; with all the drugs we have there is only a chance to partway stabilize a person who, with the right support from a community that cares, can stay stabilized for a good long time, and without that community, can't. As Pixie, a Haitian mother now living on the street without her children, staring around at the desolation surrounding her, says, "You see the skeletons of buildings, you see the skeletons of people, and . . . it's a damn shame, *tu comprends?* You know— politics sucks." Politics, not medicine, society, not doctors; *us,* not *them.*

Some people blame New York for having one of the worst problems of this kind, but in fact the streets of New York overflow with the homeless mentally ill precisely because New York has offered more—more welfare, more shelters, more free psychiatric care— than most of the rest of America. So the city becomes a magnet for people who have nowhere else to go, whose hometowns and states have abandoned them, and is blamed, in effect, for even *trying* to take care of them.

And why are they ignored and neglected elsewhere? Because the homeless mentally ill are not a voting bloc, nor have they organized a political action committee. Because the suburban homeowner doesn't want their halfway houses anywhere near his children—or his property value. Because the businesswoman in a hurry has trained herself to stare right through their sad, filthy faces framed in matted, lice-infected hair. Because they remind us far too insistently of how vulnerable we all are, and how inhumanely we too will be treated if and when we have the luck to falter.

India has the second largest and still one of the fastest-growing populations of any nation in the world, so it is no surprise that there are millions of homeless living on the streets of its cities. But if there is a shortage of homes, there is no shortage of relatives. Eighty percent of the population still lives in villages structured around extended families. That means that someone who becomes mentally ill will feel alone only to the extent that the illness itself keeps him or her psychologically out of touch. If and as recovery occurs, a family and a community will usually be there—to respond, converse, support, touch, comfort—in short, to make recovering more worth doing. Maggie's poignant appeal for company—*If I had someone to be with twenty-four hours a day*—is harder to imagine for similar patients in India. Someone is usually there.

In the holy city of Banaras, for example, on the banks of the Ganges, people make religious pilgrimages to bathe in the river's sacred water. But they make these pilgrimages as families. Akbur Puri, one of the villages near Banaras, draws such pilgrims from distant places; they come to seek the help of traditional healers, but also of modern physicians. Whether the victim is Hindu or Muslim, people believe it may help to bathe in the Ganges or actually to eat the pages of the holy Koran. But they recognize it will also help to seek Western-style treatment from Western-trained psychiatrists. Somatic, or biological, treatments are respected, so the families of patients may demand pills and even electric shock therapy, an approach that has, after long controversy, become accepted again in the United States, and is particularly esteemed in India.

Still, few are willing to forgo parallel or simultaneous spiritual treatment, and Akbur Puri is dense with specialists of this kind as well. Indeed, the mental hospital and clinic are surrounded by a vast, crowded camping ground consisting of patients, their families, and traditional adepts and spiritual healers. Just as Maggie's Indian counterpart would suffer no externally imposed isolation from other people, she would not have to look far to find many who would take her voices, her demons, very seriously. Not that they wouldn't try to help her get rid of them; just that they would set about to do so as believers, and as such, as full allies of the patient against the threatening forces in the spirit-world, not as experts clucking their tongues over the poor woman's nonexistent voices.

But perhaps most essentially, the social network that the Franciscan friars in New York had to build up so laboriously from scratch is already in place in Banaras. Patients normally do not come for treatment without their families, who stay nearby, participate in consultations with the doctors, take full responsibility for helping with the treatment, and above all provide a home and family for the patient to be discharged to—something that psychiatrists who care for the mentally ill poor of Manhattan often have no chance of finding for *their* patients.

An Indian psychiatrist, Dr. Indira Sharma, head of the department of psychiatry at Banaras Hindu University, talks about one of her patients in terms any Western physician would understand.

This lady is suffering from schizophrenia of one-year duration. There is a family history of a similar illness in her father as well. And it is nice that I find that the husband and the mother of the patient have also come in with the patient, and they also have expressed their keenness to cooperate in the treatment program. I am advising her to continue these drugs for about two weeks, and then she can come in for follow-up. She has also been told that the drug treatment is very essential and how the family should deal with her when she is at home. And in particular they must not react strongly when she is not able to do her routine duties, for example the domestic duties which she is expected to do. They should not express their resentment. Rather they should be neutral and try to explain to her in a sympathetic way that she is ill, and we do not mind if she is not able to do her work, which she would certainly be able to do when she gets well.

This is the sort of fine-tuning of a family that Jack Gorman is able to do with his patients in the research ward at Columbia, and that Alan Felix is unable to do at the Armory where there are no families to fine-tune—where people approach a homeless schizophrenic like Denis from the side where his blind eye is and take away his milk.

Dr. Sharma also advises the patient and the family to stay away from alternative spiritual or Koranic healers, but that part of the advice is not likely to be followed. If the patient and family can faithfully apply all that they are told about drug management, social support, and responsiveness, and return to the clinic for follow-up, then it may even be helpful to consult a spiritual healer as well. We know very well the power of the doctor-patient relationship to aid in healing, especially in psychiatry. If the alternative healer can actually enter the symbolic world of the psychotic person and converse about the psychotic thoughts in a serious, accepting way, the opportunity may present itself for drawing the patient out of mental and emotional isolation in novel and perhaps more effective ways.

As pointed out by one of Maggie's psychiatrists back in Manhattan, she would still be and seem psychotic in a culture that believed, as she does, in witches. For example, she might be unique in believing that witches can act from a great distance away. Psychiatrically normal people in such a culture would experience the witches in different, more predictable, and more controllable ways. So the point is not that psychosis evaporates in a world where everyone has beliefs that a Western philosopher might call delusions. Rather, the hope is that a culture that is not simply dismissive of these strange ideas might be able to meet the patient halfway. Or to put it another way, the support network around such a patient would consist not only of loving, concerned, well-prepared family and friends, but also of powerful symbols, language, and meaning.

Perhaps the closest we have gotten to this in Western culture is to have taken seriously some of the images drawn, painted, and sculpted by those among the mentally ill who have real artistic talent. Vincent van Gogh is the most famous of these, but there are many others whose work is documented by John MacGregor in *The Discovery of the Art of the Insane.* Even the process of art therapy, or the mere passing of the time in mental institutions in drawing and painting, involves the communication of images that may be visible only to those who are steeped in the pain of psychosis. Other visions, like van Gogh's *The Hospital at Arles,* may be straightforward depictions of the bleakness of life as the mentally ill experience it. As MacGregor says, "To value insights derived from psychotic experience is not to indulge in uncritical enthusiasm for insanity"—or, we might add, any enthusiasm at all. It is certainly not for us to say that their pain is worth the visions they have. But just by paying attention to those visions, we may get a little closer to Maggie's dream of having someone to really keep her company in her pain.

Siena is an ancient Italian town, set unobtrusively among the soft hills of Tuscany, that draws tourists from all the world just because it is beautiful. A decade ago one of my daughters, then three and wearing a prim blue pinafore, chased scores of pigeons across the sunlit stones of the great central piazza; not very impressed, they fluttered up to the clock tower that has tolled the passing hours for centuries. In July each year, the town—and hordes of tourists as well—descends on this piazza for a bit of centuries-old ritualized madness called the Palio.

It is an incredibly intense horse race in which each of the town's medieval guilds fields a horse and rider for a no-holds-barred series of turns around the medieval square. Before the race, each horse is taken into church to be blessed, and the jockeys are guarded day and night, forbidden to speak to anyone. During the race those same jockeys flog each other with whips made from calves' phalluses. The horses' hooves seem barely to make contact with the sand-covered stones as they career around and around, the track marked off by the density of the crowd, the guilds' colors flying under the shadow of the fourteenth-century clock tower. Violence, among the riders as well as the crowd, is not unusual. The winner sucks a pacifier, the loser takes a purge.

It seems crazy. Yet in the realm of real craziness—the disordered thought and action of schizophrenics—Siena proves to be much less of a horse race than New York, and devoid of the violence that psychotic people in Manhattan fear every day. Indeed, the mentally ill are fairly cradled by this ancient town, just as the town is cradled by the hills. They are neither figuratively nor actually the focus of the crowd, and they face no competition except perhaps with their own best idea of themselves. As to that, it fits fairly well with what is expected of normal people in the Mediterranean world: if you get up, wash, eat, go for a walk, shop a bit, chat with friends, have dinner and a glass of wine—no squeamishness here about mixing alcohol and madness—take a nap, shop or walk or talk with friends some more . . . well, you are not far from an ideal life even if they do call you crazy. If you sweep the sidewalk or wash dishes to pick up a few lire, and certainly if you go to a dance in the evening, well, you are doing very nicely, thank you. After all, this is not northern Europe or the Anglo-Saxon countries, where you have to prove your worth, your right to exist, every day.

A dance is in fact a common event at Siena's mental hospital, San Niccolò, originally run—like the welfare hotel in New York— by Franciscan friars. But despite their care, until recently it earned the quotation from Dante's *Inferno* emblazoned over its fourteenth-century arch: *Leave all hope behind, you who enter here.* Although from the time of Napoleon's conquests the hospital was officially run on rational principles, not devil-and-demon talk, in fact it was a living hell for most patients until the 1970s. Hundreds were in chains, many in solitary confinement; enormously strong nurses and orderlies had to wrestle them into some sort of submission. Their terror, their anguish, their unremitting suffering were almost beyond belief.

Psychiatric theories put forward by Cesare Lombroso in the late nineteenth century dominated the twentieth. The mentally ill, like criminals, were born, not made, and society needed protection from them. In the time of Mussolini, these ideas fit well with the Fascist mood. As elsewhere in Europe, and even in the United States, various strong measures to protect society, to set the mentally ill far apart, were deemed necessary. It was Oliver Wendell Holmes, Jr., the great American Supreme Court Justice, who upheld a sterilization order saying, "Three generations of imbeciles are enough." For the Nazis it was not enough to sterilize them and set them apart; they went on systematically to murder them.

Then the antipsychotic drugs came, to Siena as they had come most everywhere else, and suddenly real lives were thinkable for these patients—not just for patients like them, but for themselves, real lives after sometimes decades in chains. To ensure that the hospitals would not be tempted to hold on to their patients, Franca Basaglia, a senator in the parliament in Rome, who was married to a pioneering psychiatrist also involved in mental hospital reform, introduced a law that in 1978 codified the assumption that the state had no right to hold people against their will. The mental hospitals largely emptied almost overnight.

As in the United States, it was not an unreserved blessing. Dr. Livia D'Argenio, a small, determined woman who is medical director of San Niccolò, has lived through both eras; she knows they both had and have problems:

> It isn't as easy as people think. I am in sympathy with many
> of the new reformers, but you cannot just let people go out
> into a vacuum. They have to go somewhere. All of the people
> here are free to go if they wish. In fact the new law means
> that once they get outside, even if it's just for a visit to their

friends, then they can't come back inside without a court
order. It's rather a ridiculous state of affairs—the pendulum
has swung too much in the other direction. The stigma of
mental illness within our communities is still great.

They are free to leave if they want to, but most of them don't. The
hospital is their home, and with the medications available to them,
it is not a bad one. Still, the world outside the hospital, for those
less ill patients who can handle it, is far less forbidding than the
corresponding world of the schizophrenic discharged into the bow-
els of New York.

There is hardly a better way to illustrate this point than to follow
the fortunes of a group of patients who had been residents in a
Roman hospital, Santa Maria della Pietà, until 1988. Although the
combined impact of the new medications and the Basaglia law
should have given them their freedom years earlier, the hospital
administration held on to them. Then one day an art therapist and
another staff member took them for a day's outing to the country,
and they simply never came back. They remained in Bracciano,
the lakeside town, where the local general practitioner maintains
them on medication and helps take care of them in other ways.
The two dedicated and enterprising hospital staff members stay
with them, using both government and private sources to generate
funds to look after them as outpatients—as free men and women.

When interviewed, they have been out for a year, after being in
Santa Maria for ten, twenty-five, one even thirty-two years. The
art therapist, Evonne Couvert, draws them out. One, Roberto, says
with simple eloquence that "it was as if we had seen everything
for the first time . . . all at once . . . and when we have had the
opportunity to see beautiful things, we have felt a little . . . it's as
if certain things are asleep . . . but they must wake up again."
Evonne asks, "And what are the beautiful things outside?" "The
beautiful things outside . . . the nurse said, '*If you are looking for
peace, you will find peace . . . when you are dead.*' " But has he found
some peace here?

"Yes, I found a little peace here . . . of course, there are moments of sadness, but also good moments . . . when you have a little more strength . . . the body reacts better and the enthusiasms are . . . let's say . . . more satisfactory."

"I like it here," another man says. "There is more peace. The lake keeps your personality calm . . . it calms you down." He had never liked having too many people around, and in the hospital there had been too many people. With this group, he feels comfortable. Another man, Manuele, is asked what he had been looking for in the outside world. "You mean the difference between here and there? Outside it feels great! We don't depend any more, all of us, on the hospital. Each of us has his own responsibility."

At a town meeting in Bracciano, the mayor declares the incorporation of these mental patients into the town to be a source of pride. A physician, Dr. Sigillo, rises to say that "this meeting should really fill us with joy, because the community is making a great effort toward the mentally disabled people. And that means that an experiment, something new, has been carried out, conscientiously and with determintion, to solve the problem." He goes on to observe wisely that mental illness was born together with human beings, implying that it must be solved with human beings.

An older visiting physician, Professor Antonnio Iaria, medical director of Santa Maria della Pietà in Rome, has waited a long time for this unauthorized experiment. "I witness now with pleasure something that I have always maintained—that patients can leave the hospital, and they can do it well. I remember that in one of those meetings, in the year 1974–75, when we used to be angry, when I began talking about my plans, a nurse told me that I was an incurable optimist. I would like to tell the nurse now that my optimism had some results."

Dr. Tommaso Losavio, also of Santa Maria della Pietà, expresses how profound this experiment is:

> I don't think that it's enough: to find a house, where you can put people outside the psychiatric hospital, because that house itself can become a small asylum. It is important that this reality has its real location in the village, the borough where these people live, and that the community acknowl-

edges this situation, not any more as strange, alien, but a reality which belongs to that community. If these people are recognized as citizens of this village, the village itself is transformed, because it becomes conscious of a reality which belongs to it, not imposed from outside, but a *suffering* which, in one way or another, exists in the village.

The suffering itself is given a right of citizenship, and this allows the house not to be separated, excluded, but to be part of this context of life.

The suffering itself is given a right of citizenship. It recalls the dreams of Anne Waldschmidt and her friends, to the north in Bremen, Germany, dreams for the acceptance of disability as an integral part of human social life, and Dr. Eric Cassell's warning that physicians must learn to deal with suffering as well as disease, or forfeit their right to be called healers. It is also a far cry from that young mother, living on the street in New York, staring around in despair at "the skeletons of buildings, the skeletons of people," and then crawling back into the cardboard box that her "community" has forced her to call home.

A decade ago the Bracciano story would have seemed quite implausible to most psychiatrists. But ideas about chronic schizophrenia are changing. Several recent studies in Europe and the United States have followed severely ill schizophrenics for decades, and found that some of them do surprisingly well. For example, the Vermont Longitudinal Study found that of 118 patients who in the 1950s met stringent current criteria for schizophrenia, "one-half to two-thirds . . . had achieved considerable improvement or recovered" and were living in the community in the 1980s. All "were once profoundly ill, backward, chronic patients." Clearly, "chronic" schizophrenia is not always so chronic. The question is, What determines whether it is or not in individual cases?

Dr. Arthur Kleinman has devoted his career to a single overriding idea: that the cultural and social context of illness, especially mental illness, is at least as important as any process going on in the body

or brain. Not that he isn't convinced of the power of those processes too; just that he has learned through decades of professional
experience that in our time the emphasis on biological explanations
of mental illness has once again gained the ascendance. Millions
of people in Western countries, most of them close to "normal"—
whatever that means—have found that they can tinker with their
brain chemistry, not just with illicit but with safely prescribed
drugs; and as a result they can adjust to lives that otherwise would
have been deeply unsatisfactory, by virtue of flaws that used to
be thought of as philosophical or spiritual, not medical problems.
People have come to terms with their lives by splashing drug cock-
tails at their brains. Since not all human situations can be changed,
this approach is not always a bad thing.

But by inference, the same people assume that those with more
serious mental illnesses are basically medically ill, sufferers from
brain disorders, period; and, by further inference: brain disorder,
brain treatment. But as we have seen, few psychiatric illnesses,
indeed few illnesses in general, can be legitimately dealt with just
as biochemical problems. And Dr. Kleinman has done more than
anyone to lay the foundations of a new kind of psychiatry that
will be a creature neither of laboratory brain research nor of the
psychotherapist's office, but a far broader, more enlightened dis-
cipline which can set those valid approaches to work in a real-
world human context.

Kleinman is a psychiatrist who for decades has had daily responsibility for patients, including many of the most seriously ill
and many of the most desperately poor. But he is also an anthropologist with years of experience in developing countries, among
people whose ways of life and belief are so unfamiliar, so exotic,
as to baffle most psychiatrists who lack any training in anthropology. He can prescribe chlorpromazine, as it were, with the best
of them, and he draws on various standard psychotherapies in his
daily work. But when he looks at a patient his vision extends far
beyond the chemical slush of the brain and body, far beyond the
dreary walls of the consulting room, to a whole world of forces
as uncomprehended by many psychiatrists as the space-time continuum was by physicists at the dawn of the twentieth century.

These are the social and cultural forces that help to cause mental illness and that can keep making it worse or, with the help of medications and psychotherapy, turn it back toward health. They are as various as the stresses of homelessness and poverty, the humiliations of bigotry, the strength of religious faith, the isolation of loss and grief, and the fear of devils and demons. They can be as seemingly trivial as the contemptuous glance of a policeman, the backfire of a passing bus that reminds a man of war, or the trapped feeling a woman gets when her boss makes sexual jokes with her. They can be as charged as a father's rape of his child or the touch of a brother's loving hand on his sister's troubled brow. And they can be as exotic as the belief that eating pages of the Koran is curative or that a passing shadow is devastatingly harmful.

How do we know that these forces are real? One way is simply through a process of elimination. Much as we know about the force of genes, we have repeatedly proved that they are not up to the task of explaining all of mental illness. Take schizophrenia for example—a disorder in which the environment would not, offhand, seem to explain much. But if you look at identical twin pairs in which one member of the pair has schizophrenia and then take a look at his or her twin, as a number of studies have done, you will find that the other twin has the same disorder only about half the time, give or take 10 or 15 percent, depending on the study. This is a paradox for the theorist who takes an interest only in biochemistry. Because although it means that the genes are very powerful, it also means that the environment is about equally powerful. While some of this environmental effect is due to things like head injury and brain viruses, much must be due to the social and cultural forces that, after a century of psychiatric science, we still know very little about.

At least that is true of the forces that help to cause schizophrenia in the first place. As for what helps schizophrenics get better, and what helps keep them that way, hundreds of family and milieu studies have taught us quite a bit more. There is no longer any doubt, even in the minds of the most biologically oriented psychiatrists, that patterns of culture and social life within the mental institution systematically influence the time it takes an acutely ill schizophrenic to recover enough to be discharged. It is equally well established that the pattern of interaction in a family, or in any group to which the improved patient is discharged, can predict or precipitate the next breakdown; and that systematically applied family therapy can significantly postpone that breakdown, even without change in the medications.

It therefore stands to reason that the pleasant, friendly byways of the lakeside town of Bracciano will have a positive therapeutic effect compared to the empty urban canyons of New York, and that even within Manhattan the hotel run by the friars will help keep schizophrenics well far better than the Armory. By extension, it seems possible that as we survey the world, cultures with strong family traditions and broad kin ties will be better places to get sick in than cultures in which the family has been worn down to a skeleton. While this possibility is certainly suggested by what we saw in India, proving it is something else again.

The concept that psychotic patients in the developing world recover more readily than those in the industrialized world has been discussed for at least half a century, but the evidence put forward is full of problems. First and foremost is the problem of diagnosis. As recently as the early 1970s, studies showed that British and American psychiatrists differed widely on the diagnosis of the same psychotic patients, with the Americans classifying most of them as schizophrenic and the British instead labeling them manic-depressive. This was not a merely semantic dispute, since the label "schizophrenic" led to treatment mainly with antipsychotic drugs like chlorpromazine, while the "manic-depressive" label meant the patient might be stabilized on lithium, with much rarer serious side effects—a drug not often used in the United States at the time. If two countries sharing the same language and similar cultures, even similar medical traditions, could differ so drastically in their ways of categorizing psychotic people, what could be expected when comparisons arose between psychotics from really *different* cultures?

Since the American psychiatrists were to move in the direction of the British in diagnosis during the 1970s and 1980s, and since lithium proved useful for more and more of their patients, it is reasonable to conclude that the British were right. But besides the drug therapies there is another crucial difference between the two disorders: since the nineteenth century, schizophrenia has been viewed as a basically degenerative disorder, one that gets worse as the patient goes through life. But manic-depressive illness has been viewed as naturally cyclical; it is in the nature of the illness to have periods of madness alternating with periods of relative mental health.

Thus the first serious problem with the cross-cultural hypothesis of recovery: if the chronic disease in question (schizophrenia) is often confused with a naturally cyclical one (manic-depressive illness), then only the most rigorously controlled studies could convincingly show that recovery is faster and better in less developed countries. But decades of studies of the hypothesis lacked such controls.

Dr. Kleinman, together with his colleague Keh-Ming Lin of the UCLA Medical Center, recently reviewed this disappointing record and concluded that most of the studies of the hypothesis cannot be considered good evidence to support it—there are just too many uncertainties about patterns of diagnosis in all the different countries and cultures being compared. But there is yet another serious problem. True schizophrenia is a very maladaptive disorder. As we saw in New York, survival itself is threatened when a person's behavior is that impaired. If we then consider the same level of impairment in the context of an underdeveloped country, where the consequences of not eating, clothing, cleaning, and defending oneself properly may well be fatal, we can readily see that the psychiatrically sickest patients simply may not survive in that context. And if they do not survive they will not be around to be studied by researchers looking at how well they recover. The result may be an overrepresentation in developing countries in favor of patients who are less impaired to begin with, and so more likely to recover in any case.

Lin and Kleinman are aware of these problems, but are optimistic about the possibility that two major international studies conducted by the World Health Organization—one recently completed and one still in progress—may have solved them. Unfortunately this does not yet seem to be the case. The completed study followed 1,200 patients in cities in nine countries: Arhus, Denmark; Agra, India; Cali, Colombia; Ibadan, Nigeria; London, U.K.; Moscow, Russia; Prague, Czecholosvakia; Taipei, Taiwan; and Washington, D.C., U.S.A. Of the total, over 800 were classified as schizophrenic.

Two and five years later, the industrialized countries did have lower recovery rates on average, but recovery varied much more *among* the industrialized countries themselves, and also among the nonindustrial countries, than it differed *between* the two types of countries. In addition, some of the centers had high rates of dropout from their study samples. Finally, many of the "schizophrenics" in India, Colombia, Nigeria, and Russia had to be later rediagnosed as manic-depressives or other varieties of psychotics with better intrinsic prospects for recovery than true schizophrenics have. The same was *not* true of the other countries in the study, which apparently had more accurate diagnosis to begin with. Lin and Kleinman believe that forthcoming results from the second international study will provide stronger support for the cross-cultural hypothesis of recovery, but that remains to be seen.

What is beyond question, however, is that humane treatment of the mentally ill is in itself a good thing. In Banaras, India, treatment is not as humane as it could be, for the simple and sad reason that resources there are insufficient by a long way to provide really good treatment for the mentally ill poor. Strangely, the same is true in Manhattan; but in India families are often there to provide a decent milieu for recovery. They may be dirt-poor, but they are there. In New York the poor psychotic faces a lonely life in the bleakness of the Armory or on the unforgiving streets, surrounded by "skeletons of buildings." With good insurance and a supportive family one can do well in New York; but without them one might just be a bit better off in Banaras.

As for Italy, I think it would be my ideal place to have a psychotic break, especially if my financial resources were scarce. For all its imperfections, it seems the most humane of the three places. And the mental-health system there is grappling bravely with its own idea of itself, constantly reexamining its own claim to humanity. As one psychiatrist said at the meeting in Bracciano,

> Madness is a phenomenon universally recognized, but the people's attitude toward folly changes, historically and geographically. And the attitude is often based on prejudice. Prejudice is basically fear of madness. Madness . . . upsets people profoundly . . . It causes in ourselves the worry that our own folly can be awakened.

But as Arthur Kleinman points out in his book *Rethinking Psychiatry*, there is another kind of prejudice, one that is pervasive in his own medical specialty, and one that he has spent his life trying to change:

> Cross-cultural comparison, appropriately applied, can challenge the hubris in bureaucratically motivated attempts to medicalize the human condition. It can make us sensitive to the potential abuses of psychiatric labels. It encourages humility in the face of alternative cultural formulations of the same problems, which are viewed not as evidence of the ignorance of laymen, but as distinctive modes of thinking about life's problems . . . Most experienced psychiatrists learn to struggle to translate diagnostic categories into human terms so that they do not dehumanize their patients or themselves . . . Irony, paradox, ambiguity, drama, tragedy, humor—these are the elemental conditions of humanity that should humble even master diagnosticians.

Irony, paradox, ambiguity, drama, tragedy, humor: they may be the elemental conditions of humanity, but they still do not leap to our minds when we confront the mentally ill. Rather, we slap a medical label on them and confidently send them away. To be truly humane means to rise above our fears and accept the fact that the mentally disabled are not so very different from us that we could not possibly be in their shoes. It means that one way or another we have to grant citizenship to suffering.

SEVEN

LIFE SUPPORT

THE SENIOR CITIZEN is a new man in Florida!" my Uncle Herman announced one day in his broad Brooklyn accent, slapping me on the back with a big, heavy, healthy hand. "You ought to come down there and study them!" It was around 1970; he and my aunt had moved a few years earlier to a south Florida community called Century Village. There are many such communities now, each consisting of hundreds or thousands of small, rather pretty mass-produced houses owned by retired couples or individuals—given the different death rates of the sexes, usually women. Their accessible clubhouses are full of stimulating activity: card games, theater, libraries, political meetings, even community newspapers. There is dancing—square, folk, or couple dancing—swimming, golf, softball teams, bowling leagues. Nearby are affordable restaurants, markets, and the ubiquitous shopping malls. Everywhere you see vigorous, cheerful old people, ranging over a more-than-thirty-year age span from the late fifties to the nineties. And these people are glad to be alive.

My conversation with my uncle occurred at the beginning of a vast cultural change in the United States that has taken a large and increasing minority of elderly people out of the cities where they spent their lives, away from their grown children and grandchildren, and into communities filled with others like themselves. The first thing that must be understood about this movement is that it was engineered by the senior citizens themselves. No one put them away in what some might see as remote ghettos. They decided to segregate themselves.

Sun City, Arizona, is one remarkable example of such a community. It is a new, fabricated town built for exactly this purpose, and its citizens, who call themselves Sun Citians, swear by it. Grandchildren are allowed to visit only a few weeks a year, and no one under fifty-five may live there. "Dutch" Schultz, a man in his mid-seventies, is one of the town's many amateur performers; decked out in a cowboy hat and string tie, he strums his guitar and sings the unofficial anthem to an audience of other septuagenarians:

> Sun City, U.S.A.,
> It's so outstanding in every way,
> It's great in the West and we're here to stay
> In Sun City, U.S.A.

In the song, which Dutch wrote himself, he calls Sun City a "heaven on earth" and praises its founder for giving it "a heart to withstand the passage of time." It ends, significantly, on the line "Sun City will never grow old."

Later Dutch and his wife Dee, a dance performer who does routines that might daunt a person half a century younger, glide around an artificial lake on their boat and talk about life, death, and dancing. "Well," Dutch says with a smile, "the goal of all the activity [here] is to enjoy the rest of your life, whatever your aim is."

> And we enjoy dancing, my wife and I just enjoy—we teach dancing. I think Sun City people come out here to retire, but

once they get here, they just feel a lot younger by seeing the activities that's going on, and—I don't know, it's just that young breeds youngness, the thought, the thinking of it. One thing just leads to another and first thing you know everybody's acting that way. My son, who didn't know anything about Sun City, asked me when I moved out here, he said, "What are you movin' to Sun City for? You goin' out there to die?" And I says, "Heavens no, I'm goin' out there to start livin'."

Dee is at least as emphatic about her fellow citizens:

They don't have time to think about dying. The only time you think about dying is when a funeral home calls you and asks you if you've had your will made out, or if you've got your funeral plans made out. And that's the only time you think about dying. You're so busy around here—you get up in the morning and you have swimming, you've got aerobics and dance lessons, and you don't have time to think about dying. You've got a hard time just to visit your friends, we're so busy!

Oh sure, we go to church, and I sing in the choir. We have our times with God, and our devotionals, and those are the times that—no, sure we think about dying, but we don't dwell on it. We have a lot of fun out here in Sun City, and we . . . we *love life*.

But if Sun Citians don't like to think about dying, that doesn't mean they don't die, of course. And before they die most of them first, as doctors sometimes put it, "try to die"—they become critically ill. Harold Chinlund, an eighty-two-year-old retired accountant, was trying to die one day when his wife brought him into Sun City's Walter O. Boswell Memorial Hospital. As both of them knew, he was suffering from a fatal disease, pancreatic cancer; still, they had been told he would have perhaps three good months of life before becoming very ill and dying from the tumor. But now he was prostrate and suffocating because of a pneumonia superimposed on the cancer that threatened to rob him of the remaining promised months—months of golf, bridge, even bowling, and of time to really say good-bye to his wife.

Mrs. Chinlund is candid about their lack of preparation:

> I'm very ignorant in medical things. And when the two doc-tors stood there and said this is the only thing we can do to save his life at this point, they thought, I said, Well, you should do that. But I don't know what trauma he's going to be going through. Because I know so little about these things. And I think it's a shame that the public doesn't know what people have to go through to get well. Of course he won't ever be well, but they said that he would have at least three months relatively free of pain, and then they would start some other things on him.

But she continues in a vein that is more revealing:

> Harold and I never spoke about what would happen if we got in a situation like this. He seemed to think he was going to live forever. And he didn't want to talk about it. In fact he wouldn't even tell me what he wanted to do in case he did die—whether he wanted cremation, or anything. He just would not talk about it. I didn't know what I should do. But I talked it over with the doctors, and they seem to think there is a little hope of getting him through this pneumonia—if the cancer hasn't spread to his lower lungs. At the time of the op-eration ten days ago it hadn't spread anyplace but the pan-creas—which *is* fatal, I know that. Cancer of the pancreas is fatal. But according to these doctors, they can't tell how long he might live.

Not so very long ago in medicine, pneumonia used to be called "the old man's friend." If Harold were to succumb to it this time, he might lose the potential three good months. But he would also be spared months of battling an extremely painful illness, punc-tuated by painful, debilitating treatments, that would inevitably follow the three months. Could the doctors be wrong? Sure, it might be six months or even more; nothing in biology is totally precise. But it might also be fewer than three. With pancreatic cancer, the ending is never in dispute, only the timing—and there isn't much leeway in that.

Harold's adopted daughter Kate, who arrives some days later, is a critical-care nurse herself, and she regrets that aggressive treatment of the pneumonia has begun.

> I've been working in the medical profession long enough to know that the outcomes of this stuff are predictable and fairly ugly. But if you're given a chance, why not take it; I can't fault him for doing that. I wish they hadn't done what they did— put him on a ventilator. I don't think he would have wanted that. And I love the man, dearly. But I don't want him to be in pain, and I don't want him to be confused, and out of control . . . And he currently is tied down, and can't talk, and doesn't really know what's going on, I hope. And that's not my dad, that's not what his whole life has been about. And I really hate to see it.
>
> I honestly don't think that this "treatment" is going to make my dad any better. And I don't think that he's going to have any comfort in the rest of whatever life he has left, and I feel very badly that it happened. Just because we *can* do it doesn't mean we should. Technology isn't always the greatest boon to everyone.
>
> And the doctors have a lot of trouble with that, because they're doctors—they're supposed to *cure* people. and it's very difficult for a lot of the ones that I know to say, "Gee, I can't" . . . I think the medical profession needs to know that it's okay to die. We don't have to save everyone, just to make another two months on a life. You know, we can say, Gee, I've had a good life, I'm ready to go—and do that.

She talks at length with her dad's third wife—evidently there is some tension—trying to help her prepare emotionally for a loss that will come, if not in the next few days, in the next few months. Mrs. Chinlund is not adamant, but she does know some things the daughter may not know. "I've seen lots of men with cancer enjoy their lives. In fact our president of our club just died of cancer, and he went up to the last week or two enjoying himself."

A bit of anger flares between them, because they have different vantage points, different goals.

But a day or two later the treatment fails, even in its short-term goal of stabilizing his lungs and giving him the three months. Hearing this, and hearing the new tone in the doctor's voice, wife and daughter no longer have any disagreement. Mrs. Chinlund, perhaps, has needed these few days to adjust to the end coming sooner that she had hoped. But in any case there is no will on anyone's part to continue mechanical breathing, and—as Kate has put it earlier—the plug is pulled.

On the same day Betsy Nichols, another loving daughter facing a similar situation, waits with her mother as her father undergoes kidney surgery. The mother says, "Everything seems to break down at a different time. One thing is improving and something else is falling apart." The daughter's frustration with medicine's *fix-the-broken-machine* approach is painfully clear:

> It's very hard to talk with one doctor, because each doctor is a specialist, and we really are confident in his specialty. But if we talk to the kidney doctor, and he says, "Fifteen years ago we could do nothing, look how great it is now!"—I mean I realize he's doing his job, and I appreciate it. But what about the lungs? What about the liver? He's a whole person! And that's where the dilemma comes in. Because my father wants to live as a whole person. I do feel that they're overly optimistic. I think that everyone looks at their piece of the body, and how that's gonna react to their treatment—which I guess is good . . .

She even feels that her father is angry with her, because, unlike the Chinlund family, they *have* discussed how they would handle a situation like this: No prolongation of pointless pain. Betsy's mother, who was in on those discussions with her husband, is more blunt: "I spoke to his sister last night. And I told her that I will not sign for anything else. He knows that I had promised him I would not do this, I would not put him on life support for the sake of science." But since she is not sure that the situation is hopeless, and there is nothing new to sign for, life support continues.

Life expectancy at birth is increasing in most of the world—in Western industrial countries it is in the mid-seventies for men and near eighty for women. But this statistic gives little indication of what is happening late in life, since it averages the life span of people who die in infancy with that of people who make it past ninety. A statistic that reveals more about the later part of life is the naturally occurring maximum human life span: How long do the most long-lived people live? There is good evidence of a number of people who have lived to be between 110 and 115 years of age, but not longer. Reports of greater longevity have often been made for some remote human populations, such as herders in the Caucasus mountains, but these claims for a real Shangri-la invariably evaporate as scientists approach the source. For instance, in some cases a man is found to be usurping the birth date of a father or grandfather given the same name.

But even 110 is a difficult number to interpret, since so few people get there, and since the achievement seems to reflect luck as much as health. So somewhere between the late eighties and the early hundred-and-teens is the average maximum human life span—the age the average person can live to, given good health habits and good medical care. If we think of it as being in the nineties we will probably not be too far off. But this number too is a moving target. What is good medical care?—whatever it is, it can always get better.

More difficult to define in the elderly may be the meaning of disease itself. When I was a boy it used to be said that people died of old age. But in medical school in 1980 I was taught that that is a lie—that people, however old they are, only die of diseases. Cure the disease of a nonagenarian and that person will leave the hospital just as surely as the cured thirty-five-year-old. Not only that, but the quality of life in old age seems almost indefinitely improvable. Cataract surgery, hip replacement, pacemakers, hearing aids, false teeth, glasses, sleep aids, heartbeat strengtheners, and antidepressant drugs go a long way toward making ancient truisms about old age seem obsolete. And if you have quality of life, not surprisingly you want to keep extending it.

However defined, every year in every industrialized country there are more old people than there used to be, whether counted in absolute numbers or as a percentage of total population. And there will be still more with each passing decade. At the beginning of the 1980s, when optimism about the meaning of all this was still unreserved, James Fries, an authority on aging, advanced a theory known as "the rectangularization of the survivorship curve." What this mouthful of academese meant was that we would no longer have a small percentage of people dying at sixty-five, a slightly larger percentage at sixty-six, and so on into the nineties—which in the past produced a long sloping graph of the number of people still surviving. Instead we would have almost everyone living till, say, eighty-five, and dying in a great bunch in a hurry by, say, age ninety. The survivors, if graphed, would show an almost horizontal line, since few were dropping off, sloping only slightly until age eighty-five; and then a precipitous vertical drop between eighty-five and ninety. In time the graph of survivors by age would approach the shape of a rectangle.

The idea is expressed more vividly by "the wonderful one-hoss shay" or carriage, described in a comic poem by Oliver Wendell Holmes, Sr., the great nineteenth-century American physician and author. In it a deacon frustrated by flaws in every carriage he has owned invents one "that was built in such a logical way / It ran a hundred years to the day . . .":

> *You see, of course, if you're not a dunce,*
> *That it fell to pieces all at once,—*
> *All at once, and nothing first,—*
> *Just as bubbles do when they burst.*

According to this "one-hoss shay" theory, future people with optimum habits and medical care will not wear out one organ at a time, getting sick and staying sick for decades; instead they will stay healthy as they age, falling to pieces all at once, according to a genetic plan for the bursting of the organismal bubble.

Unfortunately, although Fries still defends the idea, it does not seem to be the way things are going so far. As Edward Schneider, John Rowe, and others have pointed out over the years since, we have seen instead an increased variation in the age at death, persistent variation in the state of health at any given age, and a large subgroup of people who get sick early and stay sick for a long time as they age. At the same time the group over eighty-five has been having the fastest rate of increase in numbers and the greatest decline in mortality. Most important of all, advances in medical research are making possible more and more interventions every year to deal with the diseases of the very elderly. Those people—indeed all the people over sixty-five years of age—have health needs that are colossal, constantly increasing, and theoretically, given the march of science, infinitely expandable.

Daniel Callahan, director of the Hastings Center in New York, a think tank for biomedical ethics, has spoken out frequently on this problem; although not a physician, he is a respected authority on the health-care needs of the aging in the United States. As he wrote recently,

> In 1980 people over age sixty-five—11 percent of the population—accounted for 29 percent of the total American health-care expenditures of $219.4 billion. By 1986 the elderly accounted for 31 percent of the total expenditures of $450 billion. Annual Medicare costs [the publicly paid portion of elderly health-care bills] are projected to rise from $75 billion in 1986 to $114 billion by the year 2000, and that is in current, not inflated, dollars . . . By the year 2040, it has been projected, the elderly will represent 21 percent of the population and consume 45 percent of all health-care expenditures. How can costs of that magnitude be borne?

The question seems rhetorical, but Callahan goes on at some length to show that they cannot—not without giving up many other things that we cherish, such as the health care of families with children or the education of the young.

Consider: In 1986 a liver transplant, which a few years before was an experimental treatment reserved for young people in otherwise excellent shape, was given to a seventy-six-year-old woman in Pittsburgh. Since then articles have appeared in top U.S. medical journals with titles like "Open-Heart Surgery in Octogenarians" and "Outcomes of Surgery in Patients 90 Years of Age and Older." And a 1991 report of the Institute of Medicine of the U.S. National Academy of Sciences called for greatly increased investment in research on aging and training of geriatric medical specialists. Clearly there need be no end of increasing expenses for the medical care of the elderly and for the development of new technologies.

The solution Callahan proposes is simple, radical, draconian: we must, he believes, eventually establish a cutoff at a certain age— say, eighty—after which we will no longer *allow* major, high-expense medical and surgical interventions, even if they are lifesaving. Callahan argues that at this age people have already either lived full lives or had a reasonable chance to do so. They have had not only their biblical threescore and ten, but ten more— a "natural life span"—and consequently death for them would be a "tolerable death." To support this idea he cites the fact that people usually grieve in a different way after the death of an older person than after the death of a child or a young adult—one often described as untimely.

There seems to be some cross-cultural validity to these perceptions. It has become almost proverbial to refer to the Eskimo practice of setting old people off on an ice floe. As far as we know this kind of act was done with great reluctance, in the spirit of assisted suicide, not murder. And it was done only after a good old age, or at least the best old age people like the Eskimo could afford, with full physical and emotional support, with solicitous care during illness, and above all perhaps, with respect.

Similarly, among the !Kung San, or Bushmen, hunters and gatherers whom I lived with for two years during the 1970s in the Kalahari in Botswana, elderly people were traditionally treated with the greatest attention and respect—until their infirmities became a burden that threatened the survival of their children and grandchildren. Then, in the traditional setting, and only as a last resort, an old person might separate from the rest of the group and quietly succumb to exposure and weakness in the familiar bush country where he or she had spent a lifetime. In contrast, the illness of one young mother occasioned a dangerous trip in a trance by a spiritual healer who went to the world of the spirits to tell them in no uncertain terms that this person was too young to die.

But, it must also be said, people like the Bushmen or the Eskimo— not very different in their ways of life and their options from the people who must have been our own remote ancestors—these people did not have the sort of death we often have today. The things we think of as death-defying technology, from cardio-pulmonary resuscitation to the most powerful antibiotics, from blood-pressure-raising drugs to breathing machines—all are able abruptly to stop someone from dying who has a great deal of life left to live. But unfortunately they also very often function to prolong the process of dying in a person whose time has really run out.

This problem can arise at any age—in the neonatal intensive-care unit, for example—and indeed the most celebrated cases have been people neither at the beginning nor the end of life, but in its undisputed prime. Karen Ann Quinlan, for example, was in her twenties when an auto accident put her into a coma in which a mechanical respirator was necessary to keep her alive. She had apparently lost function in the most primitive part of her brain, which controls breathing, and had definitely no remaining function in any higher parts of her brain—the parts that enable us to feel happy or sad, to recognize our loved ones, to watch television and see more than a flickering light, even to know that time is passing. She was what is technically called brain-dead.

After seven months of this inhuman existence, her father went to court to get an order for the hospital to turn off the respirator. Counterarguments held that this would be tantamount to murder.

But the petitioners argued that Quinlan's life was being wrongly extended with a technology that could not have been considered by those who designed our traditional ethics. The respirator was not saving her life, merely abusing someone who was dying—or by some definitions, already dead. The New Jersey Supreme Court was persuaded by the petition, and the respirator was turned off, but Quinlan did not die for another nine years, during which she breathed for herself very nicely. This was the first of many surprises and complications that would make thinking about these matters in real life much harder than in the abstract. But the case did give a first impetus to the notion that there might be a right to die; or at least, if one is dying in any case, a right to die unmolested by useless, even cruel, technology.

A more recent, equally celebrated case was that of Nancy Cruzan, who at twenty-five, in 1983, had a car crash that put her in a severely brain-damaged state—but not as damaged as Quinlan, and not completely brain-dead. She breathed for herself, and was not even thought to be dying. She was nourished through a feeding tube. Unlike, say, a demented person who gets pleasure out of a teddy bear, or a quadriplegic who can't speak but who can enjoy the visits of relatives, Cruzan was unable to get anything whatever out of life. Yet she might live for thirty more years. Her parents, who had grieved the loss of their daughter for years, asked the courts to permit the feeding tube to be withdrawn, which would cause her to die of starvation. A lower court said yes, but the Missouri Supreme Court said no, citing the sanctity of life.

It was generally agreed that withdrawing food and water was not the same as turning off a mechanical ventilator. But the case ultimately turned on the issue of whether Cruzan's parents could show that she would have rejected all treatment, including the feeding tube, if she could have been asked in advance what she would have wanted. The United States Supreme Court, while recognizing Cruzan's right to refuse treatment, was not persuaded that she had met Missouri's stringent criteria for doing so. But as it turned out, the state relented in its stringency, and the feeding tube was removed. Since starvation and thirst can be an unpleasant way to die, Cruzan was made as comfortable as possible with sedatives and painkillers. Her distraught parents stayed with her, and when she died they were relieved even though grief-stricken.

Thus the Supreme Court, in 1991, backhandedly confirmed the right to die. But this and other cases had to do with the right of individuals to refuse treatment, including artificial tube feeding, or at most with the right of families to protect their loved ones from unwanted treatment. It was not considered relevant that Nancy Cruzan's care was costing the state of Missouri $130,000 a year and had already gone on for eight years. The courts did not ask what medical or other services were withheld from other people in need, in this, the real world of limited resources. They decided that individuals have a right to die in certain circumstances, particularly if they have put their intentions in writing in what is called a "living will." And if they have transferred in writing a power of attorney for health care, to designate in advance someone to decide for them if and when they become incompetent, that is even better.

But the issue of a right to suicide is different from the right to die by refusing treatment, and the issue of a right to get assistance in suicide, particularly assistance from a physician, is something quite different again. All these issues are currently under active discussion in the United States. Twelve leading physicians published an article in *The New England Journal of Medicine* in March 1991 called "The Physician's Responsibility Toward Hopelessly Ill Patients." These physicians acknowledged that withdrawal of life support from such patients is quite common, that assistance in suicide is not rare, and that many physicians have knowingly given a dying patient in great pain a dose of a narcotic or sedative high enough to hasten the end of life. All but two of them believed "that it is not immoral for a physician to assist in the rational suicide of a terminally ill patient."

Dr. Carlos Gomez, an internist who also has a Ph.D. in policy studies, recently completed research in the Netherlands on the practice of euthanasia. Although, strictly speaking, it is against the law, euthanasia is common. Gomez reported the results of his study in his 1991 book *Regulating Death*. Dr. Gomez found that patients who request euthanasia or assistance in suicide may get a psychiatric evaluation, but treatment with antidepressant drugs, for example, may be too brief to really produce therapeutic success. Doctors dealing with terminal patients in pain are not always well skilled in pain management (in the United States they certainly are not)—treatment that might in some cases postpone or abolish their patients' desire to die.

Gomez also noted the moral dilemma posed by patients *demanding* that a reluctant physician assist in euthanasia or suicide. Such demands have the potential to undermine gravely the physician's most important role—that of the patient's ally in battling disease and premature death. As he says in conclusion, "the claim to a right to death at the hands of a physician is essentially a private claim on a public good . . . a claim that I doubt can be justified . . . Moreover, it needs to be shown how physicians can be allowed to kill at some patients' requests yet also be trusted not to kill when the temptation is there—either from the seeming hoplessness of the patient's condition, pressures from the family, or financial imperatives." In addition, assisted suicide or even a requested and legal withdrawal of life support is emotionally very painful for some physicians.

Here in the United States, Daniel Callahan at the Hastings Center opposes euthanasia and physician-assisted suicide. But doctors, for their part, are mostly very unfriendly to his notion of across-the-board withdrawal of major interventions after a certain age. Christine Cassel, John Rowe, and Richard Besdine, among other leading physicians who care for the elderly ill, have strongly criticized his proposal. Cassel, who is chief of medicine at the University of Chicago medical center, calls it "misleading and even dangerous," and points to a near-term probability of five million excess deaths as a result of it. While withholding treatment is very different from euthanasia, the plan is uncomfortably reminiscent of the early-twentieth-century German medical treatise *The Release and Destruction of Lives Devoid of Value*.

Yet the ice floe is not the gas chamber. Callahan argues that far from resembling Nazi killing of Jews, Gypsies, homosexuals, and "mental defectives," his plan would withhold treatment—not kill—in a completely nondiscriminatory way, because all of us, regardless of race, color, creed, sexual habits, or mental status, equally accumulate years of life. If we are still around at eighty, we have all presumably had the chance to have a life, and we could all then have a "tolerable death." Of course he understands that the *rich* octogenarians will still manage to get care one way or another, but he argues that no society can really undertake to offer all its members every chance at life that the richest can afford. For example, no one has proposed that Medicare in the United States or the National Health Service in Britain fund private jet transport for poor heart patients to the best transplant centers in the world.

Callahan's critics have been careful to separate his proposal from discussions of the right to die and the right to suicide, assisted or not. As Cassel writes eloquently, "it is one thing to let people die because their lives have become an inconvenience to them; it is quite another to let them die because their lives have become an inconvenience to us." Cassel believes that such a practice will wear through the moral fabric of our society and render us thick-skinned in relation to all kinds of wrongs. She also stresses the human cost of a blanket condemnation of the elderly to illness without intervention:

> Even if biological life span is limited to ninety-five to one hundred years, there will easily be twenty million people over age eighty [in the U.S. alone] by the year 2020. Most of them will be healthy, active people who could contribute to society if our society would allow them to do so. Treatment of a life-threatening illness in an eighty-five-year-old could save ten or fifteen years of life.

Noting that the elderly are the most diverse, least generalizable group in our society, she also says, "The current aging of society is an unprecedented event, a success of civilization . . . It is the challenge of our success that we create employment, educational and economic structures, and medical care that give all of us as we grow older a positive attitude about the future and about the people with whom we share our society."

*   *   *

But even if we decide that we must make every reasonable effort to keep the old alive and well, we will still have to decide just where and how the health care budget for them should be spent. When William Miller, for example, came to Sun City's Walter O. Boswell Memorial Hospital, he was drastically short of breath and accumulating life-threatening levels of fluid in his tissues. Like Mr. Chinlund, Mr. Miller had pneumonia; but unlike Mr. Chinlund, he had no immediate life-threatening illness, so the pneumonia was not his friend. Had he gone to his doctor a few days earlier— or if, as in the old days, his doctor had gone to him—he would not have come to the hospital as the emergency-room physician, Dr. Lauren Turley, puts it, already "knocking on the door."

> The social problems are more of an obstacle than the medical problems. Two patients live with each other, they barely are keeping each other in a living situation. One of them gets admitted, and then we immediately have a problem with the other one who can't stay alone by themselves. We have to deal with that a lot out here.

Mrs. Miller, also ill and wheelchair-bound, could offer him no assistance, and Sun City's rather weak network of volunteers was inadequate to monitor or halt his downhill slide. Even the simple act of picking a patient up off the floor of his home must often be performed by paramedics—the first and only help to come to the scene.

But in Clifden, a beautiful old seaside town in the rolling Connemara countryside of County Galway, in the extreme west of Ireland, the social problems are handled rather differently. Although for generations the youth of the west of Ireland have emigrated, mostly to the United States, enough young people have stayed so that Clifden's age composition is totally different from that of Sun City. Far from rejecting the nonelderly, the senior citizens of Clifden are happiest when their grown children decide to spend their lives there too. Far from limiting the visits of grandchildren, Clifden's elderly tend to them, and cherish that role in spite of the burden. In the community hall people come together to play on musical instruments handed down from generation to generation, and their dances have the warmth and spontaneity of movements that have been made in the same way for centuries.

In short, Clifden is everyone's idea of an old-fashioned country village, and its older citizens everyone's image of grandparents. The coming of age may be no more enjoyable than it is in Sun City, or even less; but it carries with it complex rewards of status and place. You still belong in the place you grew up in—the place where your kids grew up—and you know it. You have a crucial role to fill, caring, teaching, and being a model for the young. And as the infirmities of the last years of life creep up on you, you will do today as much as possible what you did yesterday, and the response of those around you will be what it has always been: affection, appreciation, respect.

Ireland cannot afford the kind of "heroic" hospital care that was given to Mr. Chinlund and Mr. Nichols in Sun City, so we can probably assume that when Clifden's elderly reach the point when there are only a few weeks or months left, they may not get that extra bit of time. But on the other hand, if one thinks of the last events of those men's lives in the Sun City Hospital as a kind of abuse of the elderly and dying, then Ireland's inability to match them might not seem so unfortunate. And if we look at the lives lived by Clifden's elderly, especially the kind of medical care they get in the next-to-last phase of their lives, before the end is almost upon them, we may find ourselves starting to doubt some of the choices made by Sun Citians.

Take the circumstances of William Miller's life that led to his hospitalization—circumstances that would be quite unlikely in Clifden. He found himself getting short of breath, then shorter, and shorter still. He was at home with a wife who was sicker than he was, and who was in no position to monitor his health or to take him to the doctor. Days passed, and his breathing difficulties worsened. He still did not go to the doctor. Was it too difficult to get out and get over there? Was some mental weakness contributing to his self-neglect, or was it misplaced pride? Or perhaps he had a kind of medical insurance that required him to pay for visits to his doctor, but not for being rushed to the hospital in an emergency. In any case, he did wait for an emergency, and the result was a life-threatening shortness of breath that would mean an expensive hospitalization at best, not to mention a great deal of needless anxiety and pain.

In Clifden, the whole series of events would not have been set in motion, at least not in the same way. Someone like Mary Coyne would have prevented it. She is a "home help," a kind of visiting social worker; her job is to keep tabs on William Miller's Irish counterparts, the infirm elders of Clifden.

> Older people need to be loved, to see that they are still part of the community, that they still have an input in that community, and that they won't be isolated—they will be allowed to live in their own homes, in their own communities, and virtually live and die in the communities that they were born in.

Three times a week, Mary Coyne drives to the home of Bridget and John Connealy, a couple in their eighties. She helps Bridget out of bed, gets her up and walking, helps a bit in the kitchen, has tea with the two of them, chats about politics, and laughs with them—all at the expense of the taxpayers of Ireland.

She sees her role as "mostly social," but realizes that it "crosses over" and "becomes medical" at times in the sense that she can monitor the health of these two people, and prevent deterioration that would lead to a disruptive and expensive hospitalization. Also, by running through the simplest routines of life with them three times a week, Mary Coyne helps them to maintain skills that might otherwise be eroded, resulting in a sharp increase in their dependency or in falls or other accidents that often devastate the lives and health of the elderly. *Use it or lose it* is a basic principle of life for the elderly, but if they are not independent or motivated enough to use their skills, they have the home help to stimulate them and help them keep those skills alive.

"Oh, she's better to me I think than my daughter," Bridget says in answer to a question. "Because my daughter is away from me, but she's coming every second day to me, and that means a lot to me, doesn't it." John concurs: "She means a lot to me and a lot to Bridget as well. Because when she comes here three days a week she gets her out of bed and she washes her and changes her clothes and freshens her up and that's worth a lot to me—I'm not able to do all that." By mobilizing Bridget and helping her to keep clean, Mary Coyne also helps to prevent bedsores and infections. By simply visiting and chatting with the two of them, she helps stave off the debilitating psychological depressions to which older people are easy prey.

Mary Coyne believes that her love for the elderly stems from her childhood, "where my grandparents lived with us, and they were a second family, people we could go to for advice and love and an extra cuddle and sit on their knee for longer than we could my mother, because she was busy." The culture of caring for the elders of Clifden has perpetuated itself through intact three-generation families.

For most of Clifden's senior citizens, "home helps" such as Mary Coyne are the most frequent official visitors. But there are regular visits from a nurse and a doctor as well. The nurse is another Mary—Mary Syron—and she comes once a week, also at government expense. The visits are free, as is any medicine the elderly may need. "They are also entitled to equipment if need be," the nurse explains, "like a commode, a wheelchair, or a walking frame."

> From what I can gather from my visit to America, there are no GPs who go out to the houses visiting people or who are called out to the houses; people have actually got to go to the hospital or to the emergency room to be seen. And there are probably no home helps provided by the government, or nurses working within the community. And health care is always a worry to people, that maybe they are not going to be able to afford it.

Mary Syron has noticed a lot on her visit to America, as Mary Coyne has done in her years in England; the contrast with Ireland could not be more vivid.

Here if you have a medical card, and most older people do, then they can rest assured that they are going to have whatever visits they need from whatever member of the community-care team without having to think, Well, am I going to be able to financially afford it? The older people in Ireland have entitlements that—say, if they're living alone they get an extra living-alone allowance. They have a fuel allowance just to make sure that they are adequately warm.

In short, the emphasis in Clifden is on caring rather than curing. The strategy is to spend small amounts of money on a regular basis to prevent health crises, rather than to let things slide—put bluntly, to ignore people—until such a crisis arises, and then to pull out all the stops to bring a hospitalized patient through, at a cost of thousands of pounds or dollars.

Doctors too play their roles in caring rather than curing. As the home help visits three times a week and the nurse once a week, so the local general practitioner makes a house call once a month. Dr. John Casey, or just "Doctor John," as he is affectionately known to all, readily admits that Clifden is no Shangri-la. Because of the emigration of able-bodied adults, the greater part of the population is made up of the elderly and the very young—people with the greatest health needs. In this situation the health-care delivery system must in some ways take the place of the family.

He admits too that there are many things Irish medicine can't do, because "resources are far greater in the States." For example, his patients must sometimes wait two or three years for a hip replacement operation—one of the most successful operations in all of surgery, and a life-transforming one that gives crippled people their lives back. By the time an Irish patient can get off the waiting list and have the procedure, deterioration may have gone too far in other ways. (Similarly, Dr. Julian Tudor-Hart, a leading, highly experienced general practitioner in Wales, has argued that frugal Britain, in spite of its more technological orientation than Ireland, performs far too few coronary bypass operations, leaving many of his patients—middle-aged and elderly Welsh miners—on waiting lists while years of their lives are spent in pain.)

But on the whole Doctor John much prefers the Irish system. He spent part of his training years in the States, and he came away deeply impressed with the differences in the way medicine is practiced. Although he saw many exceptions, there is little doubt in his mind that American doctors are as a rule much more interested in money that Irish doctors are. And he feels convinced as well that the result is a less caring kind of doctoring.

Despite all the arguments against overly aggressive treatment for the elderly—"flogging" the patient is one way of putting it—physicians in England and the United States do not see themselves as prolonging life for no good reason. Dr. Farid Ghebleh, an intensive care specialist who is taking care of Harold Chinlund, the accountant with pneumonia on top of his pancreatic cancer, explains succinctly how doctors think in these situations:

> My personal philosophy is that we need to give them every chance that they have, we need to work hard to save their lives. We should be very practical and not philosophize too much when you're dealing with an individual patient. I've had frequent examples of people who really looked, like, dead—they looked like they had absolutely no chance, and they came back. They're more than anecdotal cases—in my past five, six years of critical-care practice I've seen numerous of those cases.

He also feels that doctors should "do everything until we have enough objective reasons to withdraw and stop that kind of therapy."

In principle, this must be right. But on the phrase "enough objective reasons to withdraw and stop" there hangs a long tale of cultural differences, scientific ambiguities, medical traditions, and philosophies that differ not only among nations and religious groups but even among families and individuals. What would be a good death in Clifden might seem needless or even neglectful in Sun City. And what seems good and routine medical practice in Sun City might strike the Hindus of India as sacrilegious and the Irish as cruel—not to mention disastrously wasteful of precious resources. Sooner or later we have to recognize that those resources are not just pound or dollar signs ringing up in the eyes of health bureaucrats. The thousands spent trying to give Harold Chinlund three more months translate into services withheld from others. A dozen wheelchairs. A hundred visits from someone like Doctor John. A year of Mary Coyne's salary.

These are the kinds of services that would almost certainly have saved the life of Harold's neighbor William Miller, the man who was "trying to die" from an unnecessary pneumonia. The best critical care that America had to offer was not up to the task of bringing him back from the edge, and he died a few days later— a death caused in essence by a largely *social* failure, and a death far more expensive than it would have been to prevent. Something is wrong, the people of Clifden would surely say, with the social and medical philosophy that surrounded Mr. Miller's death, an untimely one for all his having lived past threescore and ten.

But one of the main fears of elderly Americans is that they will not be allowed to die when the time comes, or even when the time has long passed. Sun City has a chapter of the Hemlock Society— an international society for the promotion of death with dignity, run by Derek Humphry, a Briton who was a distinguished jour- nalist in England, then America. Consider what its members have to say about their real experiences and their equally real fears.

A plump, tired-looking woman in her mid-sixties speaks through her tears, her voice breaking, about nursing her brother, who was terminally ill back in 1975: "I made up my mind I would help if he needed, if he asked; he didn't ask, he fought it to the end. And I would have helped him, and I would just about now be getting out of jail for it. I would have done it. He died screaming."

Another woman describes her ninety-six-year-old aunt's dis- astrous condition. "She had a massive stroke when she was ninety- three, is bedridden completely, she knows nothing and all I want is the feeding tube to be removed from her, and they will not do it. The nursing home has told me to get her out of there if I want this done. The doctor has threatened me that he will get off the case and they just will not, and the poor thing is just suffering, just terribly."

A stylishly dressed and coifed sixtyish woman picks up this theme: "The best advice that I got, and it seems the best advice that doctors feel they can give, is *Do not put a terminal patient in the hospital*, bcause you lose all control over them. You have no choice in the matter then. Once they're put on survival you can't take them off." But this is a questionable assertion, as we have learned from the Karen Ann Quinlan and Nancy Cruzan cases. In fact, the nursing home has proposed an option to the niece of the ninety-six-year-old stroke patient: take her out of the institution. The niece treats it as if it were moot, because it is very hard to do emotionally, and certainly it is easier if you can avoid the nursing home in the first place.

A handsome man in his fifties speaks forcefully of his Native American roots:

> I come from an Indian background, and even back in those
> days, even then, they knew what to do. . . . The point is
> when they knew it was time to go, no one interfered with
> them. You left camp, everyone knew where you were going,
> or what area or spot you had picked ahead of time. And no
> one interfered. Call it what you want, but no one interfered.
> You decided. You knew when it was time to go. You might set
> there for several days before you finally go, but no one
> touched that spot and no one interfered. Because *you* decided
> that it was time to go. I think man is the only animal that fi-
> nally outsmarted Mother Nature. And in outsmarting Mother
> Nature I think he kind of outsmarted himself.

A tall, thin, infirm-looking man says matter-of-factly, "When my quality of life no longer is happy to me, I'm gonna leave." But a small, smiling, energetic woman with a southwestern twang understands the difficulty with his prediction: "The trouble is it has to be legalized, because you can be ready to go and you've got the medicine right there, but you can't do it." The man mistakenly thinks she is talking about will. "You can't," she goes on, "I mean if you are not physically able to reach over there and get the medication and take it, and no one can help you." "I want to go before that," the man says, but the energetic lady sees that it's not that simple. "That makes people feel they'll do it before it's really necessary, because they're afraid tomorrow . . . I mean you look at me here today—tomorrow I may by lying there comatose. You know, every one of us could, and it's too late then. Should I do it today, instead of cuttin' the grass?"

Her brilliantly funny line penetrates acidly to the heart of the problem. The decision to die is not one we want to take lightly, but the longer we put it off the greater the chance that we will be physically or mentally incapable of acting just at the moment when we clearly would most want to act. Then we have stumbled into Hamlet's "calamity of so long life." This is what frightens people who want to die with dignity, and they are afraid not so much of doctors as of hospitals and nursing homes.

A white-haired lady seems older than any of them but speaks with at least equal force:

> I don't understand. By this age I would rather be a dog.
> When there comes time, they just get a hypo. In minutes—in
> practically seconds—you're asleep, and it's finished! What is
> the big deal about human beings being dragged on and on
> with excruciating pain? It's ridiculous!

On the table in front of the room are copies of Derek Humphry's best-selling book, *Final Exit*, which gives both practical advice about and ethical justification for suicide, including assisted suicide, in the setting of painful or humiliating terminal illness. Legislative initiatives have been mounted in California, Washington State, and elsewhere to decriminalize assisted suicide and even euthanasia. Michigan has no law against assisted suicide, and so has recently become something of a haven for a nonclinical physician—a pathologist by specialty—who has invented a suicide machine. With it, Dr. Jack Kevorkian has aided in the suicide of at least four women with degenerative terminal illnesses. In the first of these cases a grand jury was convened, but it refused to indict him on any charges whatever. Although he has flaunted his disregard for court orders, assisting in several other suicides, it is still not clear that he will be punished. Although the state is appealing the decision, a Michigan court in mid-1992 dismissed murder charges against Kevorkian in two more of the deaths.

Similar exoneration closed the case of Dr. Timothy Quill in New York State, after his admission in the pages of a leading medical journal that he had acceded to the request of "Diane," a young terminal leukemia patient in pain, by placing a lethal overdose of barbiturates near her bed. It was in that same journal that twelve prominent U.S. physicians, representing different specialties and regions of the country, had previously written a paper admitting that practices such as Dr. Quill's are in fact widespread, and that most of them did not disapprove of such practices. Poll after poll among ordinary citizens shows a steadily growing public approval of them as well.

But Carlos Gomez's study in the Netherlands raises questions about such practices, questions that might be thought of as in the realm of practical ethics. Daniel Callahan, too, fears the release of an army of doctors who, feeling that they have a license to kill, may privately play God. And this is not necessarily something they will relish. For all the assurance of some patients that they have a right to demand a lethal injection from the doctor, doctors too have rights. And they may well resist such formidable demands on their consciences, having spent a lifetime learning and struggling to stave off death. We may not have the right to ask them to bring death about. But the question of whether suicide, including assisted suicide, is ethical is quite separable from the question of whether doctors should be involved in these acts. And all of these questions will be debated in the years ahead.

As for Callahan's solution—the cessation of major intervention after a universal cutoff age—few are likely to embrace it, because the differences among the elderly of a given age are simply too large. A right to die there may well be, but a duty to die is something else again. If it is a great ethical burden to discriminate among the elderly to determine who, on purely biological grounds, is the best candidate for, say, heroic resuscitation measures, it is at least an equally great ethical burden to willfully condemn them across the board to be deprived of resuscitation. Indeed, as Christine Cassel, chief of medicine at the University of Chicago, has said, it might in effect leave us morally crippled. We might find ourselves resembling those German intellectuals, a jurist and a psychiatrist, who wrote in 1920 of "lives devoid of value"—a prelude to some of the most devastating immoralities of our destructive and insensitive century.

Yet as for dying, as Ecclesiastes says, eventually there is a time for that too. The people of north India know this from their own scriptures, and so they come to Banaras, a holy city on the holy river Ganges, when they believe the time has come for them to die. This city, they believe, is the home of Lord Shiva, the high god who presides over happiness. There is a hospital of some capability in Banaras, and most people avail themselves of what it has to offer—including some fairly high-powered Western medicine not available at all twenty years ago. But that is not why they come to Banaras.

They come instead for "a good death," and somehow they know when a hospital stay is starting to interfere with that. According to Hindu belief, if you die in Banaras near the banks of the Ganges, you die in a state of grace—and your soul is released from the reincarnation cycle of life and death. You no longer have to be born and die only to be born again, as all those who die in less exalted states do. Dying in this way, you pass on to heaven. It is in effect synonymous with "a good death," and it is certainly not a death in which the body is poked full of needles and tubes surrounded by busy strangers. Indeed, such a death may be seen as a torture of the body. A good death can best occur outside the hospital, when the doctors and nurses have respectfully given up on their effort to prolong life because it is not succeeding. The patient is then discharged to the care of the family—especially the grown children.

It is their obligation to pay back their "parental debt" by making a good death possible for their mothers and fathers. For one family, the dying of their elderly mother is the second they have arranged to take place in Banaras; their father's dying had already taken place there. Mata Shukla is conscious and able to speak a little, but the doctors have said that she will not live long. They have discharged her from the hospital to a kind of hospice setting, where her family surrounds her, and in the next room religious musicians play and sing ancient chants to Krishna. Her daughter-in-law bathes her, and she awaits the imminent arrival of her eldest son. Another relative brings her sugar dissolved in water, and another fairly banters with her about food. She complains a bit about pain in her shoulders, and suggests at one point, perhaps jokingly, that she might go for a ride in a cart "to look around." No one is thinking about postponing this death, and yet no one is in the slightest hurry. Their job is to wait and watch, to make her feel comfortable, and to weave a kind of spiritual burial cloth out of love, filial obligation, and caring.

After her death—twelve days after arriving in Banaras—she is dressed in a more substantive burial cloth, one of considerable beauty, draped with garlands and with shining gold and silver trim. On a platform high on the shoulders of her relatives she is borne through the streets of Banaras. While musicians play and her loved ones cast rice up over her body, showering her with this symbol of life, the dense workaday crowd parts, bicycles make way for the procession, and she is carried down to the Ganges where, as dusk falls, cremation fires are burning in the shadows of ancient buildings on the riverbank. With the last of the sun, as her soul goes up to heaven, the ashes that are her earthly remains are taken for one last voyage over the great quiet darkening holy river. And her heirs can now return to their village and go on with their earthly lives knowing that they have done the right thing.

Presumably there is also an Irish version of "a good death," and even an American one. Whatever these may be—and they are no doubt different from a good death in Banaras—they are not likely to take place in a hospital where the dying person is being almost assaulted by well-meaning strangers brandishing medical technology, weapons against disease that may well have once been appropriate but may no longer be so. And if we hope to have a good death, whatever culture we live in, we will somehow need to know when to put an end to the assault.

EIGHT

PANDEMIC

Today AIDS is a household word, and one that inspires almost universal fear. Everyone, it seems, knows that it is incurable and irreversibly deadly. Everyone knows that average men and women can avoid it by abstaining from sex, and can reduce their chances of getting it by changing sex partners as little as possible and by using condoms in sex. Even most IV drug abusers know that they will get it by sharing needles.

Yet rates of this devastating disease are rising rapidly in almost all countries and exponentially in the world as a whole. To date in the United States, where the disease was first identified in 1981, there have been 250,000 cases and 130,000 deaths; it is projected that there will be 1 million cases by the turn of the millennium— all of which, barring a "miracle cure," will end in death by the year 2020. By that date, barring a vaccine, there may be millions of cases more. At least a fourth—perhaps as many as half—of children born to infected parents are born infected; none of these children will live to grow up.

In the world as a whole, according to recent World Health Organization estimates, there are about 12 million people infected—most not yet sick—including a million children; by the year 2000 there will be 40 million infected. These are conservative estimates; some recent private projections by scientists who think that WHO has political reasons to underestimate the problem have been up to three times higher. But let us take the lower figure, 40 million. If, as seems quite possible, this number roughly quadruples again in each of the first two decades of the twenty-first century, then around one in ten inhabitants of this planet will be infected.

For those who feel safe because they are not male homosexuals and do not "mainline" drugs, consider this: 90 percent of current cases worldwide, according to WHO, were acquired by heterosexual transmission. According to U.S. Surgeon General Antonia Novello, only one eighth as many U.S. women as men are infected—1 in 800 versus 1 in 100. This indicates only a low level of heterosexual transmission. But if you look at teenagers, more than half as many girls as boys are infected—a pattern more similar to that found in Central and East Africa, where there are no—repeat, no—groups privileged or protected from the virus, except perhaps those who are no longer sexually active. Transmission from men to women may be easier than from women to men. Unborn children are a prime risk group in Africa.

According to recent studies of teenagers entering U.S. Job Corps programs—among the poorest of U.S. teenagers, but not the most reckless—the ratio of infected girls to infected boys is about equal. This is because more than half of all teenagers become sexually active before finishing high school, and because most do not use condoms. So if you are a parent, and have been congratulating yourself on not having passed AIDS to your children at birth, you can look forward to being frightened out of your wits when they reach high-school age. Their chances of contracting it then are increasing steadily, and if they do they will almost certainly be dead before they are thirty.

In Britain, according to epidemiologist Anne M. Johnson, writing in the *British Medical Journal* in May 1992, there is also a heterosexual epidemic looming on the horizon. The British epidemic is heavily influenced by travel to Commonwealth countries, where the spread of AIDS has been predominantly heterosexual for a decade. In England, Wales, and Northern Ireland, between 1986 and 1991, "the proportion of cases of AIDS attributable to heterosexual transmission increased from 2 percent to 14 percent and diagnosed HIV infections from 4 percent to 23 percent." Of all British HIV infection acquired heterosexually, only 17 percent came through sex with someone in a high-risk category—for example, an IV drug abuser, a gay man, or someone who got the infection through a blood transfusion.

The rest—83 percent—were infected by what is called secondary or "second generation" heterosexual transmission. That is, they got it heterosexually from someone who also got it heterosexally. Although the numbers are still very small, with only 1,620 people infected in this way by the end of 1991, they are rapidly on the rise. The notion of who is at risk in the United Kingdom is constantly evolving. In the early 1980s the only group considered at risk were gay men who had had partners in the United States. Today promiscuous heterosexuals must also be seen as at risk. As Johnson concludes, "prospective sexual partners do not come with a log book of their past partners and experiences . . . Perhaps the most important lesson to be learnt from the accounts of second generation heterosexual transmission in the United Kingdom is that many of those infected did not perceive themselves as at risk."

Meanwhile in the United States, a new and different epidemic has budded off the AIDS epidemic: tuberculosis has been on the rise again since 1988—ironically, just the year when the TB unit of the Centers for Disease Control optimistically changed its name from "TB Control" to "TB Elimination." It is far from being eliminated now. Not only is the number of cases rapidly increasing, but many of the new cases are resistant to all drugs known up to now to be effective against TB. These strains evolved because of failure by some patients to comply with the full, rather long course of treatment for the older strains of TB—the kind the drugs cured. Following the process described in Chapter 3, the restless tide of resistant TB microbes surged into the gaps left by inadequate use of the old barriers.

Thus the AIDS pandemic—a term for an epidemic that persists, eventually becoming pervasive in a large population, or for parallel epidemics around the world—will now be complicated by an epidemic of one of the classsic killers of history, and one that worldwide still causes more deaths than any other infectious disease. Unlike AIDS, TB is not very difficult to get. Unlike AIDS, TB is borne through the air on tiny droplets, often coughed out by sufferers. Unlike AIDS, when TB kills (as it does most of the time if drug resistant) it kills quickly. And patients infected with AIDS may have TB yet still test *negative* for it, since it is in the nature of AIDS that patients do not have normal immune function, which is necessary for the TB test to be accurate.

And what about a cure or a vaccine for AIDS? Won't we have one of those before 2020?

Maybe. But according to the most optimistic projections, tens of millions more will contract the infection, and millions who now carry the virus will develop the disease and die before either solution comes to pass. Consider some of the obstacles to both prevention and cure.

The AIDS virus itself is remarkably hardy and adaptable. It was not discovered until the 1980s, but two cases have been identified as likely to have been AIDS as early as the 1950s. The virus probably lay dormant in a nonepidemic state long before that, possibly for centuries, probably in central African monkeys. By the time the human epidemic was getting under way, the virus was able to exist in many slightly different forms. This indeed appears to be an important key to its success: the body's immune system is essentially outrun by the virus's changeability. Various forms of the virus are present in about equal numbers during the early stages of the disease; but as the body's immune system becomes exhausted, the forms of the virus that reproduce fastest begin to predominate and can no longer be contained. Drugs like AZT and DDI, both of which at first looked very promising, are outrun in a similar way and amount in the end to temporary delaying tactics. Many conceivable future vaccines can probably be circumvented by this remarkable virus in a similar way.

The situation is not hopeless; many new tactics are being tried, and an effective cure or vaccine may eventually be discovered. But the AIDS virus itself is a prime example of the "restless tide" metaphor for the microbial world, and it has already dashed the hopes of many infected people who had thought they might outlive the epidemic. The virus's evolution under natural conditions prepared it to fight off many forces arrayed against it, and the forces deployed by medical science so far have apparently not afforded it any surprises. There will be no magic bullet for AIDS anytime soon.

That means quite simply that the only way to really save lives is to slow the spread of the virus from person to person. As columnist Charles Krauthammer has said, AIDS is the quintessential behavioral epidemic. With the exception of the unborn, and those who in the early 1980s got the virus iatrogenically—from doctors, by blood transfusion—almost all cases have resulted from sexual activity (especially unprotected vaginal or anal intercourse) or from needle sharing among IV drug users. These patterns have predictably resulted in some religious groups concluding that AIDS is a punishment for sin—Don't sin, they claim, and you won't get it. Jehovah's Witnesses are even able to include transfusion in this concept, since they are forbidden to accept that frequently life-saving intervention.

This blame-the-victim moralizing needs some rethinking. If AIDS is God's punishment for male homosexuals, then lesbians must be God's chosen people, since they have lower rates of infection than heterosexuals. And the countless people throughout history who have died for want of a blood transfusion might also differ with this theory. But translating the religious idea into public health terms, we do have to recognize—not blame, but recognize—the role of human action in this disease.

AIDS is the first epidemic in which civil rights have taken clear precedence over at least some public health considerations for so long. A number of legitimate voices have been raised in the medical and public health communities calling for more widespread testing, as well as for modifications of confidentiality when the infected individual is placing others at risk.

In every epidemic of the past, control has been achieved partly through measures that today are made impossible—solely for AIDS—by civil liberties arguments. Many have claimed that abrogating civil liberties would in every instance worsen the public health picture by driving victims underground; but in fact this is a scientific question to which there is really no answer as yet. Such a risk must be weighed against other risks, and against the benefits to be gained by measures that some object to as antilibertarian. It is highly likely that this debate will intensify in the future, especially given the ancillary epidemic of multiply-drug-resistant TB.

Still, regardless of how this debate evolves, the fundamental causes of the epidemic lie in conditions that are outside the control of those who contract the virus and spread it. In fact the situation is very similar to that encountered by Rudolph Virchow and other physicians in the social medicine movement during the nineteenth century, as they tried to make sense of the epidemics of that era. They were dealing with diseases that they sensed were caused by microbes—and that eventually were proven as such—but it was clear that social conditions played an essential role in favoring the spread of the diseases.

What these conditions had in common was poverty. Living in circumstances of overcrowding, poor nutrition, ignorance, and hopelessness favored alcohol and drug abuse then as it does now. The countless humiliations of being poor in that society as in ours left sex, drinking, and drugs as the only affordable pleasures that could blot out the hopelessness of poverty, a prison with no exit. Then as now some sanctimonious people who had never had to deal with real poverty themselves insisted on blaming the victims, and so a broad religious coalition in that self-satisfied time concluded that the root cause of epidemics was sin. As the century drew to a close the microbe theorists were in the ascendance and the sin theorists on the wane. But in fact both microbial spread and sin were trunks that stemmed from the same causal roots: poverty, overcrowding, malnutrition, ignorance, and despair.

Thailand is a case in point. Like most Asian countries it is overcrowded and struggling to overcome the problems of underdevelopment. Like most countries, rich and poor, anywhere in the world, it has always had a sex trade. But during the war in Vietnam, when men serving in the U.S. and allied forces in the region went to Thailand for "R & R"—some called it "I & I," for Intoxication and Intercourse—sex for sale became routine, and in the years since it became deeply entrenched and institutionalized. Prostitution reached down through the teenage years to enlist twelve-year-olds. Rural poverty and desperation disgorged thousands of such children into the cities, there to be bought and sold not just night by night or trick by trick, but on a very long-term basis, as indentured servants with little hope of release from the brothels holding their bonds—for most intents and purposes, almost as slaves.

By the late 1980s, with AIDS on the rise in most of the world, Bangkok was a mecca for sex tourists—Japanese, Australian, and European men who flew there expressly to purchase the favors of Thailand's increasingly famous prostitutes, including preteens. The infection rate at that time is not known. In 1988 there was hardly a symptomatic case of AIDS recorded in the country, and even IV drug abusers showed only a 1 or 2 percent rate of infection with the virus. There were many advance warnings but few precautions were taken, and so Thailand today has one of the highest rates of HIV positivity in the world.

Approximately 400,000 people are infected in this nation of about 50 million. Projections are that by 1996 the country will be treating some 90,000 full-blown cases of AIDS—and that will be just the beginning. But there are now only 100,000 hospital beds, period, in the entire country. Buddhist monks are distributing condoms and getting set to care for thousands of AIDS patients in their monasteries. In some regions 60 percent of the busy prostitutes are HIV positive, and they will serve as a reservoir for the spread of the epidemic throughout the country, and to Japan, Australia, and Europe, which send some five million men a year to Bangkok looking for illicit sex. As one observer aptly described the public health situation with respect to AIDS in Thailand, it is like an air raid in which the sirens have sounded but the bombs have not yet dropped.

Dr. Praphan Phanuphak, of the Chulalongkhorn Hospital in Bangkok, saw the first case of AIDS in Thailand in an American homosexual man, early in 1985. Today he sees fifty to sixty people a day in his HIV clinic. In the early years most cases were homosexual or bisexual, but by the late 1980s the great majority of cases were acquired through intravenous drug abuse; today, Dr. Praphan estimates, about 90 percent of the new cases stem from heterosexual intercourse. Thus Thailand in three or four years has run through a cycle that is taking over a decade in Western countries.

Since the poor are the ones more often forced by circumstance to become sex workers, and since the poorer customers are more likely to frequent poorer prostitutes—in turn more likely to be infected—AIDS is spreading most rapidly among the poor. Yet there are recent hints of some slowing of the rate of spread of the infection. Prostitutes when interviewed showed considerable understanding of how AIDS is transmitted, and they know that condoms can reduce the chance of transmission. Some claim to be asking, and getting, their clients to use protection—although since the government economizes by not giving out jelly with the condoms, repeated intercourse becomes abrasive and painful, discouraging condom use. These small positive signs are the result of what, for a poor country, has been a massive government effort at education for prevention. An architect of the program, Dr. Werisit Sititrai sums it up eloquently:

> We're probably the first in the world to pull in the police to
> help campaign against AIDS and promote condoms. We're
> probably the first in the world to have the biggest campaign
> on changing sexual culture. In terms of medicine itself we
> have gone through a lot, educating medical personnel and
> trying to change the philosophy of medicine, to move from
> just medicine into society; move from the virus into the
> human being.

As a result, many have come to think of Thailand as "the biggest classroom on AIDS prevention in the world."

In the north, toward the Burmese border, pleasant, terraced green hills slope down and level off in vast rice paddies; men and women stand knee-deep in cool water and tend the plants that have kept them alive for thousands of years, while water buffalo plod by in the service of that same ancient goal. Women here have always played a key role in providing economic support for their families. So it is easy to understand how young girls may find it difficult to resist ensuring the survival of their families by selling their bodies for what must seem to them great riches. Dr. Wat Uthaivoravit, Chief of Preventive Medicine of the region's Chiang Rai Hospital, takes prostitution for granted as he tries to think of ways to slow the spread of AIDS in his country.

A remarkably dedicated and compassionate man—he has taken in three children orphaned by AIDS—Dr. Wat pursues the general practice of medicine in this beautiful countryside where, he knows, the population goes about its daily business unaware that it is about to be ravaged by AIDS. He tries to convince young women infected with the virus to have their tubes tied, so as not to give birth to children who, even if they are lucky enough to escape the disease, will certainly be orphaned when they are less than half grown. He patiently cares for the early victims of the epidemic, who have developed the burdensome symptoms and begun the long, painful process of dying. But in keeping with his belief that "every doctor should be involved in prevention," he spends a surprising amount of time hanging around brothels.

These are not as unwieldy or dangerous in Chiang Rai as in Bangkok, and the one where he practices has an almost festive atmosphere. Girls—they are mostly in their teens, and sex alone can't make them women—attend a kind of survival school at the brothel, and Dr. Wat and his colleagues give the lessons. The uneasy laughter of embarrassment turns to a more relaxed enjoyment as the girls banter and giggle about the toys they have been given to play with. Yes, toys; but these particular ones give new meaning to the phrase "educational playthings." They are crude, stick-like wooden dolls with carved, removable barrels around them. The barrel, the girls learn, is like the clothes on one of their customers—entirely superficial. To get any real idea of what is underneath the clothes—of the real man—you pull off the barrel, and . . .

Out pop a couple of stick arms and a penis even larger and thicker than the arms. Near the tip of the penis on some of the dolls is a big red spot, vivid against the dull wood color of the rest of the doll. That spot represents the invisible disease that the well-dressed man with the fistful of money can give you—a disease that will cause you and your children to die, slowly, painfully, hopelessly.

Other "toys" are used to teach girls how to use condoms to try to avert this fate, and according to Dr. Wat, condom use has reached very high levels—he believes 100 percent—in this particular brothel. While this may be overly optimistic, it is likely that his program has had an impact. In the face of such a rapidly growing menace, even a slowing down of the rate of spread is a goal that deserves to be eagerly sought; one must be grateful for small victories.

Unfortunately, the Thai government is about to do an end run around these dedicated physicians by greatly toning down the already successful AIDS awareness campaign. At issue is the country's tourist industry, worth about $4 billion annually. The number of tourists dropped to 5.1 million in 1991, alarming some government officials, and leading to the conclusion that the AIDS awareness campaign had been *too* successful. The sex industry itself, only part of which is tourist-supported, is a billion-dollar-a-year business. It is estimated that 90 percent of Thai men participate in it at some point in their lives.

Yet given the Bangkok Metropolitan Association estimate that 37 percent of the city's prostitutes are infected, a figure that rises to 60 percent in the north, it seems amazing that AIDS awareness would be deliberately curtailed at this time. Even in purely economic terms, it seems irrational to try to protect a $6-billion-per-year economic sector in ways that will ultimately threaten the entire economy of what has been until now one of the most effective of all developing countries. But it is happening, and is only one among many instances in which AIDS confronts us with baffling paradoxes.

*   *   *

One such paradox is the fact that sometimes great insights arise from the greatest human disasters. In the case of AIDS, the disaster has forced physicians and public health officials to take an approach to prevention that has not really been seen since the heyday of the social medicine movement of the nineteenth century. As Dr. Jonathan Mann, former director of the World Health Organization's AIDS prevention programs, put it in 1990, at the Sixth International Conference on AIDS, "AIDS is catalyzing a revolution in health care."

> No one set out to make a revolution . . . Yet, in carrying forward this work, the deficiencies of our health care and social systems worldwide have been so starkly and painfully revealed that the pre–AIDS era paradigm of health care, its philosophy and practice, has been challenged and found to be desperately inadequate and, therefore, fatally obsolete . . . The emphasis was medical and technological, involving experts and engineers, and, for certain purposes, this approach was quite effective. However, this paradigm envisioned a fundamental dichotomy between individual and social interests . . . Attention to behavioral, social, and societal considerations was often rudimentary and naive.

He went on to describe the enormous impact that the worldwide fight against AIDS had made on this old approach. "The key to the new paradigm is the recognition that behavior, both individual and collective, is the major public health challenge of the future."

Dr. Mann also noted—and he embodies the principle—that AIDS had shrunk the worldwide network of medicine and health, because the epidemic itself was the product of a shrunken world. "For example," he pointed out, "international travel has increased fifteen-fold since 1950," reflecting "an increasingly global linkage and interdependence. This also offers infectious agents an unparalleled opportunity for rapid pandemic spread; HIV may be the first virus to take advantage of this situation, but it is unlikely to be the last."

This global solidarity, for better or for worse, helps bring thousands of tourists a month to Thailand, where their wealthy-nation pocket change buys sybaritic pleasures beyond—well, maybe not beyond—their wildest dreams. It also buys them AIDS. However, this international commerce in viruses is not a one-way street. On the contrary, the microbe was brought to Thailand as yet another example of the rich countries' flair for exporting things to the poor ones. We send them cigarettes that give them epidemics of heart disease and lung cancer. We send them weapons that make possible wholesale slaughter of their own and neighboring peoples. And we sent tourists who, in the mid-1980s, brought them their first cases of AIDS.

These particular tourists almost certainly came from the United States and Australia. Australia, in fact, helped pioneer the AIDS pandemic, with rates in the mid-1980s that were higher than in almost any other country. Sydney, a city with all the ills of any modern metropolis—poverty, drug abuse, prostitution, violent crime—was initially a center of AIDS prevalence because, like San Francisco in the United States, it had a large gay population. Many of these men had become infected before 1985, just as among American gays.

Yet, despite the proximity of gay communities to heterosexual prostitution and IV drug abuse, Australia has not had a second phase of the AIDS epidemic nearly as large as that in the United States. This second phase consists of spread among poor IV drug abusers through the sharing of contaminated needles, followed by heterosexual spread to non-drug-using partners—often by prostitutes who are also drug abusers. These are all marginalized people, people with less access than most to health care, money, information, psychological and social support—everything. They have grown up less educated, more abused and neglected, less well nourished, impoverished in every way when compared to their middle-class counterparts. They care less about risk and danger because they have less to live for, and because risky pleasures take them away, at least for a moment, from the depressing conditions of their lives.

They also tend not to believe what they are told about those dangers. A study released in 1992 of poor black youth in the United States at risk for AIDS showed that they mistrust establishment figures, indeed all adults, so much that what they hear from them about the threat of AIDS is often simply discounted—especially when it conflicts with what they hear from their risk-prone, frequently ignorant peers. The study predicts that even "Magic" Johnson, the great basketball player who is their long-standing hero and who is HIV positive himself, will not be believed by the kids on the street; they see even him as playing a role as an entertainer, not as a believable member of their community.

So how is it that their counterparts in Australia—mainly white, it is true, but otherwise similar in background, deprivation, marginalization, and risk—are not traveling the same fast road toward a high prevalence of AIDS?

The answer may lie with the actions of a surprisingly small number of dedicated, courageous physicians and other health-care workers who have gone into the streets and somehow made these kids believe them. One of them is Dr. Alex Wodak, a primary-care internist who treated some of the first AIDS cases in Australia in 1982. He still finds clinical medicine—treatment, the medical care of the ill—to be the most satisfying work he does. Yet, confronted with the growing number of AIDS victims in Sydney, he concluded that he had to do more. He explains why by telling the story of one of his own heroes:

It just seemed not enough to look after individual patients. There's a very great figure in public health called John Snow, who was involved in trying to control the cholera epidemic in London. He traced the epidemic down to a particular water pump in Soho. And when he worked out what was going on—worked out that the cholera was spreading from that water pump—he pulled the handle off that pump so that people couldn't use the well, and that stopped the epidemic. And

he's really held up as a model by people like me, who think
that it's not enough to treat the diarrhea of people who have
cholera. You've got to do something about controlling epidemics at their source.

So for me it was very clear that we had to distribute clean
needles and syringes.

He makes this transition from cholera to AIDS, from John Snow's
water-pump handle to his own needle-exchange program, sound
easy. But no one accused Snow of debasing the morals of London's
poor by disabling a contaminated water pump. Dr. Wodak had to
confront, first, the entire police force of Sydney, and then the
government of Australia. He was accused of corrupting public
morals, just as Paul Ehrlich had been for trying to cure syphilis
almost a century earlier. Many were convinced that needle exchange would only increase the number of addicts—a prediction
since contradicted by evidence from many countries. All it does
is slow the spread of AIDS. Wodak is a mild-looking, soft-spoken
man, and it is hard to imagine this confrontation, yet it happened.
Like most physicians not the sort to become a lawbreaker, he and
his colleagues at the hospital went through channels—and more
channels, and still more channels:

> Finally, I got frustrated with all this sort of committee work
> and writing more and more reports and documents. So I went
> to my colleagues in my department and I said, "We're getting
> nowhere, and everyone's afraid to break the ice, and some-
> body's going to have to do it without any permission. Let's do
> it—let's do it with our own money, let's do it on our own
> time." So that's what we did . . . We put a notice on the door
> November the thirteenth, 1986. And we started, and people
> came, and we handed out needles and syringes, and the
> press came in droves. . . .
>
> And then the next year they changed the law so that what
> we were doing was no longer illegal.

Asked if he thinks it the role of the doctor to break the law, he
says nervously, "No, I—I'd only do it in epidemics . . . I just fig-

ured that a doctor has a lot of privileges, and if you can't use your position in . . . in society . . . now and then, when it really matters, if you can't use your position to force something that has to happen, then you shouldn't really have those privileges." He speaks too of "a totally different form of medicine than we would have been practicing a generation or two generations ago."

> We're now dealing mainly with lifestyle problems over which individuals have at least some control, and we have to maximise that control . . . We're also dealing now, more and more in Western medicine, with chronic diseases which relapse, and remitting diseases that come and go. We're not dealing with sort of flash-point acute episodes where the doctor comes in on the white horse and lances the boil and everything's alright.

Over a century ago Rudolf Virchow said, "Politics is only medicine on a grand scale." Today Alex Wodak says, "You can't separate medicine and politics. They are sides of the same coin." He recognizes that politics, even if it is a form of medicine, is not a satisfying or appealing form; but he stresses the need for changes in medical training. Indeed, he seems to be calling for a new kind of doctor. What he says is not so different from what Johns Hopkins intern John Townes said after treating Isabel Humbles at the end of her long course of alcohol and drug abuse: It is not enough to be there at the end point, in the crisis; the problem won't be solved there, it has to be solved earlier, before things get that bad. But Wodak, an experienced physician, practicing in an environment more conducive to change, sounds far more hopeful.

And he is not alone. Dr. Rachael Buckley and Dr. Ingrid Van Beek practice the new kind of medicine at the Kirketon Road Clinic in "the Cross"—the King's Cross section of Sydney, where male and female prostitution and intravenous drug abuse converge with droves of middle-class suburban youth out on the town for a thrill. And not just youth: according to one HIV-positive male prostitute hanging out at "the Wall," a center of sex-for-sale in the city, more than half of the men who do business with him have children's car seats in their vehicles. These middle-class youth, these family men, have the potential to carry the AIDS epidemic throughout Australian society.

Yet so far that spread is not happening. Dr. Buckley, who looks a bit like a street kid herself, and Dr. Van Beek, who in contrast is graceful and elegant, along with others staffing the Centre are effectively standing in its way. They never thought, when they went into medicine, that this was what they would be doing. Yet night after night they climb aboard the AIDS Bus—it sallies forth in the wee hours seven nights a week—and go to the source of the problem, like John Snow homing in on the Soho water pump. They give out five thousand clean needles and syringes a week. They stock condoms too by the thousands. They teach ignorant teenagers toying with their lives how to stay alive a few years longer—maybe long enough so that they come to their senses and turn to lifestyles less likely to destroy them. They teach them how to persuade customers to use condoms. They try to convince already infected young women not to become pregnant and pass the disease on to an unborn child.

What they don't do is judge, having learned that that is no way to slow an epidemic. Their strategy is called *harm minimization* or *harm reduction*. The assumption is that these young people will keep on doing harmful things, that they cannot be prohibited from doing them, and that in many cases they cannot even be cured of doing them; all a physician can hope to do is reduce the harm they will do themselves by engaging in these behaviors. Harm reduction is not as satisfying as lancing boils, but where AIDS is concerned it saves a lot more lives. Doctors don't have the gratification of effecting a simple cure, but they can watch the number of AIDS cases in Australia begin to level off, while the number in the United States continues to rise and rise again.

Dr. Van Beek even tries to convince patients who inject cocaine to switch to heroin. It seems an odd role for a doctor. But an IV heroin abuser may need to inject only once or twice a day, while an IV cocaine abuser may need to inject twenty times. If she persuades her patient to switch, she reduces that person's risk of contracting AIDS from a dirty needle by 90 or 95 percent—harm reduction indeed.

In Perth, the Western Australian Health Department is paying unemployment and health benefits to prostitutes who carry the AIDS virus, on condition that they stop selling sex. The Australian national government distributes highly explicit, even obscene comic books called *Streetwize*. It assumes that young people are mainlining drugs and having all kinds and combinations of licit and illicit sex. Despite being a government publication, *Streetwize* speaks the kids' language, improper and often unpleasant though it may be. It does not preach to them; it teaches them, painlessly, to exchange dirty needles for clean ones, or to clean them properly with bleach before passing them on, and to use a condom effectively. It gives them role models who are "cool" and "down and dirty" but who use bleach and condoms because they intend to stay alive, and it portrays those who don't as uncool numskulls. A prison version of the comic, *Gaolwize*, directs similar information and persuasion at inmates who often are engaging in homosexual sex and drug injection while in prison.

All these efforts at education are carried out at Australian government expense. They could not conceivably be done in the United States. Reward prostitutes by paying them to avoid sex? Teach lawbreaking addicts how to do injections safely? Openly admit that there is sex in prisons? Impossible! Any of these actions would condone crime and immorality; better to pretend and preach. Accordingly, American prostitutes will continue to ply their trade, spreading the virus far and wide. Needle sharing without precautions will go on apace—Louis Sullivan, the U.S. secretary of health and human services, has in mid-1992 just shortsightedly killed another attempt to fund clean-needle programs—and the second phase of the epidemic will accelerate. And the prisons will discharge tens of thousands of AIDS-infected convicts into the community over the next few years.

Meanwhile evidence mounts that harm-reduction strategies work. For example, in 1986, Allan Parry and his colleagues instituted a free needle exchange program that virtually halted the spread of AIDS among drug users in Liverpool, while Edinburgh, an otherwise comparable setting where needle exchange was out-lawed, experienced an explosion of drug-related AIDS cases. The cost of running the Liverpool program for a year is less than the cost of treating one AIDS patient. In Amsterdam, needle exchange was begun in 1984. Ernst Buning, writing in *The International Journal of the Addictions* in 1991, showed that "ample data are available to support the role of the needle exchange in facilitating drug injec-tors to use drugs in a safer way: no increase in drug use could be validated, participants of the exchange schemes were less involved in needle sharing, the supply of large quantities of needles to drug users did not lead to an increase in needle stick accidents by the general public, and, finally, the HIV prevalence among drug in-jectors has remained stable since 1986, while the incidence of acute hepatitis B had gone down."

In 1989 the percentage of all AIDS cases attributable to drug injection was 3 percent in the United Kingdom, 7 in the Nether-lands, and at least 22 percent—and rapidly rising—in the United States. New York, our largest center of drug abuse, instituted needle exchange programs under Mayor Ed Koch, but these were stopped by the new mayor, David Dinkins. He has since shown more flexibility with regard to trial programs, but these remain very inadequate. New Haven has maintained such programs; ac-cording to a 1991 study by the Institute of Management Sciences in Providence, Rhode Island, the programs have reduced the spread of AIDS by 33 percent in the first year. As with almost all programs that have been studied, the vast majority of dispensed needles are returned within weeks or even sooner. In addition, the percentage of returned needles contaminted by the AIDS virus dropped from 63 to 26 percent in the first four months of the program. Back in New York, Judge Gustin Reichbach has collab-orated with AIDS crusader Dr. Joyce Wallace to develop a new type of sentencing for prostitutes and minor drug offenders, where AIDS education replaces jail. But they have had to fight a recal-citrant system every step of the way, and Judge Reichbach was reassigned to civil court in 1991 to prevent him from interfering with business-as-usual in the criminal courts.

Somehow the facts have been lost on our health leaders nationally, who continue to prefer moralizing. This is what might be called the ostrich strategy, which we carry forward while the Australian and other governments practice harm reduction. We will have hundreds of thousands of unnecessary cases of AIDS, it is true, while Australia, which once had a worse AIDS problem than we do, largely escaped the second phase of the epidemic, now rampant in the United States. But we will have the gratification of knowing that we held firm to our high moral standards, and that we did nothing to even hint at condoning unacceptable inclinations, unconscionable behavior.

Dade County, where Miami is located, has perhaps the highest rate of HIV infection in the United States. It is 50 percent black, 20 percent Hispanic, and 30 percent "Anglo"—which really means "other," and includes a lot more variation besides. Dr. Pedro J. Greer, a Cuban-American who is director of the Camillus Health Concern for the Homeless, serves a particular subgroup of the Dade County poor—those who have nothing to call home except a space on a street, under a bridge, on a bench, or in an alleyway. In the late 1980s these people had no health services, or for that matter other services, of any kind. But by the early 1990s, thanks to Dr. Greer and a few other people generous with their time, skill, medical equipment, furniture, and hard cash, the Dade County homeless has some threadbare but badly needed clinics devoted exclusively to them.

Greer himself goes prowling under the bridges and in the alleyways, wearing his white coat and stethoscope. He is a large, charismatic, genuine man. Everyone seems to know him, and he certainly knows them. They greet him unthreateningly, as a valued friend. He asks about one's children, another's surprisingly advanced reading. Not only is he making house calls, he is making house calls to people who have no house. While others use similar skills to amass personal wealth, Dr. Greer does colonoscopies on paying customers—the well-insured—part-time, so that he can find time to tend to homeless people for free.

Among other serious diseases, many of these people are going to get AIDS. More than 12 percent of the adults were HIV positive in 1990. Yet the homeless no longer fit the old generalizations about them—male bums or hoboes who have hit the skids. A surprising number are educated, some even college graduates. Of the estimated eight thousand homeless people in Miami alone, approximately a third are women; but contrary to the bag-lady stereotype, their average age is twenty-three. Many are pregnant, or caring for dependent children; roughly half of those children are under five years old, and many already have established chronic illnesses. The population of homeless nationally may be increasing as fast as 25 percent a year. At that rate of compounded interest, given the high rate of AIDS infections, in no time there will be a vast harvest of death.

And it will be nondiscriminating. As Dr. Greer writes of his AIDS research, "We showed no difference statistically for HIV infection in the homeless, regardless of race, ethnicity, risk groups (intravenous drug abuse, prostitutes, and homosexuals), or lack of risk groups. Poverty was the only common denominator." Commenting on this, he says,

> So what does that tell you? That this disease is the same here as it is in Haiti and other regions of the world, in third-world countries. So in the United States of America we have our own little third-world country. Yet we're not willing to do anything about it. We're not willing to do the prevention.

AIDS is the entity that scares us, because it is the easiest to visualize spreading throughout society from a reservoir among the homeless. But many, many other diseases are rampant among them. Hepatitis—transmitted in ways similar to AIDS—and other sexually transmitted diseases as well as the new forms of tuberculosis are highly correlated with AIDS in this population.

Moreover, the homeless nationally have three times as much hypertension, twice as many gastrointestinal disorders, five times as many neurological disorders, and ten times as much peripheral vascular disease, including gangrene and varicose veins—a surprising amount of which stems from abnormal sleeping postures. "In effect," Greer says in conclusion, "a third-world country of disease is superimposed over first-world-country diseases. What we don't pay for today, we'll pay for tomorrow, not only economically but in the future of this country."

Like his Australian counterparts Alex Wodak and Ingrid Van Beek, Dr. Greer does not care about fixing blame, or about moralizing against behavior he disapproves of. He cares about harm reduction. And like them, he does not do it alone. Bessie Garrett, for example, is an intensive-care nurse who also spends a lot of time on the street, and has a remarkable way with the homeless people she finds there. She knows things about those people that are counterintuitive. For instance, most people think that women are the right target for education about condoms; that certainly seems to be the way it works in Australia and Thailand. But Bessie Garrett has discovered that if she gives out condoms to women, and the men they are with discover the condoms—which presumably they must if the devices are to be used—the men will beat the women up, seeing the condoms as a sign of infidelity. So she talks to men, not women, about safe sex.

But Dade County needs dozens of professionals like Pedro Greer and Bessie Garrett. Yet Americans do not want to pay for them to do what they do. While it is inspiring to see individuals like these, who have the courage and dedication to buck the system and give of themselves in ways that few people anywhere are prepared to emulate, what is needed is a systematic approach to training and rewarding such people. What is needed is a response from us as a society—a willingness to make sacrifices to help those people to keep on doing their work. And what is needed even more is some attention to the root causes of illness, the conditions favoring it, in the culture of poverty and despair.

Dr. Greer is a frank, plainspoken man who likes to use the grim analogy of bodies floating in the river to bring out the illogic of how we approach these problems:

Now a body floats by and you resuscitate it—as the person at the edge of the river. Five, you get tired; ten, society says,

Hey, there's a problem, build a clinic. A thousand, they say,
Wait a second, build a hospital. A million, they say, Hold it,
hold it, hold it—we need a big giant public tertiary referral
center. Two million float by and then you have a bond or tax
that says, Look, we need to pay for it *more*. . . .
    These people are falling off a bridge somewhere. That
bridge is society. It's urban poverty. It has to be repaired.

A number of recent analyses, including some that have survived
vigorous criticism without losing their force, have shown that during the 1980s the richest few percent of people in the United States
became substantially richer, while the poor became poorer. Unemployment worsened dramatically, directly affecting the middle
class, forcing many in this group down into poverty. Every serious
study of the homeless in America has shown them greatly increasing in number during the past dozen years.

The disparity between black and white, different from and superimposed on the one between rich and poor, has remained very
great during these years according to most major measures, no-
tably excepting the number of black actors on television. Infant
mortality, maternal mortality, rates of death from all major diseases, victimization by violence, joblessness, poverty, homelessness, school segregation—all show a continuing pattern of
inequality and discrimination best summarized in the title of a
recent book by distinguished sociologist Andrew Hacker—*Two
Nations: Black and White, Separate, Hostile, Unequal*.

A century and a half ago French historian Alexis de Tocqueville,
visiting and reporting on democracy in the United States, wrote
that "the danger of a conflict between the white and the black
inhabitants perpetually haunts the imagination of Americans, like
a painful dream." He may have been thinking of events like the
notorious and violent (but perfectly understandable) Nat Turner
rebellion against slavery in 1831. But in the mid-1960s race riots
in many American cities showed that the nation was still haunted
by the same painful dream. And despite an official government
report in 1968 recommending many changes to prevent such violence in the future, few changes were implemented. So it was not

surprising that this nightmarish recurring dream identified by de Tocqueville returned yet again with race rioting in 1992.

But race is not the only or even perhaps the central problem dividing Americans. At the beginning of the 1980s a swing in public opinion—really a change in philosophy—made selfishness not just acceptable but downright admirable. It was justified in terms of the "trickle-down" concept in economics; for the rich to get much richer was supposedly good for everyone, since their greed would serve as the engine of economic growth that, when fired up, would power the whole country, benefiting the middle class and eventually the poor. George Bush in 1980 called this "voodoo economics," which it turned out to be; it was without merit then and it is without merit now. But Mr. Bush practiced it and defended it himself for twelve years, soothing his nation with cynical bromides about "a thousand points of light" and "a kinder, gentler America." Rarely have such assurances been more at variance with reality.

As Kevin P. Phillips, author of *The Politics of Rich and Poor*, said in a recent interview, "By the end of the 1980s, Horatio Alger got replaced by Charles Keating, Michael Milken, and Leona Helmsley." These three criminals, convicted of pocketing millions of dollars that could have gone to help the poor, were punished in the end—while others practicing less criminal forms of selfishness, like Donald Trump and Robert Maxwell, merely fell into failure and disgrace. But countless unknown others, one of whom turned out to be the President's son, were equally effective during this period in amassing wealth at the expense of the less fortunate. Unlike Keating and Trump, they were usually able to keep their gains, protected by ire raised against these weightier scapegoats, and by a national philosophy that somehow condoned the almost complete absence of compassion.

Among the consequences is the fact that in an era when every other Western industrialized nation has accepted the necessity of building a solid floor under the poor—minimally, with universal health insurance—the United States has not only allowed the poor to languish in their squalor, but has forced millions more newly poor people to share that squalor with them. In an era in which

the Communist world has almost universally recognized the superiority of capitalism, only the United States has failed to recognize that capitalism without compassion is a system that must
ultimately humiliate and sicken those who benefit from it, filling
them with hesitancy and shame. And hesitancy and shame, of
course, will prove no sort of recipe for success.

Despite the attention we give it, the drama that drives our discussions of it, and the unquestionable cloud it forms on the horizon, AIDS is not the most important preventable threat to health
in either the developed or the underdeveloped world today. More
than 70 percent of premature deaths—deaths preventable with
present knowledge—in the United States are attributable to three
causes: tobacco abuse, inadequately treated high blood pressure,
and overnutrition. Another 10 percent or so are attributable to
injuries, including violence. Looking at years of life lost before age
sixty-five, injuries loom much larger, accounting for more than 40
percent, with a major contribution from injuries caused by alcohol
abuse; tobacco abuse still accounts for 18 percent.

Lung cancer alone, an almost completely preventable behavorial
epidemic encouraged by social, economic, political, and cultural
forces, will cause more than 150,000 deaths in 1992—more than
the total number of AIDS deaths from 1981 to the present. This
epidemic, like AIDS, affects the poor much more than it does the
well-to-do; and it is only one of the major deadly diseases caused
by smoking.

In general, the amount of money the United States spends on
AIDS research is not uncontroversial. As Dr. Robert Wachter of
the University of California at San Francisco wrote in the *New
England Journal of Medicine* in January 1992, "federal spending for
AIDS was $1.6 billion in 1990, a year after 40,000 Americans died
of the disease. During the same year, federal spending for cancer,
a disease that killed 500,000 in 1989, was $1.5 billion, and spending
for heart disease, which killed 750,000, was less than $1 bil-
lion . . . in fact overall spending for health care research remained
essentially fixed; it was self-evident that money spent on AIDS
was money not spent on something else." That money—or, pref-

erably, other money—could be spent fighting cancer and heart disease, through research and prevention. Many gaps in the prevention of these two groups of diseases are in desperate need of funds for programs to fill them.

Other gaps in prevention leading to needless illness and death include inadequate prenatal care, inadequate childhood immunization, inadequate mental health services, inadequate addiction rehabilitation services, inadequate health education, and inadequate health screening.

Without exception, each of these causes of loss of life is much more damaging to the poor than to the more well-off, and the poor have higher mortality rates in virtually every comparison. These differences are due to the same disparities of health care, knowledge, opportunity, and optimism that led to large differences in mortality and illness from quite other diseases during centuries past. Then, as now, specific diseases are the mediators of the generic process: the devastating effect of poverty on health. This effect, these disparities, have been known since ancient times. We like to think that we have conquered them, put them behind us, but we certainly have not.

As for the rest, the underdeveloped world, AIDS is scarcely the most important killer there either. Tuberculosis, for instance—not the new, AIDS-related kind, just the old standby killer of history— takes far more lives throughout the world than AIDS will for years to come. Since it slowly chokes you to death, it too isn't exactly an ideal way to die. Malaria, with its spiking fevers and swollen bellies, comes to at least a hundred million new people a year, and millions of these die untreated or with strains resistant to the treatments we have. Tens of millions more are gravely debilitated, robbed of the vitality that makes life and work worthwhile.

Schistosomiasis, caused by an insidious, snail-borne parasite absorbed through the feet in countless bodies of water, is likewise a hopeless obstacle to vigorous life. But it is a chronic, essentially downhill one; two hundred million people are affected worldwide. Bleeding occurs in internal organs ranging from liver to bladder, the victim loses weight, and—as in AIDS—resistance to many other diseases is lowered. As with tuberculosis, there are drugs that help, but the course of treatment is so long that completion by the illiterate poor is very unlikely.

The situation of the mother with her infant is one that evokes almost universal tenderness; it has been a major theme in religion, art, and literature. Yet we allow about half a million women to die each year worldwide in connection with pregnancy and childbirth, most from childbed fever. This alone is still more than the number of people who will die this year from AIDS worldwide, and it has occurred without stirring much excitement, year in and year out since long before the AIDS problem started.

There are other major diseases far exceeding AIDS in their impact on human options in the underdeveloped world; but this is not the place for a litany of these ancient and ongoing collective human catastrophes. Still, it is worth mentioning three other points.

First, we are now actively and vigorously involved in spreading tobacco addiction to the developing world—much more rapidly and with more devastating effect than we did AIDS. In the foreseeable future many more deaths will occur in Colombia from American tobacco than will occur in America from Colombian cocaine. There are 350,000 tobacco-related deaths each year in the United States and 500,000 in Europe; now we are eagerly trying to spread this plague to developing countries. Tobacco companies, increasingly hampered by American and European health law, are shifting their focus to a vast and vulnerable populace in the third world, where health-education programs are too impoverished to counterbalance cigarette advertising.

In Bangkok, where tobacco may ultimately do even more damage than AIDS, one ad reads "Winston, Style of the U.S.A." American government intervention? Not likely, given the trade deficit. As Los Angeles congressional representative Mel Levine has said, for Washington "Asian lungs [are] more expendable than American lungs." In China, women are viewing smoking as a sign of liberation—just as their European and American counterparts did in the post–World War II era, with continuing tragic consequences. Like AIDS, the behavioral epidemic of tobacco-caused diseases is still in an early stage in most of the developing world; unlike AIDS, nothing much is being done to slow it down.

Second, starvation—the full-blown clinical syndrome of malnutrition—affects five hundred million people a year at a minimum; some estimates range much higher. This too, like AIDS, is not a pleasant way to die; this too reduces resistance to many other diseases.

It is easy to say: they have produced more people than they can feed; therefore many of them must starve. But this conveniently glosses over the fact that the absence of family planning is also a public health problem, one that has been gravely exacerbated during the past decade by ignorant Western, especially American, politicians and institutions. It is quite possible that a century hence the only thing that in retrospect will matter about our era is that, through pathetically ignorant and misguided leadership, we systematically impeded the worldwide effort to slow population growth. The virtual absence of discussion of this subject at the much-vaunted Earth Summit of 1992 rendered that event almost useless and ludicrous, dwarfing in importance the other criticisms leveled against it.

Third, we have virtually abandoned the world's children—many to die of diseases that are trivially easy to prevent with a small expenditure of funds. Worldwide, about fifteen million children die each year, and many millions more survive the onslaught of illness with permanent impairment and dreadful pain. More than ten million of these fifteen million deaths are preventable with readily available measures. Diarrhea treated with inexpensive oral rehydration salts—which an illiterate mother can easily learn to supply—would not, as it now does, lead to millions of children dying each year by simply drying up. Bacterial pneumonia and other respiratory infections, easily treatable with everyday antibiotics, would not steal the breath of life from millions more. And whooping cough, measles, and tetanus—all vaccine-preventable and almost abolished from Western countries—would not ravage and kill still more millions.

Roughly 150 million—40 percent—of the underdeveloped world's children are in the process of starving, but some other things they need are much cheaper than food. A quarter million a year go blind from simple vitamin A deficiency; a capsule worth two U.S. cents, given twice a year, would leave those children the light. Untold millions suffer brain damage from iodine deficiency; for a few cents' worth of iodized salt, each of them could keep the great mental and emotional powers nature has set in store for almost every human child.

But, you say, it's overpopulation again! They produce so many of these babies, we in the West can't be expected to mop up after their indiscretions, can we?

Fine, but at least be consistent. If you believe that in this situation neglect is acceptable, have the decency to propose euthanasia for ten million or so children a year. At least spare them the humiliation of blindness and mental retardation, the protracted despair of death by starvation, the seizures and rigidity of tetanus, pneumonia's gasping for breath, malaria's roller coaster of feverish delirium—the callous natural variety of deaths caused by diseases that, unlike the irreversible process of AIDS, we know how to stop right now, today.

So why does AIDS get so much intense attention, when all these other scourges that we lack the will to wipe away remain, one generation after another, dull, expectable statistics that mock our insistence on calling ourselves humane?

Simply put, it is because AIDS can get to *us*. It is not compassion at all, but fear. Annie Crowe, a nonphysician who works the streets of Sydney night after night saving the lives of youngsters who don't even care to be saved, puts it very plainly:

> In the years from 1977 to the early eighties there were no, no real supports for the street level at all . . . I mean, you're talking about young people who are living on the streets with virtually no social supports at all, no family, no school . . . no nothing, no GP, no one at all . . . We had kids who were overdosing, who were suiciding, who had the most incredible range of medical problems you've ever seen, from infected tattoos through to throat infections, lung infections that turned into pneumnia before our very eyes . . .

Prior to AIDS I don't think anybody cared at all about street people or junkies or gays, or young street kids . . . But then AIDS came and all of a sudden because of AIDS everybody got scared. Suddenly AIDS was the big virus with the street people and the money came pouring in.

Annie goes on to put these observations in an even darker light:

Nothing, nothing in the world is worth AIDS, nothing. But the truth is that these streets and the resources that we've been able to put on these streets would not be here but for AIDS . . .

I mean everybody hopes and prays for a cure for AIDS. But in one sense a cure might bring our death knell here. I mean it may be that the resources do dry up if a cure was found for AIDS tomorrow . . .

It is not easy to think of something sadder. Here is a person who dedicates her life, at considerable risk with minuscule reward, to helping those whom no one else cares about—including saving them from AIDS; yet she *fears* a cure for this horrible scourge because she knows that it is not the most important threat to them. And she knows too that without AIDS no one would give a second thought to them, and she would be back watching them languish and die with no resources to help them, just as she was in 1980.

Although he is much less bitter and cynical than Annie Crowe, Dr. Jonathan Mann, the former WHO AIDS program director, clearly has made a similar calculus. As in the United States alone, worldwide spending for AIDS has for years now been far out of proportion to the share of illness and death attributable to AIDS. Strong arguments can be made based on projected mortality a decade from now; but even those projections do not justify the relative neglect of other causes of premature death—many of which, even in the worst-case AIDS scenario, will still be more important and more damaging than AIDS after the year 2000. Yet WHO's budget for AIDS is at least double that for the next largest program in the organization, the Tropical Disease Research Program, which subsumes not one but a number of intrinsically more important diseases.

Mann, like Annie Crowe, is not naive. He knows that the main reason developed countries are willing to spend so much on AIDS is that they are scared to death of it. And he also knows that for decades before AIDS the developed countries basically didn't give a second thought to disease and death in the developing world.

So although he is much more diplomatic than Crowe, he secretly thinks something similar on a worldwide scale to what she thinks in relation to downtown Sydney. The terror of AIDS has awakened uncaring well-to-do people from their comfortable slumber, and induced them to pull a few more coins—that's all it is, really— from their fashionable pockets, to toss at the world's continuing crisis of health. Mann and others like him are not playing tricks with the coins; they are using them to set up structures for AIDS control and prevention like the one that is working at least for now in Thailand. But they are putting these structures in places that have never had any sort of health care before, and organizing them in a new network that covers the world; and they believe that they will permanently change the process of disease control, so that long after the AIDS problem is solved the structures will go on preventing other dreaded diseases, different needless deaths.

Let us hope that they are right. One would hope, too, that we could bring ourselves to feel ashamed that only a fear for our own safety could separate us from our pocket change—that the specter of millions of painful early deaths that annually dwarfs the human impact of AIDS would alone suffice to stir our consciences. It is not quite compatible with our lofty view of ourselves to have been incapable of responding to this challenge. But that appears to be the way it is. At least, then, let us help others out of self-interest, if we cannot bring ourselves to help them out of compassion.

EPILOGUE

THIS BOOK HAS surveyed real current situations of doctors and other health workers carrying out policy, in eight spheres of medicine, throughout much of the world. By this means I have tried to develop a sense of what we in the United States need to think about, and what we need to do.

First, we must try to restore trust between doctor and patient. This will entail changes in medical training, and renewed emphasis on the physician's task in alleviating suffering—a complex spiritual task—and not just fixing the broken machine. But it will also entail a much greater public understanding of the limits of what doctors can do, and a renewed tolerance by patients for the human failings of their doctors. Both doctors and patients must make the considerable effort needed to increase patients' understanding of their illnesses, so that the doctor-patient relationship becomes a true collaboration for healing. Where the doctor's conception of the illness differs greatly from that of the patient, as in the case of widely differing cultural backgrounds, economic levels, or education, both must make a serious effort to bridge the gap.

Second, a massive shift in emphasis, through both training and reimbursement, must restore a healthier balance between primary care and specialization, between low-tech and high-tech interventions. Major new incentives must draw young people into primary-care medicine. The status and role of nurses and nurse-practitioners must be enhanced. Preventive medicine, including measures to be taken before illness begins as well as in its earliest stages, must become central in education and practice, and must be rewarded accordingly. Doctors-in-training must no longer be used just as low-wage labor for crisis intervention among the acutely ill poor. Young doctors and their poor patients both deserve better, but in addition, the society that is paying for these services can find more cost-effective ways of allocating resources. For the sake of humaneness as well as of training, we should establish a network of clinics outside of hospitals to deliver preventive medicine and primary care. Imaginative new strategies and tactics for outreach and education must be aggressively mounted.

Third, we must overcome the tendency to see drugs as miracle cures. Drugs used against microbes and parasites must be jealously guarded and used extremely sparingly, as if they were a precious nonrenewable resource—which they are. Drug evaluation for consumer protection must identify not only dangerous or ineffective drugs but also those that, at greater expense, accomplish no more than already proven ones. Drug-company advertising and marketing tactics must be much more carefully monitored. At the same time, there must be new incentives for companies to develop drugs that may not have great commercial success or that may present liability risks. As with malpractice litigation against doctors, we need to understand that our irrational expectation of perfection from drug companies will hamper the fight against illness.

Fourth, the promise of mastery over human biology presented by the new science of genes must be pursued with exceptional caution. Unprecedented and welcome advances will certainly come out of this science. But an excessive zeal for perfection may lead us to tamper with the pool of human genes in ways that—perhaps inadvertently—reduce not just negative aspects of human variation but positive ones as well. The experience of twentieth-century authoritarian regimes teaches us to fear abuse of this new power to alter the human species. At the individual level, decisions about fertility and pregnancy have been transformed in only a decade. Advances in the control of the genes and of reproduction will relentlessly challenge the human ethical sensibility. Will we rise to this challenge?

Fifth, the role of surgery and related interventions in the body must be reevaluated. The postwar refinement of medical science has been marred by overenthusiasm for certain surgical procedures, some of which had to be abandoned when they were found to be useless. A distressingly high proportion of the types of operations we do have no firm foundation in scientific research. Even those that do are often performed unnecessarily—some of them thousands or tens of thousands of times more often than necessary every year—because there are incentives to perform them. The incentives must be changed. Evaluation of the outcomes of surgery, in terms of both the overall value of certain operations and the quality of practice in particular hospitals as opposed to others, is woefully inadequate. Outcomes research must be given the highest priority.

Sixth, our treatment of serious mental illness is both inhumane and wasteful. It is also indicative of some things that are wrong with our whole health-care system. Remarkably effective psychiatric drugs drastically reduced mental-hospital populations beginning in the 1950s. But hundreds of thousands of patients were discharged to grossly inadequate out-of-hospital situations. As with chronic physical illnesses like heart disease and hypertension, we are not prepared to pay for services, such as halfway houses for chronic schizophrenics, that will keep patients in stable functional condition. We allow them to sink or swim, and they usually sink—into homelessness, alcoholism and drug abuse, needless infectious disease, victimization by violence, and other severe stresses that put them back into the mental hospital. Aside from being a moral disgrace, this approach costs more than would a humane approach of timely preventive intervention.

Seventh, the aging of our population is certain to supply an unending source of new and greater medical expenditures unless we begin to face some hard choices. But these choices are only more frequent for the elderly, not limited to them. The question is not, Who is too old to deserve care? but, Who is too sick to benefit enough from costly intervention?—a question that starts in the neonatal intensive care unit and ends in the nursing home or geriatric hospital. As with mental illness, aging forms a continuum from health to severe disease, and timely, humane intervention in the community and the home can prevent both suffering and expense. But too many of our resources for health care are devoted to the last months of life. We need to face the fact that all life must end. To expect doctors to make the decisions for us, under the pressure of emergency or crisis, is nothing but a sign of immaturity. These decisions must be made by society, which is a fancy way of saying us.

Finally, we face a new pandemic—a global epidemic, AIDS—that has frightened every thoughtful person. As with the great epidemics of the past, social conditions are central to its spread. Few things highlight our failure to recognize the connection between social life and disease as strongly as does this uncontrolled worldwide threat to health. Any nation that fails to see the connection now will face economic and human costs almost beyond description. Yet ironically, both the dismaying social conditions and the major threat to health, within the United States and throughout the world, have long preceded AIDS. Many diseases, both infectious (like tuberculosis) and degenerative (like heart disease), are in large part the result of poverty and its concomitants. True, they are often mediated by what we think of as bad habits, like smoking or risky sex. But to consign people to circumstances that take away any rational hope for the future while making most healthy pleasures inaccessible, and then to blame them for indulging in unhealthy ones, is something approaching the height of cynicism. If we can't afford to or won't address the central problems of poverty, the least we can do is mount specific programs of treatment and prevention aimed at poverty's victims.

The idea of a national health plan is one whose time has come. Leading physicians as different as C. Everett Koop, the conservative former surgeon general, and Marcia Angell, the liberal executive editor of *The New England Journal of Medicine*, agree that neither major party in the 1992 election year had a credible plan for addressing the crisis. Each, along with the American College of Physicians, the American Nurses Association, and many other responsible bodies, believes that much more must be done.

More than 12 percent of the U.S. gross national product, or about $800 billion in current dollars, is spent on health care each year, and further increases are on the way. Everett Dirksen, the late Republican senator from Illinois, used to joke, "A billion here, a billion there, and pretty soon you're talking about real money." We're not just talking about real money, we're spending it; and not the billions of the Dirksen era, but hundreds of billions. Yet catastrophic illness routinely impoverishes middle-class families, and the poor cannot beg, borrow, or steal decent health care.

Meanwhile, doctors are growing ever more bitter about the interference of bureaucrats who have never learned or practiced medicine, and who never have to face patients or their families, yet who tell physicians how they may care for the very ill. The same physicians must endure, work, and sacrifice under the constant threat of personal ruin by lawyers in this most litigious of societies—lawyers who often confuse malpractice with natural accident, or with the fact that medical science is not yet perfect.

With medical costs running far ahead of inflation, people who pay taxes, medical insurance premiums, and doctors' and hospitals' bills can be forgiven for wondering whether they are getting their money's worth. The reasons for escalating costs are varied, but rising expectations are a major one. People will no longer let doctors fail. We sue at the drop of a stethoscope, and a doctor's best protection in court is to have left no stone unturned, to have ordered every possible test and done every procedure that could remotely be considered relevant. People will cluck their tongues about costs right up to the hospital door; but as soon as we or our loved ones are rolled across that threshold on a stretcher, nothing is too dear. We will cheerfully spend thousands of dollars of someone else's money for a gain of 1 percent in knowledge, one slim ray of hope.

The lure of technology—the hope of pulling clear of crises that would have been last year's hopeless cases—is irresistible. The trouble is that new procedures tend to be less certain and more expensive than those that have been in use for many years. Always, care is distributed unequally according to social status, wealth, and power. Women may receive less treatment than men for the same diseases. And as for prevention, it is rarely covered at all by third-party payers; we work from a principle something like "a dollar's worth of cure is better than a penny's worth of prevention." So if you want an inoculation, a prenatal exam, a cholesterol check, a mammogram, or health counseling, you're often on your own—even though these measures save money and eliminate untold suffering. The Roman orator Cicero was a lawyer, not a physician, but he had experienced serious illness himself, and he spoke to us with a fully current relevance when he said, "The competent physician, before he attempts to give medicine to his patient, makes himself acquainted not only with the disease which he wishes to cure, but also with the habits and constitution of the sick man."

A national health plan would not be a panacea. Fears about such plans abound. Could costs continue to escalate? (Yes, but much more slowly, and controllably.) Could we end with explicit rationing of health care? (We already have rationing, just not *explicit* rationing.) Could the patient's choice of physician and the right of redress in the event of malpractice become more limited? (Not necessarily; Canada's system retains physician choice, and with the right approach both compensation and restriction of malpractice could become more likely.) Would a shadow world of private medicine arise, allowing a two-tiered system of care to reemerge? (Probably, but no one would be left out and the floor would be higher for the poor.) Transplants and other exceptional procedures could become the Rolls-Royces of medical care, affordable only for the privileged few. The only power patients have over their doctors, short of lawsuits, is payment for services, and this power could perhaps be weakened. Finally, medicine-for-profit would not be as easy to pursue, thus removing a key incentive that helps motivate some doctors to keep on doing one of the most demanding jobs in the world.

Yet a variety of national programs work in Britain, Canada, and other countries with health statistics we can envy. Over half the doctors in Britain remain general practitioners. For about twenty years now American medical educators have tried everything they could think of to increase the number of graduating medical students who elect and stay in primary-care specialties—general internal medicine, general pediatrics, and family medicine—the latter being our rough equivalent of British general practice. (It says a good deal about the difference between the two countries that in America family medicine is considered a specialty, and one not chosen very often.) Yet despite this effort, the trend in America toward high-tech, procedure-oriented specialization and subspecialization and away from every form of primary care has continued unabated.

This alone puts British medicine at an enormous advantage. Unnecessary procedures and tests are kept to a minimum, as are multiple consultations and multiple billings. The American notion that everything must ideally be done by a specialist is simply wrong. Specialists and their procedures—including hospitalization itself—are dangerous. They should never be invoked unless absolutely necessary. Very often the best care money can buy is the less expensive kind provided by a primary-care physician who knows the patient, and who has the time and knowledge to invoke interventions less dramatic than high-tech procedures and surgery. This level of care does not always have to be provided by a physician. For example, nurse-practitioners are an elite corps of specially trained nurses whose duties overlap, in important ways, the functions of primary-care physicians. In family practice, internal medicine, pediatrics, and obstetrics and gynecology, nurse-practitioners can play a larger and more crucial role. Yet it is unlikely that they can succeed fully without the collaboration of primary-care doctors, who are trained in a different way and who are their link to more specialized levels of care.

Equally important, primary-care doctors are specialists too. Here is what *they* have done thousands of times: rapidly distinguish between life-threatening and merely frightening situations; take people with cardiac arrest or drug overdose, or children with severe bleeding or epiglottitis—an inflammation that stops breathing—and prevent them from dying, which they are otherwise highly likely to do; sew minor lacerations in injured children without traumatizing them psychologically; persuade patients with simple colds that they don't need antibiotics; persuade busy mothers that their children do need immunizations on schedule; talk cigarettes out of the lives and lungs of a small but significant minority of patients; and not least, exercise day after day an increasingly learned and sophisticated judgment that refers some patients on to more specialized doctors and keeps others under a simpler regime of care. The impact of these last sorts of judgments is emphatically *not* just to save money, regardless of who is paying. It is also to save patients the enormous time, trouble, discomfort, boredom, pain, side effects, and physician-induced illness that can often result from the most sophisticated and specialized medical care.

If the British system is not the envy of the world—if even those in the United States who favor radical reform do not advertise the successes of that system—it is not mainly because the British have chosen the wrong type of organization for their national health system, but because they spend only 6 percent of their gross domestic product paying for it. The proportion of GDP spent in the United States is more than double that. Although some of the difference is due the fact that we perform a larger number of needed medical and surgical procedures, most is due to our enormous administrative inefficiency—plus substantial health-care fraud, unnecessary procedures, cash-register physicians, and heedless malpractice litigation.

One of the most impressive things about Britain's 1992 national election, aside from how blessedly quick it was, was that Prime

Minister John Major promised faithfully that nothing, not the slightest hint of effort by his administration, would be directed toward restoring in Britain the privately organized medicine of half a century ago. Granted, given politics as usual, this was not a completely ingenuous statement. But it reflects the fact that the British people love the National Health Service more than they dislike "creeping socialism," even now, as well as the reality that the NHS must simply be working, and working very well. Because only when a public institution is functioning well do people forget that it is run by government, and so violates their cherished conservative or middle-of-the-road political principles.

As for the Canadian system, we have heard administration representatives from President Bush on down claim that Americans would never put up with it, that it would have the efficiency of the Postal Service and the compassion of the IRS. Actually, it has the prices of the Postal Service and the efficiency of our army in the Persian Gulf—good enough for government work or any other sort of work. It has far more compassion than our system does. And it would be far more compatible with Americans' aggressive free-enterprise philosophy than the British system would be. It performs needed procedures and defers needless ones, rationing by medical appropriateness instead of our rationing by income, or by the availability and inclinations of specialists seeking fees. It gives patients free choice of doctors and leaves doctors independent and, on average, well paid. It covers every man, woman, and child, and it even allows the rich to buy private care if they want to. It replaces private insurers with a single-payer system, enormously reducing the cost of paperwork and freeing doctors to do what they love best: doctoring.

It is no coincidence that the Canadian proportion of GDP spent on health care—like, in fact, the German and French proportions—is roughly midway between the British and American levels: around 9 percent. Canada accomplishes less in the realm of high-technology care than the United States, but that is not because it has a national health program. It is because it has universal coverage, while the United States has chosen to leave over 35 million people without insurance coverage for basic health care. Britain, like Canada, has universal coverage; but because it spends only about two thirds of what the Canadians spend, it remains substantially behind Canada in the availability of procedures on or near the technological frontier of medicine. As for out-of-control bureaucracy, large-volume needless surgery, malpractice-suit shenanigans, and other peculiarly American problems, Britain and Canada have both succeeded remarkably well in avoiding them.

Granted, emergency rooms in Britain and Canada do not look anything like ours. AIDS and drug abuse are less prevalent, and strict gun control laws prevent most violent trauma. Their populations remain less ethnically heterogeneous than ours, and for this and other reasons preventive medicine is more effective in those countries. More important, however, is that most other advanced countries have either abolished or stringently regulated the private insurance business, which has only a questionable function in health-care delivery. They have found far better ways of regulating medical malpractice and compensating its victims than the haphazard, hit-or-miss, frequently ignorant flailing at doctors by private trial lawyers with nothing to lose. And they have reined in medical greed, whether by doctors with their hearts in the wrong place or by corporations that are trying to turn the care of the ill into a spectacle that looks and acts increasingly like a stock market trading floor.

Equally important, other nations have set limits on what they *will* do in medicine that deliberately fall short of what they *can* do. We still insist on doing everything that can be done for almost every patient. We want to save one-pound premature babies, at a cost of $100,000 to $1 million each, with results that often require a lifetime of additional costs for the permanent part of the damage. We want to give eighty-year-old people kidney dialysis, organ transplants, and other extremely expensive treatments, even while we withhold vaccinations from poor children on the grounds that we're out of money. We want to subject a demented octogenarian to heart-lung resuscitation over and over again, even though all this does is prolong and intensify pain—even, in some cases, where the patient has left clear instructions to prevent such measures from being performed.

In medical school I helped to resuscitate an eighty-three-year-old woman who was dying of a lung disease. She was not in, nor could she be returned to, a mental condition that permitted judgment, and there were no close kin. So the person in charge of the decision was the lawyer representing the nursing home where she lived. In the middle of the resuscitation a young doctor, the house officer in charge, ran out into the hall to phone the hospital's lawyer, who had the nursing home's lawyer on another line. The lady had to be revived. At the cost of thousands more—and great pain for the patient, who was probably aware of little else—she was kept alive for three more weeks.

But we have even harder choices to make. The state of Oregon has pioneered them, listing hundreds of medical and surgical procedures according to their estimated cost-effectiveness, and drawing a line below which state Medicare and Medicaid funds will not be available for coverage. One result, for example, would be to reject most transplants in favor of preventive measures like immunization. We can argue about exactly where to draw the line between reimbursed and nonreimbursed procedures, or about the ordering of priorities in the list. But it is clear that something like this must be done, and the plan has bipartisan support in the state legislature, where it was designed in part by physician legislators.

In the summer of 1992 the Bush administration blocked the Oregon plan, evidently for political reasons in an election year. The plan tries to ensure the greatest good for the greatest number, and to do this we have got to learn to say no to some interventions. When you see a picture of Coby Howard, a seven-year-old boy who died because he was $10,000 short of the $90,000 he needed for his liver transplant—when you look into the eyes of his grieving family members—it becomes very difficult to say no again. But somehow we have to learn to visualize the untold children whose deaths are averted when we shift to preventive measures. Perhaps we need to see pictures of them too, saying, "We didn't die of measles because of the government's vaccine." Or perhaps we need to know the name and see the face of one of the children who *did* die of measles in an epidemic in the United States in 1989 and 1990—an epidemic that should never have happened, and never would have if we had immunization programs comparable to those in other industrial countries.

In a 1987 Harris poll 90 percent of Americans agreed that everyone deserves "as good as a millionaire gets" in health care. But this same public wants costs to come down, and much of it wants the government to stay out of health care. At the copy service I use, there is a cartoon of a man laughing into a telephone, saying, "You want it good, you want it cheap, and you want it fast? Pick two and call me back." The same can be said of equal access, freedom from government intervention, and cost control in health care—pick two (at most) and call me back. But Americans want all three, plus the right to sue for vast sums in damages every time a doctor makes an honest mistake.

A national health plan will not solve all these problems. What it will do is mitigate our national disgrace: the inability of tens of millions of poor people to get any decent care at all. The price tag will depend on how much we decide we are willing to pay for health care. If we want that price tag to stay the same or even come down, we will have to do several things. And we have to do them as citizens, not just wait for the government to do them.

First, we must simplify the bureaucracy of private and public insurers. The most straightforward way to do this is to institute a national health program with a single pool of funds and a single mechanism of disbursement. Some physicians and economists favor a straightforward imitation of the Canadian system. Contrary to common belief, a single-payer system does not have to be based on disbursements from one national pool—the specter of the long arm of Washington meddling in every doctor-patient encounter. In some countries the single payer is at the regional level. In Canada it is at the provincial level—Ottawa's involvement is minor. The equivalent for us would be a state-by-state single-payer plan subject to some regulation and coordination at the federal level. Each of us would have a health insurance card as standardized as a Social Security card or a driver's license. Presentation of the card would cover all needed medical expenses. This change will require votes, and also sacrifice from some of us who work for or hold shares in private insurance companies or for-profit medical organizations. As of 1992, neither major party in the United States has had the political courage to try to move Americans in the direction of such a plan. Yet it is clearly the most humane as well as the most sensible choice.

Second, we must move to limit the rapid growth of for-profit medicine. As Dr. Arnold Relman, a leading physician and the former editor-in-chief of *The New England Journal of Medicine*, has written, "The growth of the medical-industrial complex continues unabated." Dr. Relman is by no stretch of the imagination any sort of socialist. He believes that medicine "flourishes best in the private sector but it needs public support, and it cannot meet its responsibilities to society if it is dominated by business interests. . . . If most of our physicians become entrepreneurs and most of our hospitals and health-care facilities become businesses, paying patients will get more care than they need and poor patients will get less . . . [physicians] will be seen as self-interested businessmen and will lose many of the privileges they now enjoy as . . . trusted professionals." Patient dumping—the dreadful and sometimes deadly practice of turning the very ill away from the hospital door—is only the most obvious and painful consequence of turning medicine, once a private craft, into a large-scale, aggressively competitive business. There are many others, subtle and manifest, trivial and serious. The Canadian plan keeps doctors in the private sector but puts payment of doctors in the public sector. This combination makes it the best compromise for the United States.

Third, we must change the structure of incentives that causes an ever-increasing excess of overspecialization. Third-party payers, especially government payers, must move farther and faster than they have to reduce reimbursements for procedures and increase those for primary-care medicine— including preventive care and counseling of patients, not necessarily by doctors. Medical students in a national health system should be on full scholarships at public expense, but until we have such a system they should be offered such support in exchange for limited commitment to a national health corps. Dr. Gerald Weissman, chief of medicine at

New York University School of Medicine and editor of *MD* magazine, has suggested that such a corps could be built from and modeled on our already existing national corps of Veterans Administration Hospital physicians, Native American reservation physicians, and Public Health Service doctors. His plan deserves attention.

Fourth, we must drastically reduce malpractice litigation and provide a fairer process for victim compensation and physician oversight. Sweden and Canada provide models of excellent health-care systems in which doctors practice responsibly without the goad of the lawsuit threat. Outrageously high malpractice insurance premiums—some doctors pay over $100,000 a year—end up largely in the pockets of lawyers. A society that continues to use lawyers as the vanguard of an assault on doctors will continue to have doctors who act defensively and resentfully in their own self-interest.

Here we come to the most difficult point: What is really needed? Unless we want our health-care bill to drift farther upward, we will have to stop doing everything we can do. Some things must be deemed too costly for their level of effectiveness. Some people who could be saved for a while must be allowed to die. Some patients—particularly at the beginning of life, in the intensive-care nursery, and at the end, in the geriatric ward—must be lost. It sounds unfeeling, but we are already doing it. It's just that the lives we give up on now are different. Their story is not the dramatic one of the heart transplants in the nick of time, or the one-pound baby finally brought through. It is the mundane one of excess ordinary mortality, day in and day out, among the uncared-for poor throughout the land.

Perhaps the concept of medical triage can serve as a model. It comes from the French word *triager*, to sort. It applies usually to disasters affecting many people—earthquakes, bus accidents, wars—when there are too many injured for the available doctors to handle. The doctors must decide, sometimes very rapidly, who will get the care. Ethics permit such decisions to be made, and some lives are deliberately let go of. Doctors usually try to save not necessarily the most serious cases, but the ones who can profit most from efficient and timely care. Depending on how urgently we feel we must cut costs, we may already be in a situation of triage at the national level. But of course, if we are willing to spend more, we can do more; that option remains open as well.

These questions will not disappear, no matter how we solve our health-care problems. Still, the thought of indigent people in pain, dying without the safety net the rest of us take for granted, ought to suffice to move us to action. A national health plan works in every other industrialized nation, with the sole exception of South Africa—and that isn't good company. As Aneurin Bevan, the founder of the British National Health Service, once wrote, "No society can legitimately call itself civilized if a sick person is denied aid because of lack of means." We need to go forward now, with trial programs in a few states—Hawaii has one that is enormously progressive and works very well—careful monitoring, and meticulous attention to the problems and solutions found by others who are ahead of us in this particular scale of human decency. Or, in plain American English: Just do it.

And then of course there is the offering of comfort: what the doctor can always do, even when there is no hope; what doctors have always been able to do since the dawn of human time. It is something that is possible under virtually any health-care system, yet something that modern doctors seem to be forgetting. A patient I knew in medical school was left virtually brain-dead when she had an unexplained stroke after routine abdominal surgery. A resident came in and said to the devastated family, "She has beautiful blood gases." A senior neurologist I knew went to the bedside of a man to give him bad news. The television playing in the background, he told the man he had an aggressively malignant brain tumor that would soon be fatal, and then he just left, saying that the third-year medical student with him would stay behind to answer any questions. And when a twenty-six-year-old woman died of ovarian cancer, she was by far the youngest patient to have died on that ward in years. Half the nursing staff was crying with the family. But the attending physician, with six medical students in tow, was almost chipper as she signed the death certificate—a brief detour from the diagnostic game she was involved in with the students, to whom she said not a word about the death.

These examples illustrate a social system that has lost its human dimension, that has allowed science, technology, and bureaucracy to seem sufficient. Yet they are only part of the story. A thousand times a day in every hospital acts of kindness and thoughtfulness aid in the process of healing. We must design a system that encourages such acts; the system we have now too often inhibits them. Some think that a doctor is only another kind of technician; they are wrong. Regardless of what decisions we make in the end about how to organize health care, we need somehow to restore the role of the human voice and touch, to create conditions in which doctors will be able to relate freely to their patients without fear or resentment on either side. Only then can we ensure that medicine will be the respected, valued, and noble profession in the future that it has been for so much of the past.

NOTES

INTRODUCTION

ix "Some claim . . . that America has the best health care . . .": For example, Dr. Louis Sullivan, secretary of health and human services, stated that "the United States health care system is the most advanced in the world" on the *MacNeil/Lehrer NewsHour,* show no. 4248, January 15, 1992; transcript by Strictly Business, Overland Park, Kansas.

ix "Men in Harlem . . .": Colin McCord and Harold Freeman, "Excess Mortality in Harlem," *The New England Journal of Medicine* 322:173–77 (1990).

x "John Wennberg and David Eddy": See chapter 5 for full discussion.

x "Women . . . receive inadequate treatment": The National Institutes of Health, under the able leadership of Dr. Bernadine Healy, has begun to try to redress this imbalance. See her editorial, "The Yentl Syndrome," *The New England Journal of Medicine* 325: 274–76 (1991), for some of her views and innovations. A recent issue of a major journal was devoted entirely to women's medical problems, as summarized by Carolyn M. Clancy and Charlea T. Massion, "American Women's Health Care: A Patchwork Quilt with Gaps," *Journal of the American Medical Association* 268: 1918–20 (1992), and Vivian W. Pinn, "Women's Health Research: Prescribing Change and Addressing the Issues," ibid., 1921–22. Some see a need for a new specialty (other than gynecology) specifically devoted to women's medicine: Tamar Lewin, "Doctors Consider a Specialty Focusing on Women's Health," *The New York Times,* November 7, 1992, p. A1.

xi "a vast parasitic bureaucracy": Steffie Woolhandler and David Himmelstein, "The Deteriorating Administrative Efficiency of the U.S. Health Care System," *The New England Journal of Medicine* 324:1253–58 (1991).

xi " 'the monstrous game' of adverse selection": Personal communication from Paul Starr, October 1991.

xi " 'policy churning' ": Gina Kolata, "New Insurance Practice: Dividing Sick from Well," *The New York Times*, March 4, 1992, p. A1.

xi "cheat the system outright": Gordon Witkin, with Dorian Friedman and Monika Guttman, "Health Care Fraud," *U.S. News and World Report*, February 24, 1992.

xi "evil practice of patient dumping": George J. Annas, "Your Money or Your Life: 'Dumping' Uninsured Patients from Hospital Emergency Wards," *American Journal of Public Health* 76:74–77 (1986). For a dramatic account of recent consequences in one state, see Rebecca Perl, " 'Patient Dumping': Law Doing Little to End Hospital Practice," *Atlanta Journal-Constitution*, September 29, 1991, p. 1.

xi "a malpractice redress system . . . in utter failure": Barry M. Manuel, "Professional Liability—A No-Fault Solution," *The New England Journal of Medicine* 322:627–31 (1990); with accompanying editorial by Arnold S. Relman, pp. 626–27.

xi "study in New York State": A. Russell Localio and others, "Relation Between Malpractice Claims and Adverse Events Due to Negligence: Results of the Harvard Medical Practice Study III," *The New England Journal of Medicine* 325:245–51 (1991).

xii "In Sweden . . . the mechanism for compensating patients": Marilynn Rosenthal, *Dealing with Medical Malpractice—The British and Swedish Experience* (London and Durham, N.C.: Tavistock and Duke University Press, 1988).

xii "costs are out of control": George J. Schieber, Jean-Pierre Pouillier, and Leslie M. Greenwald, "Health Care Systems in Twenty-four Countries," *Health Affairs* 10:22–38 (1991).

xiii "the cost of bureaucracy alone": Woolhandler and Himmelstein, "Deteriorating Administrative Efficiency of U.S. Health Care."

xiii "damage to the morale of physicians": Anthony Astrachan and Gerald Weissman, "The Hassle Factor"; series of six articles in *MD* magazine, May–December 1991.

xiii " 'Shut out the future . . .' ": From a 1913 address by Osler to medical students at Yale, published in *A Way of Life and Selected Writings of Sir William Osler* (New York: Dover Publications, 1958). See chapter 2 for discussion.

xiii " 'Medicine is a social science . . .' " (Virchow): George Rosen, "What Is Social Medicine?: A Genetic Analysis of the Concept," *Bulletin of the History of Medicine* 21:674–733 (1947), p. 676. For a poignant account of one doctor's unsuccessful struggle with the truth of Virchow's statement, see Jack L. Mayer, "Time Out," *The New York Times Magazine*, October 18, 1986, p. 96.

xiv " 'In terms of gross national product . . .' ": Roger M. Battistella and Richard McK. F. Southby, "Crisis in American Medicine," *Lancet 1*: 581–86, March 16, 1968. I have rendered the word "Negroes" in the original as "African-Americans."

xiv "Few of us take the simple . . . actions": Willard G. Manning, Emmett

B. Keeler, Joseph P. Newhouse, Elizabeth M. Sloss and Jeffrey Wasserman, *The Costs of Poor Health Habits* (Cambridge, Mass.: Harvard University Press, 1991). See also Robert M. Veatch, "Voluntary Risks to Health: The Ethical Issues," *Journal of the American Medical Association* 243:50–55 (1980); and Daniel Wikler, "Who Should Be Blamed for Being Sick?" *Health Education Quarterly* 14:11–25 (1987).

xiv "a complex ritual dance": Melvin Konner, "Transcendental Medication," *The Sciences* 25:2–4 (1985); repr. in Konner, *Why the Reckless Survive, and Other Secrets of Human Nature* (New York: Viking, 1989), pp. 19–28.

xv " '. . . curing the stupidity and indifference of humanity . . .' ": T. Billroth, *The Medical Sciences in the German Universities: A Study in the History of Civilization*, trans. from the German with an intr. by William H. Welch (New York: Macmillan, 1924), p. 90. Quoted in Kerr White, *Healing the Schism* (New York and Berlin: Springer-Verlag, 1991), p. 85.

xv " 'It is not up to you . . .' " Rabbi Joseph H. Hertz, *Sayings of the Fathers: Pirke Aboth* (West Orange, N.J.: Behrman House Publishers, 1945), p. 44.

xv "majority of . . . diagnosis comes from the history": J. R. Hampton, M. J. G. Harrison, J. R. A. Mitchell, J. S. Prichard, and Carol Seymour, "Relative Contributions of History-taking, Physical Examination, and Laboratory Investigation to Diagnosis and Management of Medical Outpatients," *British Medical Journal* 2:486–89 (1975).

xvi "universal tendency to postpone intervention": Elisabeth Rosenthal, "Hurdle for Preventive Medicine: Insurance," *The New York Times*, April 19, 1990. Some physicians are optimistic about this preventive role: see Henry Wechsler, Sol Levine, Roberta K. Idelson, Mary Rohman, and James O. Taylor, "The Physician's Role in Health Promotion: A Survey of Primary-Care Practitioners," *The New England Journal of Medicine* 308:97–100 (1983).

xvii "a system—a society and culture of medicine": Robert A. Hahn and Atwood D. Gaines, eds., *Physicians of Western Medicine: Anthropological Approaches to Theory and Practice* (Boston: D. Reidel, 1985). For a survey of leading physicians' views on the role of medical sociology, see Robert G. Petersdorf and Alvan R. Feinstein, "An Informal Appraisal of the Current Status of 'Medical Sociology,' " *Journal of the American Medical Association* 245:943–50 (1981).

xix "like that of many physicians . . . not so impressed with the human side": Robert A. Hahn, "Between Two Worlds: Physicians as Patients," *Medical Anthropology Quarterly* 16:87–98 (1985); Martha Weinman Lear, *Heartsounds* (New York: Simon and Schuster, 1980); Harvey Mandell and Howard Spiro, eds., *When Doctors Get Sick* (New York: Plenum Books, 1987); Edward E. Rosenbaum, *A Taste of My Own Medicine* (New York: Random House, 1988).

xix "many medical schools . . . have instituted new programs": Lisa Belkin, "In Lessons on Empathy, Doctors Become Patients," *The New York Times*, June 4, 1992, p. Al.

CHAPTER 1: THE CODE OF SILENCE

3 "pageantry of dance and trance": Melvin Konner, "Transcendental Medication."

4 "endlessly proved by placebo effects": Howard L. Fields and Jon D. Levine, "Biology of Placebo Analgesia," *American Journal of Medicine* 70:745–46 (1981).

4 "recovery time from heart attack": William Ruberman and others, "Psychosocial Influences on Mortality After Myocardial Infarction," *The New England Journal of Medicine* 311:552–59 (1984).

4 "lessen suffering . . . in radiation treatment": Bruce Forester, Donald S. Kornfeld, and Joseph L. Fleiss, "Psychotherapy During Radiotherapy: Effects on Emotional and Physical Distress," *American Journal of Psychiatry* 142:22–27 (1985).

4 "a pleasant view through a window": Roger S. Ulrich, "View Through a Window May Influence Recovery from Surgery," *Science* 224:420–21 (1984).

4 "Consider this passage from *Decorum*": Hippocrates, *Decorum*, excerpted in Ann G. Carmichael and Richard M. Ratzan, eds., *Medicine: A Treasury of Art and Literature* (New York: Macmillan/Hugh Lauter Levin, 1991), pp. 36–39.

5 "the medico-legal doctrine of informed consent": Caroline L. Kaufman, "Informed Consent and Patient Decision Making: Two Decades of Research," *Social Science and Medicine* 17:1657–64, 1983.

6 " 'It is not the job of the physician . . .' ": Ned H. Cassem, M.D., personal communication, Harvard Medical School, 1981. But see also his chapter "Treating the Person Confronting Death" in Armand M. Nicholi, Jr., *The Harvard Guide to Modern Psychiatry*, pp. 579–606, which among other things summarizes empirical studies of truth telling.

7 "The Japanese 'believe very strongly . . .' ": Filmed interview with Professor Margaret Lock, BBC Science/Features, 1991. See also Edward Norbeck and Margaret M. Lock, eds., *Health, Illness, and Medical Care in Japan: Cultural and Social Dimensions* (Honolulu: University of Hawaii Press, 1987).

9 " 'When an old person dies' . . . ": Filmed interview with Dr. Taizan Mikawa, BBC Science/Features, 1991.

10 "some . . . relationship between mind and body": James Gorman and Steven Locke, "Neural, Endocrine, and Immune Interactions," in Harold Kaplan and Benjamin Sadock, eds., *Comprehensive Textbook of Psychiatry*, 5th ed. (Baltimore: Williams and Wilkins, 1989), pp. 111–25; and Steven Locke and James Gorman, "Behavior and Immunity," in Kaplan and Sadock, pp. 1240–49.

11 " 'Why did you need this illness?' ": Bernie Siegel, *Love, Medicine, and Miracles* (New York: Harper and Row, 1986).

11 "When I wrote . . . criticizing Siegel": Melvin Konner, "Laughter and Hope," *The New York Times Magazine*, March 13, 1988, pp. 49–50.

11 " 'The trouble with this explanation . . .' " Alice Stewart Trillin, "Of Dragons and Garden Peas: A Cancer Patient Talks to Doctors," *The New England Journal of Medicine* 304:699–701 (1981), p. 701. See also Arthur Frank, *At the Will of the Body: Reflections on Illness* (Boston: Houghton Mifflin, 1991).

12 "seriously ill people fight their illnesses bravely": Barrie R. Cassileth and others, "Psychosocial Status in Chronic Illness: A Comparative Analysis of Six Diagnostic Groups," *The New England Journal of Medicine* 311:506–11 (1984).

12 "Norman Cousins . . . believed he had cured his own potentially fatal illness": Norman Cousins, *Anatomy of an Illness as Perceived by the Patient* (New York: Norton, 1979).

12 "an important, supportive psychological adviser": Norman Cousins, *Head First: The Biology of Hope* (New York: E. P. Dutton, 1989).

13 "hundreds of experiments with animals": Gorman and Locke, "Neural, Endocrine, and Immune Interactions."

13 "every patient needs to believe": Shelley E. Taylor, *Positive Illusions: Creative Self-Deception and the Healthy Mind* (New York: Basic Books, 1989).

13 "[Cassell's] 1991 book": Eric J. Cassell, *The Nature of Suffering and the Goals of Medicine* (New York: Oxford University Press, 1991).

14 "Suffering is experienced by persons . . .": Eric J. Cassell, "The Nature of Suffering and the Goals of Medicine," *The New England Journal of Medicine* 306:639–45, p. 639. For a sophisticated history of the cultural context and meaning of suffering and pain, see David B. Morris, *The Culture of Pain* (Berkeley, Calif.: University of California Press, 1991).

14 "the 'patient-as-colleague' model": Julian Tudor Hart, *A New Kind of Doctor: The General Practitioner's Part in the Health of the Community* (London: Merlin Press, 1988), p. 316.

15 "They are not taught any of the skills": Melvin Konner, *Becoming a Doctor: A Journey of Initiation in Medical School* (New York: Viking, 1987). Some new programs are beginning to change this: See Lisa Belkin "In Lessons on Empathy, Doctors Become Patients," *The New York Times*, June 4, 1992, p. 1. For an account of the role of medical humanities in humanizing medical students, see John Stone, "Medicine and the Arts," *Theoretical Medicine* 6: 309–25 (1985).

15 ". . . that patients have their own theories . . .": Arthur J. Rubel and Michael R. Hass, "Ethnomedicine," in Thomas M. Johnson and Carolyn F. Sargent, eds., *Medical Anthropology: Contemporary Theory and Method* (New York: Praeger, 1990).

17 "pursue 'alternative medicine'—unorthodox methods of healing": Raymond H. Murray and Arthur J. Rubel, "Physicians and Healers: Unwitting Partners in Healing," *The New England Journal of Medicine* 326:61–64 (1992); Stephen J. Fulder and Robin E. Munro, "Complementary Medicine in the United Kingdom: Patients, Practitioners, and Consultations," *The Lancet* 2:542–45 (1985).

17 "chiropractic manipulation for low back pain": Paul G. Shekelle, Alan H. Adams, Mark R. Chassin, Eric L. Hurwitz, and Robert H. Brook, "Spinal Manipulation for Low-Back Pain" (review article), *Annals of Internal Medicine* 117: 590–98 (1992).

17 "study of 660 cancer patients": Barrie R. Cassileth, Edward J. Lusk, Thomas B. Strouse, and Brenda J. Bodenheimer, "Contemporary Unorthodox Treatments in Cancer Medicine: A Study of Patients, Treatments, and Practitioners," *Annals of Internal Medicine* 101:105–12 (1984).

17 "In France . . . alternative healers": "French Foundation to Study 'Soft Medicine,' " *American Medical News*, April 11, 1986.

18 "a tolerant attitude . . . toward alternative healing": Nevertheless, it must be recognized that it would be easy for the tolerance toward alternative medicine to go too far. For its long and undistinguished modern history, see Young, James Harvey, *American Health Quackery: Collected Essays of James Harvey Young* (New York: Princeton University Press, 1992).

18 "by registering a claim of malpractice": Barry M. Manuel, "Professional Liability—A No-Fault Solution," *The New England Journal of Medicine*

322:627–31 (1990); with accompanying editorial by Arnold S. Relman, pp. 626–27.

18 " 'the malpractice equivalent of Beirut' ": Filmed interview with Robert White, Jr., Physician's Protective Trust Fund, Miami, Florida, BBC Science/ Features, 1991.

19 "only a small fraction of doctors' acts of negligence": Localio et al., "Relation Between Malpractice Claims and Adverse Events Due to Negligence."

20 "trust between doctors and patients has . . . broken down": G. Timothy Johnson, "Restoring Trust Between Patient and Doctor," *The New England Journal of Medicine* 322:195–97 (1990). See also John C. Burnham, "American Medicine's Golden Age: What Happened to It?" *Science 215:* 1474–79 (1982).

22 "his or her own survival is at stake": Konner, *Becoming a Doctor.*

22 "Among other things, a nurse's job . . .": Patricia Benner, as quoted by Suzanne Gordon, "What Nurses Know," *Mother Jones,* September/October 1992, pp. 40–46. See also Benner and Wrubel, *The Primacy of Caring,* 1989. The literature on sexism in traditional medicine and subordination of nurses, 97 percent of whom are still women, was reviewed by Richard Levinson, "Sexism in Medicine," *American Journal of Nursing* 76:425–31 (1976). A still-applicable classic account is Leonard I. Stein's "The Doctor-Nurse Game," *Archives of General Psychiatry* 16:699–703 (1967).

22 "Doctors change inside during training": Howard S. Becker, Blanche Geer, Everett C. Hughes, and Anselm L. Strauss, *Boys in White: Student Culture in Medical School* (Chicago: University of Chicago, 1961).

23 " 'You start regarding patients as the enemy . . .' ": Terry Mizrahi, *Getting Rid of Patients: Contradictions in the Socialization of Physicians* (New Brunswick, N.J.: Rutgers University Press, 1986).

23 "the great influx of women into medicine": Carola Eisenberg, "Medicine Is No Longer a Man's Profession," *The New England Journal of Medicine* 321:1542–44 (1989). See also Natalie Angier, "Bedside Manners Improve as More Women Enter Medicine," *The New York Times,* June 21, 1992, p. A16.

24 " 'There are times when I'm stymied . . .' ": Filmed interview with Dr. Ian Nisonson, 1991.

25 "how many decisions are 'a toss-up' ": Jerome P. Kassirer and Stephen G. Pauker, "The Toss-Up," *The New England Journal of Medicine* 305:1467–69 (1981).

26 "Surely the collaboration . . . does not have to go this far": For a fascinating account of a current conflict in Italy similar to the one in Japan, see Antonella Surbone, "Letter from Italy: Truth Telling to the Patient," *Annals of Internal Medicine* 268:1661–62 (1992) and the accompanying editorial by Edward Pelligrino, "Is Truth Telling to the Patient a Cultural Artifact?" pp. 1734–35, which considers the implications for the United States, and the limits of the concept of doctor-patient collaboration.

26 "Big Daddy": Tennessee Williams, *Cat on a Hot Tin Roof* (New York: New American Library, 1955).

26 " 'twenty-eight thousand acres of th' richest land . . .' ": *Cat on a Hot Tin Roof, p. 154.*

27 "what Anatole Broyard . . . called for": Anatole Broyard, "Doctor, Talk to Me," *The New York Times Magazine,* August 26, 1990.

27 "what doctors . . . wish . . . when *they* get sick": See the last five references for the Introduction.

CHAPTER 2: THE TEMPLE OF SCIENCE

29 "Unlike at many hospitals today . . .": George J. Annas, "Your Money or Your Life: 'Dumping' Uninsured Patients from Hospital Emergency Wards," *American Journal of Public Health* 76:74–77 (1986). See also Rebecca Perl, " 'Patient Dumping': Law Doing Little to End Hospital Practice," *Atlanta Journal-Constitution*, September 29, 1991, p. 1.

30 " 'I desire no other epitaph . . .' ": William Osler, *Aequanimitas: With Other Addresses to Medical Students, Nurses, and Practitioners of Medicine,* 3rd ed. (Philadelphia: Blakiston, 1943), p. 390; as quoted by Edward C. Atwater in "Internal Medicine," in Ronald L. Numbers, *The Education of American Physicians: Historical Essays* (Berkeley: University of California Press, 1980), p. 167.

31 "it is likely that they will learn it from nurses": Benner and Wrubel, *The Primacy of Caring,* 1989. See also Gordon, "What Nurses Know."

31 "one of Osler's famous speeches": Osler, *Aequanimitas.*

32 "skeptical voices are being raised": Gerald Weissman, "Against Aequanimitas," *Hospital Practice,* June 1984, pp. 159–69.

32 " 'The first essential . . .' ": Quoted in Weissman, "Against Aequanimitas," p. 162.

32 " 'If the goal . . . is to lead to *aequanimitas* . . .' ": Weissman, "Against Aequanimitas," p. 169.

33 "Tudor-Hart challenges the Osler legacy": Julian Tudor-Hart, *A New Kind of Doctor,* chapter 3.

33 "in the reality of training": See, for example, Jack D. McCue, "The Distress of Internship: Causes and Prevention," *The New England Journal of Medicine* 312:449–52 (1985). See also Nicole Lurie, Brian Rank, Connie Parenti, Tony Woolley, and William Snoke, "How Do House Officers Spend Their Nights?: A Time Study of Internal Medicine House Staff On Call," *The New England Journal of Medicine* 320:1673–77 (1989). A proposal for reform was made by the American College of Physicians, "Working Conditions and Supervision for Residents in Internal Medicine Programs: Recommendations," *Annals of Internal Medicine* 110:657–63 (1989).

35 " 'Shut out the future . . .' ": From a 1913 address by Osler to Yale medical students, published in *A Way of Life and Selected Writings of Sir William Osler.*

35 "the uninsured": Emily Friedman, "The Uninsured: From Dilemma to Crisis," *Journal of the American Medical Association* 265:2491–95 (1991); part of a special issue of the journal devoted to "Caring for the Uninsured and Underinsured."

35 "America's peculiar system of payment": John K. Inglehart, "The American Health Care System: Private Insurance," *The New England Journal of Medicine* 326:1715–20 (1992). For a brief comparative history see Paul Starr and Ellen Immergut, "Health Care and the Boundaries of Politics," in Charles S. Maier, ed., *Changing Boundaries of the Political* (Cambridge, Eng.: Cambridge University Press, 1986).

36 "We have rationing now . . .": Recent studies have shown both that the

uninsured and Medicaid patients are more likely than others to be hospitalized for conditions that could have been avoided with timely outpatient care, and that they are more likely to receive substandard care once
hospitalized. See Joel S. Weissman, Constantine Gatsonis, and Arnold M.
Epstein, "Rates of Avoidable Hospitalization by Insurance Status in Massachusetts and Maryland," *Journal of the American Medical Association*
268:2388–94 (1992), and Helen R. Burstin, Stuart R. Lipsitz, and Troyen
A. Brennan, "Socioeconomic Status and Risk for Substandard Medical
Care," *Journal of the American Medical Association* 268:2383–87; with accompanying editorial by Andrew B. Bindman and Kevin Grumbach, "America's Safety Net: The Wrong Place at the Wrong Time?" pp. 2426–27.

36 " 'This is really acute medicine . . .' ": Filmed interview with Dr. Kenneth
Covinsky, Baltimore, BBC Science/Features, 1991.

37 " 'As an intern . . .' ": Filmed interview with Dr. Alicia Fry, Baltimore,
BBC Science/Features, 1991.

38 " 'This woman has liver disease . . .' ": Filmed interview with Dr. John
Townes, Baltimore, BBC Science/Features, 1991.

39 "The answers lie in the history of the hospital": Roderick E. McGrew,
Encyclopedia of Medical History (London: Macmillan Press, 1985), pp. 134–
42.

40 "Pantocrator, a famous hospital in Constantinople": George Rosen, "Hospitals," entry in *Encyclopedia Americana,* international ed. (Danbury, Conn.:
Grolier International, 1991), pp. 437–43.

40 " '. . . the wards for the insane . . .' ": McGrew, p. 135.

41 " '. . . too much of an emphasis on the very, very sick' ": Filmed interview
with Dr. Daniel P. Sulmasy, Baltimore, BBC Science/Features, 1991. Dr.
Sulmasy presents his views on the ethics of health-care delivery in "Physicians, Cost Control, and Ethics," *Annals of Internal Medicine* 116:920–26
(1992).

42 " 'The way we educate physicians . . .' ": Filmed interview with Dr. Jack
Stobo, Baltimore, BBC Science/Features, 1991.

43 "part of a growing nationwide trend": Daniel Federman, "Medical Education in Outpatient Settings," *The New England Journal of Medicine*
320:1556–57 (1989).

43 " '. . . focused far too much on acute medical care . . .' ": Filmed interview with Dr. Robert Heyssel, Baltimore, BBC Science/Features, 1991.

44 " 'When I brought her here initially . . .' ": Filmed interview with Carla
Supik, R.N., Baltimore, BBC Science/Features, 1991.

44 " '. . . the more-than-million-dollar workup . . .' ": Filmed interview
with Dr. Craig Basson, Baltimore, BBC Science/Features, 1991.

46 " 'It's just so overwhelming . . .' ": Filmed interview with Lynn Simpson
and Carla Supik, Baltimore, BBC Science/Features, 1991.

48 "New York's Harlem Hospital": Colin McCord and Harold Freeman, "Excess Mortality in Harlem," *The New England Journal of Medicine* 322:173–
77 (1990).

48 "worse than they seem at first": Melvin Konner, "Still Invisible, and Dying,
in Harlem," *The New York Times* Op-Ed Page, February 24, 1990. Revised
and expanded for physician readers as the lead editorial in *Hospital Practice*
25(4):13–16 (April 15, 1990).

48 "according to World Bank Statistics": Christopher J. L. Murray, "Mortality
Among Black Men," *The New England Journal of Medicine* 322:205–6 (1990).

49 " 'The closer you get to Johns Hopkins . . .' ": Filmed interview with Rev. Melvin B. Tuggle, BBC Science/Features, 1991.

49 " 'Walking time bombs waiting to go off' ": Filmed interview with Dr. Louis Becker, BBC Science/Features, 1991.

51 "too much is spent on hospital-based treatments": Jack M. Colwill, "Where Have All the Primary Care Applicants Gone?" *The New England Journal of Medicine* 326:387–93 (1992); with accompanying editorial by Robert G. Petersdorf: 408–9. See also Joel S. Weissman et al., 1992, "Rates of Avoidable Hospitalization."

52 " 'hospitals have never been ideal places . . .' ": Charles E. Rosenberg, *The Care of Strangers: The Rise of America's Hospital System* (New York: Basic Books, 1987), p.11.

53 "nurses, not doctors, determine the quality": ibid., chapter 9.

53 "Clarence Blake, a Harvard-educated physician": ibid., pp. 166–68.

55 " 'Concerned observers . . . pointed to a growing coldness' ": ibid., p. 6.

55 " 'He contrasted the histories of two patients . . .' ": Rosen, "Hospitals," p. 443.

56 "an army without infantry": Colwill, "Where Have All the Primary Care Applicants Gone?"; Howard W. French, "Panel Seeks More Family Doctors," *The New York Times*, March 5, 1989.

57 "in an issue of *Time* magazine": Claudia Wallis, "Med School, Heal Thyself: New Studies Prescribe Better Ways of Training Doctors," *Time*, May 23, 1983, pp. 54–56.

57 "These forces include . . .": For further discussion see the closing chapter of Konner, *Becoming a Doctor*.

58 "when considering how to allocate health care": Robert W. Amler and H. Bruce Dull, eds., *Closing the Gap: The Burden of Unnecessary Illness* (New York: Oxford University Press, 1987).

CHAPTER 3: THE MAGIC BULLET

61 "laying the foundations of . . . chemotherapy": McGrew, *Encyclopedia of Medical History*, pp. 54–56, 246–58; M. Weatherall, *In Search of a Cure: A History of Pharmaceutical Discovery* (New York: Oxford University Press, 1990).

65 " 'I can honestly say . . .' ": Filmed interviews with Mr. and Mrs. James Nelson, BBC Science/Features, 1991.

67 " 'the clearest possible proof . . .' ": McGrew, *Encyclopedia of Medical History*, p. 344.

67 "By about a year later . . .": ibid., p. 250.

68 "a restless, nameless, formless tide": Richard Krause, *The Restless Tide: The Persistent Challenge of the Microbial World* (Washington, D.C.: National Foundation for Infectious Diseases, 1981).

68 ". . . the more the bacteria adapted": Mitchell L. Cohen, "Epidemiology of Drug Resistance: Implications for a Post-Antimicrobial Era," *Science* 257:1050–55 (1992). First of five articles in an issue devoted to the threat of antibiotic-resistant diseases.

69 ". . . one of the leading pharmaceutical houses in France": The history of Roussel-Uclaf is based on filmed interviews with Edouard Sakiz, BBC Science/Features, 1991.

71 "Resistance to penicillin . . .": Harold C. Neu, "The Crisis in Antibiotic Resistance,"*Science* 257:1064–73 (1992).
71 "these 'nosocomial' diseases . . .": Cohen, "Epidemiology of Drug Resistance." A study published in 1985 showed that more than 5 percent of patients who stay in American hospitals acquire such an infection, far exceeding previous estimates: Robert W. Haley, David H. Culver, John W. White, W. Meade Morgan, and T. Grace Emori, "The Nationwide Nosocomial Infection Rate: A New Need for Vital Statistics," *American Journal of Epidemiology* 121:159–67 (1985).
72 "American men and women serving in the Gulf War": Kenneth C. Hyams and others, "Diarrheal Disease During Operation Desert Shield," *The New England Journal of Medicine* 325:1423–28 (1991).
72 "Centoxin . . . costs $3,800 a dose": Janice Castro, in *Time*, November 25, 1991, p. 42.
72 " 'a particularly virulent, bad form of tuberculosis . . .' ": Filmed interviews with Dr. George Grant and Mary Harding, Jarrow BBC Science/Features, 1991.
74 "high-pressure sales techniques": Mary-Margaret Chren, Seth Landefeld, and Thomas H. Murray, "Doctors, Drug Companies, and Gifts," *Journal of the American Medical Association* 262:3448–51 (1989).
75 "cyclophosphamide and nitrogen mustard": Marjorie A. Duffy and others, eds., *Physicians' Desk Reference*, 46th ed. (Montvale, N.J.: Medical Economics Data, 1992).
76 "the drug, diethylstilbestrol, or DES": Kenneth L. Noller, "In Utero Exposure to Diethylstilbestrol," in Howard W. Jones, III, Anne Colston Wentz, and Lonnie S. Burnett, *Novak's Textbook of Gynecology*, 11th ed. (Baltimore, London, and Sydney: Williams and Wilkins, 1988), pp. 623–42.
77 " 'We don't call it the practice of medicine for nothing . . .' ": Filmed interview with Candice Tedeschi, R.N., New York, BBC Science/Features, 1992.
77 "These oral contraceptives . . .": Carl Djerassi, *The Pill, Pygmy Chimps, and Degas' Horse: The Autobiography of Carl Djerassi* (New York: Basic Books, 1992). First-person account by the discoverer of "the pill."
78 "By this time a highly creative physician scientist": See Joseph Palca and Jeremy Cherfas, "The Pill of Choice?"; "Etienne-Emile Baulieu: In the Eye of the Storm"; and related articles, in *Science* 245:1319–24 (1989); also Etienne-Emile Baulieu, with Mort Rosenblum, *The "Abortion Pill"* (New York: Simon and Schuster, 1992). These references are also the source of the subsequent history.
78 "a molecule that blocked progesterone powerfully": Andre Ulmann, George Teutsch, and Daniel Philibert, "RU 486," *Scientific American* 262:42–48 (1990); Etienne-Emile Baulieu, "Contragestion and Other Clinical Applications of RU 486, an Antiprogesterone at the Receptor," *Science* 245:1351–57 (1989).
78 "This treatment had proved very safe": Louise Silvestre and others, "Voluntary Interruption of Pregnancy with Mifepristone (RU 486) and a Prostaglandin Analogue: A Large-Scale French Experience," *The New England Journal of Medicine* 322:625–48 (1990); with accompanying editorial by Sheldon Segal, pp. 691–93.
79 " 'I am a medical doctor who does science' ": Filmed interview with Etienne-Emile Baulieu, BBC Science/Features, 1991.

80 "I saw a twenty-year-old woman die . . .": Filmed interview with Mme. Aubeny, BCC Science/Features, 1991.

80 "not even permitted to be tested . . .": Tamar Lewin, "U.S. Barriers to Abortion Pill Remain," *The New York Times*, July 24, 1992. For a recent review of the legal status of RU 486, see Suzanna S. Banwell and John M. Paxman, "The Search for Meaning: RU 486 and the Law of Abortion." *American Journal of Public Health 82*: 1399–1406 (1992).

82 "that *social* conditions foster disease": Rosen, "What Is Social Medicine?"

82 "Rudolf Virchow of Vienna": Leon Eisenberg, "Rudolf Karl Ludwig Virchow: Where Are You Now That We Need You?" *American Journal of Medicine 77*:524–32 (1984).

82 " 'Don't we see that epidemics . . .' ": Rosen, "What Is Social Medicine?," p. 680.

82 "a health survey of the island of Sakhalin": Henri Troyat, *Chekhov*, trans. by Michael Henry Heim (New York: Ballantine, 1986), pp. 113–30 and p. 140.

83 "half a century of changing medical thought": For an account of this change, see Kerr White, *Healing the Schism*, chapter 3.

84 "Today TB is rising again fast": Barry R. Bloom and Christopher J. L. Murray, "Tuberculosis: Commentary on a Reemergent Killer," *Science* 257:1055–64 (1992); Dixie E. Snider and William L. Roper, "The New Tuberculosis," *The New England Journal of Medicine 326*:703–5 (1992). See also Geoffrey Cowley, "Tuberculosis: A Deadly Return," *Newsweek*, March 16, 1992, pp. 53–57; and Michael Specter, "Neglected for Years, TB Is Back with Strains That Are Deadlier," *The New York Times*, October 11, 1992; first of five articles on five consecutive days in a series, "Tuberculosis: A Killer Returns."

84 "Poverty today brings with it . . .": Amler and Dull, *Closing the Gap.*

84 "As for East Baltimore . . . the rate of blindness . . .": Alfred Sommer and others, "Racial Differences in the Cause-Specific Prevalence of Blindness in East Baltimore," *The New England Journal of Medicine 325*:1412–22 (1991); with accompanying editorial by Johanna M. Seddon, pp. 1440–42.

86 " 'I don't want to come across negative against drugs' ": Filmed interview with Candice Tedeschi, R. N., New York, BBC Science/Features, 1992.

86 "A large proportion of . . . drugs for the elderly": Sidney M. Wolfe, Lisa Fugate, Elizabeth P. Hulstrand, Laurie E. Kamimoto, and others, *Worst Pills, Best Pills: The Older Adult's Guide to Avoiding Drug-Induced Death or Illness* (Washington, D.C.: Public Citizen Health Research Group, 1988).

86 "study . . . examined 109 . . . pharmaceutical advertisements": Michael S. Wilkes, Bruce H. Doblin, and Martin F. Shapiro, "Pharmaceutical Advertisements in Leading Medical Journals: Experts' Assessments." *Annals of Internal Medicine 116*:912–19 (1992); with accompanying editorials by David A. Kessler and by Robert and Suzanne Fletcher.

87 "FDA . . . standards . . . difficult to enforce": David A. Kessler, "Drug Promotion and Scientific Exchange: The Role of the Clinical Investigator," *The New England Journal of Medicine 325*:201–3 (1991).

87 "Misprescribing . . . a major factor in . . . waste": Elizabeth Rosenthal, "As Costs of New Drugs Rise, Hospitals Stick by Old Ones," *The New York Times*, December 18, 1991, p. A1.

87 "a network of illegal pharmacies": Gina Kolata, "Patients Turning to Illegal Pharmacies," *The New York Times*, November 4, 1991, p. A1.

CHAPTER 4: CONCEIVING THE FUTURE

91 "an unsettling vision of the future": Aldous Huxley, *Brave New World* (New York: Bantam Books, 1946).

92 "growth hormone . . . in shorter children not at all deficient": Barry Werth, "How Short Is Too Short?: Marketing Human Growth Hormone," *The New York Times Magazine*, June 16, 1991, p. 14. See also Louise E. Underwood, "Report of the Conference on Uses and Possible Abuses of Biosynthetic Human Growth Hormone," *The New England Journal of Medicine 311*:606–8 (1984).

92 "already deeply engaged in a technological revolution": Daniel Kevles and Leroy Hood, eds., *The Code of Codes: Scientific and Social Issues in the Human Genome Project* (Cambridge, Mass.: Harvard University Press, 1992); Bernard D. Davis, *The Genetic Revolution: Scientific Prospects and Public Perceptions* (Baltimore and London: Johns Hopkins University Press, 1991).

94 "Thalassemia, or Mediterranean anemia . . .": Edward J. Benz, Jr., "The Hemoglobinopathies," in William N. Kelley, *Textbook of Internal Medicine*. (Philadelphia: J. B. Lippincott, 1989).

95 "Dr. Antonio Cao is planning to outfox the genes": A. Cao and others, "Control of Homozygous-Thalassemia by Carrier Screening and Antenatal Diagnosis in Sardinia," *Birth Defects: Original Articles Series 18*:303–11 (1982) (a volume in the March of Dimes series, ed. by Dr. Cao, pub. by Alan R. Liss, New York). The program was recently demonstrated to reduce thalassemia births by 90 percent: A. Cao and others, "The Prevention of Thalassemia in Sardinia," *Clinical Genetics 36*: 277–85 (1989).

95 " 'to overcome . . . thalassemia in Sardinia' ": Filmed interview with Dr. Antonio Cao Cagliari, Sardinia, BBC Science/Features, 1991.

97 " 'Degeneracy means . . .' ": H. H. Laughlin, *Eugenical Sterilization in the United States* (Chicago: Psychopathic Laboratory of the Municipal Court of Chicago, 1922), pp. 324–25; as quoted by Kamin, *The Science and Politics of I.Q.*, p. 11.

97 "Eugenic ideas became prominent": Daniel Kevles, *In the Name of Eugenics: Genetics and the Uses of Human Heredity* (New York: Viking, 1985); Stephan Chorover, *From Genesis to Genocide* (Cambridge, Mass.: MIT Press, 1979); Leon Kamin, *The Science and Politics of I.Q.* (Potomac, Md.: Lawrence Erlbaum, 1974).

97 "Leading American psychologists": Kevles, *In the Name of Eugenics*; Kamin, *The Science and Politics of I.Q.*

98 "Lives Devoid of Value": See Chorover, *From Genesis to Genocide*, p. 97. See also Robert Proctor, *Racial Hygiene: Medicine Under the Nazis* (Cambridge, Mass.: Harvard University Press, 1988).

98 " 'What we racial hygienists promote . . .' ": Chorover, p. 98. Chorover's discussion is based on a 1973 Harvard College bachelor's thesis, Robert J. Waldinger, *The High Priests of Nature*, which cites the original documents kept at the Bundesarchiv in Koblenz, Germany.

98 "consistent with advances in medical science": Proctor, *Racial Hygiene*.

98 "officially, medically certified . . . for the gas chambers": Robert Jay Lifton, *The Nazi Doctors: Medical Killing and the Psychology of Genocide* (New York: Basic Books, 1988).

99 "One British obstetrician . . .": Celia Hall, "Instruments in Body Top Obstetrics Settlement Bill," *The Independent* (London), June 3, 1991.

99 "resistance . . . to prenatal testing": Recently a widely used method of prenatal testing, chorionic villus sampling, has come under severe medical criticism, confirming some of CARA's skepticism. See Gina Kolata, "As Fears About a Fetal Test Grow, Many Doctors Are Advising Against It," *The New York Times*, July 15, 1992, p. B7.

100 " 'Medicine reflects our culture . . .' ": Filmed interview with Anne Waldschmidt, Bremen, Germany, BBC Science/Features, 1991.

100 "Two provinces . . . promulgated compulsory sterilization": David R. Schweisberg, "China Province Issues Sterilization Law," United Press International, February 23, 1990.

100 "Three other provinces followed . . .": Nicholas D. Kristof, "Some Chinese Provinces Forcing Sterilization of Retarded Couples," *The New York Times*, August 15, 1991. " 'Couples who have serious hereditary diseases including psychosis, mental deficiency, and deformity must not be allowed to bear children,' reads the Sichaun law, which is fairly typical. 'Those already pregnant must terminate the pregnancy.' " In practice, little effort is made to establish that the cause of the deficiency is in fact hereditary.

101 "If these laws are emulated at the national level . . .": Associated Press, "Health Minister Issues Warning on Hereditary Diseases, Illiteracy," Associated Press, January 24, 1990, A.M. Cycle.

101 " 'to raise the population quality' ": Schweisberg, "China Province Issues Sterilization Law."

101 " 'a heavy millstone around our neck' ": Associated Press, "Health Minister Issues Warning."

101 "thousands of compulsory sterilizations": Associated Press, "Province in China Sterilizes the Retarded," *Chicago Tribune*, May 22, 1990, final edition, p. 4.

102 "Virtually all girls are aborted": Melvin Konner, "The Gender Option," *The Sciences* 27(6):2–4 (1987); repr. in *Why the Reckless Survive*. See the latter for further references.

102 "the Human Genome Project": Kevles and Hood, *The Code of Codes*.

103 "Gilbert invites us to think of it . . .": Walter Gilbert, "A Vision of the Grail," chapter 3 in Kevles and Hood, p. 84.

105 "a smallish region of . . . chromosome 4": James Gusella, Nancy Wexler, Michael P. Conneally et al., "A Polymorphic DNA Marker Genetically Linked to Huntington's Disease," *Nature* 306:234–38 (1983). See also Nancy Wexler, "Clairvoyance and Caution," chapter 10 in Kevles and Hood, pp. 211–43.

106 "much more is known about . . . Alzheimer's": D. Goldgaber, M. I. Lerman, O. W. McBride et al., "Characterization and Chromosomal Localization of a cDNA Encoding Brain Amyloid of Alzheimer's Disease," *Science* 235:877–80 (1987); R. E. Tanzi, J. F. Gusella, P. C. Watkins et al., "Amyloid Beta-Protein Gene: cDNA, mRNA Distribution, and Genetic Linkage near the Alzheimer Locus," *Science* 235:880–83 (1987).

106 "PKU, or phenylketonuria": Charles R. Scriver and Carol L. Clow, "Phenylketonuria: Epitome of Human Biochemical Genetics" (two parts), *The New England Journal of Medicine* 303:1336–42 and 1394–1400 (1980).

107 "no longer defects at all": For further discussion see Melvin Konner, *The Tangled Wing: Biological Constraints on the Human Spirit* (New York: Henry Holt, 1989)(orig. 1982), chapter 5.

108 "possibility clearly exists . . . in manic-depressive illness": Melvin Kon-
     ner, "Art of Darkness," *The Sciences* 29(6):2–5 (1989); repr. in Konner,
     Why the Reckless Survive.
108 " 'My mind's not right' ": Robert Lowell, "Skunk Hour," in *Selected
     Poems*, rev. ed. (New York: Farrar, Straus, and Giroux, 1977).
108 " 'I hear/My spirit sob . . .' ": ibid.
108 "it clearly has an inherited component": Elliot Gershon, "Genetics,"
     chapter 15 in Frederick K. Goodwin and Kay Redfield Jamison, *Manic-
     Depressive Illness* (New York and Oxford: Oxford University Press, 1990),
     pp. 373–401.
108 "One attempt . . . to locate the gene for manic-depressive illness": Mi-
     randa Robertson, "False Start on Manic Depression," *Nature* 342:222
     (1989).
108 "studies linking it to the X chromosome": M. Baron, N. Risch, R. Ham-
     burger et al., "Genetic Linkage Between X-chromosome Markers and
     Bipolar Affective Illness," *Nature* 326:289–92 (1987).
109 "Aristotle no doubt exaggerated": S. W. Jackson, *Melancholia and Depres-
     sion: From Hippocratic Times to Modern Times* (New Haven: Yale University
     Press, 1986), p. 31.
109 "forty-seven eminent British writers and artists": Kay Redfield Jamison,
     "Mood Disorders and Patterns of Creativity in British Writers and Art-
     ists," *Psychiatry* 52:125–34 (1989); see also chapter 14 in Goodwin and
     Jamison, *Manic-Depressive Illness.*
109 "the renowned University of Iowa Writer's Workshop": Nancy C. An-
     dreasen, "Creativity and Mental Illness: Prevalence Rates in Writers and
     Their First Degree Relatives," *American Journal of Psychiatry* 144:1288–92
     (1987).
110 "painters, sculptors . . . writers . . . and blues musicians": Hagop S.
     Akiskal and Kareen Akiskal, "Reassessing the Prevalence of Bipolar Dis-
     orders: Clinical Significance and Artistic Creativity," *Psychiatry and Psy-
     chobiology* 3:29S–36S (1988).
110 "also among their relatives": Ruth Richards and others, "Creativity in
     Manic-Depressives, Cyclothymes, Their Normal Relatives, and Control
     Subjects," *Journal of Abnormal Psychology* 97:281–88 (1988).
110 "some of the most revered creators": Kay Jamison, "Manic-Depressive
     Illness, Creativity, and Leadership," chapter 14 in Goodwin and Jamison,
     Manic-Depressive Illness, pp. 332–67.
111 "a Tourette's patient, David Janzen": David L. Wheeler, "Hunting the
     Tourette-Syndrome Gene: A Study in the Rigors of Scientific Detective
     Work," *Chronicle of Higher Education*, September 23, 1987.
112 "much new information about the disorder": Roger Kurlan and others,
     "Severity of Tourette's Syndrome in One Large Kindred," *Archives of
     Neurology* 44:268–69 (1987).
112 "Tourette's syndrome patients in Connecticut": David L. Pauls and James
     F. Leckman, "The Inheritance of Giles de la Tourette's Syndrome and
     Associated Behaviors," *The New England Journal of Medicine* 315:993–97
     (1986).
112 "convinced of a quite different genetic pattern": D. E. Comings and
     B. G. Comings, "Tourette Syndrome: Clinical and Psychological Aspects
     of 250 Cases," *American Journal of Human Genetics* 37:435–50 (1985).

112 " 'It's often been felt that there are separate genes . . .' ": Filmed interview with Dr. David Comings, BBC Science/Features, 1991.

113 " 'the case is definitely not proven . . .' ": Filmed interview with Dr. Kenneth Kidd, BBC Science/Features, 1991.

114 " 'folks with Tourette's syndrome . . .' ": Filmed interview with Sue Levi-Pearl, BBC Science/Features, 1991.

114 " 'clonidine is only rarely effective' ": Arthur Shapiro and Elaine Shapiro, "Tic Disorders," in Kaplan and Sadock, *Comprehensive Textbook of Psychiatry*, p. 1876.

114 " 'the best people . . . see the child as a whole person' ": Filmed interview with Dr. Donald Cohen, BBC Science/Features, 1991.

116 " 'the capacity to blunder slightly is the real marvel' ": Lewis Thomas, "The Wonderful Mistake," in *The Medusa and the Snail* (New York: Viking, 1979), pp. 27–30.

CHAPTER 5: RANDOM CUTS

118 "In 1934 a study . . . in New York City": American Child Health Association, *Physical Defects: The Pathway to Correction*. (New York, American Health Association, 1934), chapter 8. As discussed by John E. Wennberg, John P. Bunker, and Benjamin Barnes, "The Need for Assessing Outcomes of Medical Practices," *Annual Review of Public Health* 1:277–95 (1980), p. 280.

119 "the rates of tonsil removal in thirteen Vermont . . . Areas": John E. Wennberg, Lewis Blowers, Robert Parker, and Alan M. Gittelsohn, "Changes in Tonsillectomy Rates Associated with Feedback and Review," *Pediatrics* 59:821–26 (1977). See also John Wennberg and Alan Gittelsohn, "Variation in Medical Care among Small Areas," *Scientific American* 246:120–34 (1982).

119 " 'a decline in the popularity of tonsillectomies . . .' ": Wennberg et al., "Changes in Tonsillectomy Rates," p. 825.

120 "half again as many operations in Canada": Eugene Vayda, William R. Mindell, and Ira M. Rutkow, "A Decade of Surgery in Canada, England and Wales, and the United States," *Archives of Surgery* 117:846–53 (1982).

120 "Differences *among* Canadian provinces": Eugene Vayda and William R. Mindell, "Variations in Operative Rates: What Do They Mean?" *Surgical Clinics of North America* 62:627–39 (1982).

120 "As for gaps within the United States": M. R. Chassin and others, "Variations in the Use of Medical and Surgical Services by the Medicare Population," *The New England Journal of Medicine* 314:285–90 (1986), with accompanying editorial by John Wennberg, "Which Rate Is Right?," p. 310.

121 "forty-four counties in Ontario": Vayda and Mindell, "Variations in Operative Rates," p. 630.

121 "Similar local variation . . . in the United States . . .": Klim McPherson, John E. Wennberg, Ole B. Hovind, and Peter Clifford, "Small-Area Variations in the Use of Common Surgical Procedures: An International Comparison of New England, England, and Norway," *The New England Journal of Medicine* 307:1310–14 (1982).

121 "Cesarean section makes a good case study": Jack Pritchard, Paul MacDonald, and Norman Gant, *Williams Obstetrics*, 17th ed. (New York: Appleton-Century-Crofts, 1985), p. 867–70. See also Gregory L. Goyert, Sidney F. Bottoms, Marjorie C. Treadwell, and Paul C. Nehra, "The Physician Factor in Cesarean Birth Rates," *The New England Journal of Medicine 320*:706–9 (1989).

122 "More compelling is . . . Ireland": Kieran O'Driscoll and Michael Foley, "Correlation of Decrease in Perinatal Mortality and Increase in Cesarean Section Rates," *Obstetrics and Gynecology 61*:1–5 (1983). For an account of the method by which this result was achieved, see Kieran O'Driscoll, Michael Foley, and Dermot MacDonald, "Active Management of Labor as an Alternative to Cesarean Section for Dystocia," *Obstetrics and Gynecology 63*:485–90 (1984).

122 "Every culture has its follklore about health": Lynn Payer, *Medicine and Culture: Notions of Health and Sickness* (London: Victor Gollancz, 1990). For discussion of the German medical culture and for references, see pp. 74–100.

123 "due to economic, social, and lifestyle changes": See Thomas McKeown, *The Role of Medicine: Dream, Mirage, or Nemesis?*, 2nd ed. (Princeton: Princeton University Press, 1979); J. B. McKinlay and S. M. McKinlay, "The Questionable Contribution of Medical Measures to the Decline of Mortality," *Milbank Memorial Fund Quarterly/Health and Society 55*:405–28 (1977).

123 " 'I worry about the big-pocket medicine . . .' ": Filmed interview with Prof. Lothar Heinemann, East Berlin, BBC Science/Features, 1991.

124 "Consider . . . the artificial heart": Thomas A. Preston, "The Case Against the Artificial Heart," *Utah Holiday*, June 1983, pp. 39–42; "The Artificial Heart and the Public Purse," *Medical World News*, September 10, 1984, p. 94; and "The Artificial Heart Controversy: Research, Rationing, and Regulation," *Medical World News*, February 11, 1985, p. 37. For a more recent summary of the argument, see Preston's chapter, "The Artificial Heart," in Diana B. Dutton, with contributions by Thomas A. Preston and Nancy E. Pfund, *Worse Than the Disease: Pitfalls of Medical Progress* (New York: Cambridge University Press, 1988), pp. 91–126.

124 "Pressure . . . led to resumption of the program": Barbara J. Culliton, "Politics of the Heart," *Science 241*:283 (1988).

126 "a large international study": The EC/IC Bypass Group, "Failure of Extracranial-Intracranial Arterial Bypass to Reduce the Risk of Ischemic Stroke: Results of an International Randomized Trial," *The New England Journal of Medicine 313*:1191–1200 (1985); and follow-up article with reply to critics, *316*:817–24.

126 "the U.S. government stopped paying for it": Health Care Financing Administration, Department of Health and Human Services, "Medicare Program; Withdrawal of Coverage of Extracranial-Intracranial Arterial Bypass Surgery for the Treatment or Prevention of Stroke," *Federal Register 55*(69):13321–22, April 10, 1990.

127 " 'This stunning reversal of what everybody thought' ": Filmed interview with Dr. Henry Barnett, BBC Science/Features, January 1992.

127 "such legal standards *do not exist*": "Guiding the Knife: The Surgeon's Knife Is a Strong Medicine. Why Isn't It Regulated Like One?" *The Economist*, May 4, 1991, pp. 83–85; Seymour Perry, "Technology Assessment:

Continuing Uncertainty," *The New England Journal of Medicine* 314:240–43 (1986).

128 "The infamous frontal lobotomy": Elliot S. Valenstein, *Great and Desperate Cures: The Rise and Decline of Psychosurgery and Other Radical Treatments for Mental Illness* (New York: Basic Books, 1986).

128 "the hysterectomy fad": Frank J. Dyck and others, "Effect of Surveillance on the Number of Hysterectomies in the Province of Saskatchewan," *The New England Journal of Medicine* 296:1326–28 (1977).

129 "systematic evaluation of medical technology": Victor R. Fuchs and Alan M. Garber, "The New Technology Assessment," *The New England Journal of Medicine* 325:373–77 (1992).

129 "Cesarean section . . .": Gregory L. Goyert, Sidney F. Bottoms, Marjorie C. Treadwell, and Paul C. Nehra, "The Physician Factor in Cesarean Birth Rates," *The New England Journal of Medicine* 320:706–9 (1989).

129 ". . . and cardiac pacemaker implantation": Allan M. Greenspan and others, "Incidence of Unwarranted Implantation of Permanent Cardiac Pacemakers in a Large Medical Population," *The New England Journal of Medicine* 318:158–63 (1988).

129 "the field has . . . had its share of fiascos": Thomas A. Preston, *Coronary Artery Surgery: A Critical Review* (New York: Raven Press, 1977). See also John H. Vansant and William H. Muller, "Surgical Procedures to Revascularize the Heart: A Review of the Literature," *American Journal of Surgery* 100:572–83 (1960); W. Gerald Austen and Graeme L. Hammond, "Research Progress in the Surgery of Coronary Occlusive Disease," *Journal of Surgical Research* 7:188–97 (1967). For a more recent if uneven critical history of this field, see Thomas J. Moore, *Heart Failure: A Critical Inquiry into American Medicine and the Revolution in Heart Care* (New York: Random House, 1989).

129 "The Beck operation, for instance": Claude Beck, D. S. Leighninger, B. L. Brofman, and J. F. Bond, "Some New Concepts of Coronary Heart Disease," *Journal of the American Medical Association* 168:2110–17 (1958).

130 "cutting the nerve that carried anginal pain": Vansant and Muller, "Surgical Procedures to Revascularize the Heart," p. 576.

130 "removal of the thyroid gland": ibid., p. 577.

131 "Compare your experimental group with a control group": Leonard Cobb, G. I. Thomas, D. H. Dillard, K. A. Merendino, and R. A. Bruce, "An Evaluation of Internal Mammary Ligation by a Double Blind Technic," *The New England Journal of Medicine* 260:1115–18 (1959). The Cobb finding was confirmed by E. Grey Dimond, C. Frederick Kittle, and James E. Crockett, "Comparison of Internal Mammary Artery Ligation and Sham Operation for Angina Pectoris," *American Journal of Cardiology* 5:483–86 (1960).

131 "a procedure even more drastic than Beck's": Arthur Vineberg, "Experimental Background of Myocardial Revascularization by Internal Mammary Artery Implantation and Supplementary Technics, with Its Clinical Application in 125 Patients," *Annals of Surgery* 159:185–207 (1964).

132 "by 1987, about 230,000": Thomas Killip, "Twenty Years of Coronary Bypass Surgery," *The New England Journal of Medicine* 319:316–18 (1988).

132 "Two large American trials": Veterans Administration Coronary Artery Bypass Surgery Cooperative Study Group, "Eleven-Year Survival in the Veterans Administration Randomized Trial of Coronary Bypass Surgery

for Stable Angina," *The New England Journal of Medicine* 311:1333–39 (1984); CASS Principal Investigators and Their Associates, "Myocardial Infarction and Mortality in the Coronary Artery Surgery Study (CASS) Randomized Trial," *The New England Journal of Medicine* 310:750–58 (1984).

132 "a 10 percent greater five-year survival": European Coronary Surgery Study Group, "Long-term Results of Prospective Randomised Study of Coronary Artery Bypass Surgery in Stable Angina Pectoris," *The Lancet* 2:1173–1180 (1982).

132 "declined further by the twelve-year follow-up": Edvardas Varnauskas and the European Coronary Surgery Study Group, "Twelve-Year Follow-up of Survival in the Randomized European Coronary Surgery Study," *The New England Journal of Medicine* 319:332–37 (1988); M. C. Petch, "Coronary Bypasses Ten Years On: About Two in Five Will Occlude," *British Medical Journal 303,* September 21, 1991.

132 "Heart surgeons responded . . .": Gerald M. Lawrie and Michael E. DeBakey, "The Coronary Artery Surgery Study," *Journal of the American Medical Association* 252:2609–11 (1984).

133 "when the key measure is . . . pain": N. Caine, S. C. W. Harrison, L. D. Sharples, and J. Wallwork, "Prospective Study of Quality of Life Before and After Coronary Artery Bypass Grafting," *British Medical Journal* 302:511–16 (1991).

133 "hinged on damage done by silicone": Philip J. Hilts, "Experts Suggest U.S. Sharply Limit Breast Implants: Panel Seeks Vast Testing," *The New York Times,* February 21, 1992, p. A1.

133 "Substances are regulated; operations are not": "Guiding the Knife," *The Economist,* May 4, 1991.

133 "another procedure, PTCA": Andreas R. Gruentzig, Spencer B. King, III, Maria Schlumpf, and Walter Siegenthaler, "Long-term Follow-up After Percutaneous Transluminal Coronary Angioplasty," *The New England Journal of Medicine* 316:1127–32 (1987).

134 "suggests . . . an excess of angioplasties": Michael S. Norell and Raphael Balcon, "The Current Place of Coronary Angioplasty," *British Journal of Hospital Medicine,* March 1988, pp. 216–20; "BARI, CABRI, EAST, GABI, and RITA: Coronary Angioplasty on Trial," *The Lancet* 335:1315–16 (1990).

134 "some patients' arteries close up again": Harvey G. Kemp, "Coronary Angioplasty and the Persistent Problem of Restenosis," *Journal of the American College of Cardiology* 8:1277–78 (1986).

134 "rotoblation has been catching on": Samuel S. Ahn, David Auth, Daniel R. Marcus, and Wesley S. Moore, "Removal of Focal Atheromatous Lesions by Angioscopically Guided High-Speed Atherectomy: Preliminary Experimental Observations," *Journal of Vascular Surgery* 7:292–300 (1988).

135 "other new techniques": Sandra Blakeslee, "Race Is On to Develop Nonsurgical Ways to Unclog Arteries," *The New York Times,* July 28, 1992.

136 "carefully crafted, hard-hitting columns": David M. Eddy, "Clinical Decision Making: From Theory to Practice," *Journal of the American Medical Association 263:*287–90, 441–43, 877–80, 1265–75, 1839–41, 2239–43, 2493–2505, 3077–84 (1990); 264:389–91, 1161–70, 1737–39 (1990); 265:105–8, 782–88, 1446–50, 2399–2406 (1991); 266:417–20, 2135–41, 2439–45 (1991).

137 " 'In fact very little of medicine . . .' ": Filmed interview with Dr. David Eddy, BBC Science/Features, Jan. 1992.

139 " 'we should also contribute to it' ": Julian Tudor Hart, written personal

communication to *Medicine at the Crossroads* producers, BBC Science/Features, 1991.

139 " 'prepared to measure . . . how bad they are' ": Julian Tudor Hart, *A New Kind of Doctor*, p. 207.

140 "Dr. Esselstyn's new mission": Caldwell B. Esselstyn, "Beyond Surgery: Presidential Address to the American Association of Endocrine Surgeons," *Surgery* 110:923–27 (1991).

140 "Dr. Dean Ornish . . . is conducting a study": Dean Ornish and others in The Lifestyle Heart Trial, "Can Lifestyle Changes Reverse Coronary Heart Disease?" *The Lancet* 336:129–33 (1990). See also Joanne Silberner, "Reversing Heart Disease," *U.S. News and World Report*, August 6, 1990.

141 " 'life-style changes alone . . . without drugs' ": Claude L'Enfant, quoted in Sandra Blakeslee, "Arteries Are Unblocked Without Drugs in Study," *The New York Times*, July 21, 1990.

141 " 'We can't go on merely buying . . . time' ": Alexander Leaf quoted in Daniel Goleman, "Life-Style Shift Can Unclog Ailing Arteries, Study Finds," *The New York Times*, November 14, 1989.

CHAPTER 6: DISORDERED STATES

143 "medicine's neglected stepchild": Ralph Colp, "History of Psychiatry," in Kaplan and Sadock, *Comprehensive Textbook of Psychiatry*, pp. 2132–53.

144 "two psychiatrists in France": ibid., p. 2141.

145 "almost two thirds . . . had been discharged": Ellen L. Bassuk, "The Homelessness Problem," *Scientific American* 251:40–45 (1984).

145 "the thousands who were discharged needed . . .": Jon E. Gudeman and Miles F. Shore, "Beyond Deinstitutionalization: A New Class of Facilities for the Mentally Ill," *The New England Journal of Medicine* 311:832–36 (1984).

145 "But the taxpayers . . .": David Mechanic and Linda H. Aiken, "Improving the Care of Patients with Chronic Mental Illness," *The New England Journal of Medicine* 317:1634–38 (1987).

146 " 'I take in very few homeless schizophrenics' ": Filmed interviews within the New York State Psychiatric Institute, New York City, BBC Science/Features, 1991 and 1992.

147 " 'I'm stuck here with voices' ": Filmed interview with Maggie, a patient of Dr. Jack Gorman, New York City, BBC Science/Features, 1991.

147 "supportive relationships . . . have therapeutic value": Robert Paul Liberman and Kim T. Mueser, "Schizophrenia: Psychosocial Treatment," in Kaplan and Sadock, pp. 792–806.

147 "if . . . people . . . saw things her way": Arthur G. Kleinman, *Rethinking Psychiatry: From Cultural Category to Personal Experience* (London: Collier Macmillan Publishers, 1988).

148 " 'I think that having an understanding . . .' ": Filmed interview with Dr. Alan Felix, Medical Director, Columbia Presbyterian Psychiatry Shelter Program, New York City, BBC Science/Features, Sept. 1991.

149 " 'It is a frightening experience' ": Filmed interview with Denis, a patient of Dr. Alan Felix, New York City, BBC Science/Features, Sept. 1991.

150 " 'I heard stories about shelters . . .' ": Filmed interview with Florence,

a patient at the 350 Lafayette Street shelter, New York City, BBC Science/ Features, Sept. 1991.

150 " 'You know, sometimes you feel . . . isolation' ": Filmed interview with a patient at the 350 Lafayette Street shelter, New York City, BBC Science/ Features, Sept. 1991.

151 " 'I stumbled into this . . . hotel . . .' ": Filmed interview with Father John McVean, New York City, BBC Science/Features, Sept. 1991.

152 "their resources are gone, done, finished": Bassuk, "The Homelessness Problem"; Gudeman and Shore, "Beyond Institutionalization."

152 " 'You see the skeletons of buildings . . .' ": Filmed interview with Pixie, a homeless woman living on the street, New York City, BBC Science/ Features, 1991.

153 "harder to imagine for similar patients in India": Michael Nunley, *The Mind Doctors' Dharma: On the Social Construction of Hospital Psychiatry in Eastern Uttar Pradesh, India* (Ph.D. dissertation, medical anthropology, University of California, San Francisco, 1992).

154 "full allies . . . against . . . the spirit world": For discussion of the role of culture in mental illness, see Kleinman, *Rethinking Psychiatry*, and Melvin Konner, "Anthropology and Psychiatry," in Kaplan and Sadock, pp. 283–98.

154 " 'This lady is suffering from schizophrenia . . .' ": Filmed interview with Dr. Indira Sharma, Banaras, India, BBC Science/Features, 1991.

156 "images drawn, painted, and sculpted by . . . the mentally ill": John M. MacGregor, *The Discovery of the Art of the Insane* (Princeton: Princeton University Press, 1989).

156 " 'To value insights . . .' ": ibid., p. 310.

156 "an incredibly intense horse race": Alan Dundes and Alessandro Falassi, *La Terra in Piazza: An Interpretation of the Palio of Siena* (Berkeley, Calif.: University of California Press, 1975).

158 "various strong measures to protect society": Kevles, *In the Name of Eugenics*; Chorover, *From Genesis to Genocide*.

158 " 'Three generations of imbeciles . . .' ": Kevles, p. 111.

158 "Franca Basaglia . . . introduced a law": For the history of these events in Italy, see Franca Ongaro Basaglia, "Preface," pp. 11–25, and Franco Basaglia and Maria Grazia Gianichedda, "Problems of Law and Psychiatry: The Italian Experience," pp. 271–91, both in Nancy Scheper-Hughes and Anne M. Lovell, eds., *Psychiatry Inside Out: Selected Writings of Franco Basaglia*, with a preface by Franca Ongaro Basaglia and a foreword by Robert Coles (New York: Columbia University Press, 1987). The volume also includes a copy of Law 180, the legislation leading to deinstitutionalization (pp. 292–98), and a commentary on its current impact on psychiatry by Dr. Franco Basaglia (pp. 299–304).

158 " 'It isn't as easy as people think' ": Filmed interview with Dr. Livia D'Argenio, Siena, Italy, BBC Science/Features, 1991.

159 " 'as if we had seen everything for the first time' ": Filmed interviews with three patients and Evonne Couvert, Bracciano, BBC Science/Features, 1991.

160 "At a town meeting in Bracciano": The quotations from Drs. Sigillo, Iaria, and Losavio are transcribed from a film of the meeting, BBC Science/ Features, 1991.

161 " 'one-half to two-thirds . . . had achieved considerable improvement":
Courtenay M. Harding, George W. Brooks, Takamaru Ashikaga, John S.
Strauss, and Alan Breier, "The Vermont Longitudinal Study of Persons
with Severe Mental Illness, II: Long-Term Outcome of Subjects Who
Retrospectively Met *DSM-III* Criteria for Schizophrenia," *American Journal
of Psychiatry 144*: 727–35 (1987), p. 727.

161 " 'were once profoundly ill . . .' ": ibid., p. 732.

162 "the foundations of a new kind of psychiatry": Kleinman, *Rethinking
Psychiatry*; Arthur Kleinman and Byron Good, eds., *Culture and Depres-
sion: Studies in the Anthropology and Cross-Cultural Psychiatry of Affective
Disorder* (Berkeley: University of California Press, 1985).

163 "if you look at identical twin pairs": Irving Gottesman and James Shields,
Schizophrenia: The Epigenetic Puzzle (New York: Cambridge University
Press, 1982).

163 "things like head injury and brain viruses": Brain abnormalities, not
necessarily the result of these two factors, have been found in a sample
of schizophrenics but not in their nonschizophrenic identical twins: see
Richard L. Suddath and others, "Anatomical Abnormalities in the Brains
of Monozygotic Twins Discordant for Schizophrenia," *The New England
Journal of Medicine 322*:789–94 (1990).

163 "hundreds of family and milieu studies": Liberman and Mueser, "Schizophrenia: Psychosocial Treatment."

164 "British and American psychiatrists differed widely": Harrison Pope and
Joseph Lipinski, "Diagnosis in Schizophrenia and Manic-Depressive Illness," *Archives of General Psychiatry 35*:811–28 (1978); for further discussion and references, see Melvin Konner, "The Many Faces of Madness,"
in *Why the Reckless Survive*.

165 "uncertainties about patterns of diagnosis": Keh-Ming Lin and Arthur
M. Kleinman, "Psychopathology and the Clinical Course of Schizophrenia: A Cross-Cultural Perspective," *Schizophrenia Bulletin 14*:555–67 (1988).

167 " 'Cross-cultural comparison . . .' ": Kleinman, *Rethinking Psychiatry*,
p. 17.

CHAPTER 7: LIFE SUPPORT

170 " 'Well, the goal all the activity here . . .' ": Filmed interview with Dutch
and Dee Schultz, Sun City, Arizona, BBC Science/Features, Dec. 1991.

172 " 'I'm very ignorant in medical things' ": Filmed interview with Mrs.
Harold Chinlund, Sun City, Arizona, BBC Science/Features, Dec. 1991.

173 " 'I've been working in the medical profession . . .' ": Filmed interview
with Kate Chinlund, R.N., Sun City, Arizona, BBC Science/Features, Dec.
1991.

173 "She talks at length . . .": Filmed conversation, Sun City, BBC Science/
Features, Dec. 1991.

174 " 'Everything seems to break down . . .' ": Interviews with Betsy and
Sylvia Nichols, Sun City, BBC Science/Features, Dec. 1991.

175 "Life expectancy at birth . . .": For a general discussion of life span concepts, see James Fries and L. M. Crapo, *Vitality and Aging* (New York:
Freeman, 1981).

176 " 'the rectangularization of the survivorship curve' ": James F. Fries, "Aging, Natural Death, and the Compression of Morbidity," *The New England Journal of Medicine* 303:130–36 (1980).

176 " 'the wonderful one-hoss shay' ": Quoted by Fries and Crapo in *Vitality and Aging,* pp. xiv and 134.

177 "Fries still defends the idea": James F. Fries, "Aging, Illness and Health Policy: Implications of the Compression of Morbidity," *Perspectives in Biology and Medicine* 31:407–28 (1988).

177 "increased variation in the age at death": E. L. Schneider and J. A. Brody, "Aging, Natural Death, and the Compression of Morbidity: Another View," *The New England Journal of Medicine* 309:854–56 (1983).

177 "persistent variation in the state of health": Jacob A. Brody, "Prospects for an Aging Population," *Nature* 315:463–66 (1985); John W. Rowe, "Health Care of the Elderly," *The New England Journal of Medicine* 312:827–35 (1985).

177 " 'In 1980 people over age sixty-five . . .' ": Daniel Callahan, "Why We Must Set Limits," in Paul Homer and Martha Holstein, eds., *A Good Old Age?: The Paradox of Setting Limits* (New York: Simon and Schuster, 1990), p. 23. (This book collects articles in the debate on Callahan's radical proposal.)

177 "to show that they cannot": "Afterword: Daniel Callahan Responds to His Critics," in Homer and Holstein, pp. 299–319.

178 "liver transplant . . . to a seventy-six-year-old woman": Gregory de Lissovoy, "Medicare and Heart Transplants: Will Lightning Strike Twice?" *Health Affairs* 7: 61–72 (1988).

178 "articles . . . in top U.S. medical journals": L. Henry Edmunds et al., "Open-Heart Surgery in Octogenarians," *The New England Journal of Medicine* 319:131–36 (1988); Michael Hosking et al., "Outcomes of Surgery in Patients 90 Years of Age and Older," *Journal of the American Medical Association* 261:1909–15 (1989).

178 "simple, radical, draconian": Daniel Callahan, *Setting Limits: Medical Goals in an Aging Society* (New York: Simon and Schuster, 1987).

178 "the Eskimo practice of setting old people off . . .": Asen Balikci, *The Netsilik Eskimo* (Garden City, N.Y.: Natural History Press), pp. 163–72; E. M. Weyer, *The Eskimos* (New Haven: Yale University Press, 1932).

179 "an old person might separate . . . ": Harriet G. Rosenberg, "Complaint Discourse, Aging, and Caregiving Among the !Kung San of Botswana," in Jay Sokolovsky, ed., *The Cultural Context of Aging: World-Wide Perspectives* (Boston: Bergin and Garvey, 1990).

179 "the most celebrated cases": Nancy Gibbs, "Love and Let Die," *Time,* March 19, 1990, pp. 62–71; overview of American "right-to-die" cases.

180 "A more recent, equally celebrated case": David Orentlicher, "The Right to Die After *Cruzan,*" *Journal of the American Medical Association* 264:2442–46 (1990).

181 "backhandedly confirmed the right to die": George J. Annas, "Nancy Cruzan and the Right to Die," *The New England Journal of Medicine* 323:670–77 (1992); George J. Annas and others, "Bioethicists' Statement on the U.S. Supreme Court's *Cruzan* Decision," *The New England Journal of Medicine* 323:686–87.

181 "put their intentions in writing": Marian Danis and others, "A Prospective Study of Advance Directives for Life-Sustaining Care," *The New*

England Journal of Medicine 324:882–88 (1991); Linda L. Emanuel, Michael J. Barry, John D. Stoeckle, Lucy M. Ettelson, and Ezekial J. Emanuel, *The New England Journal of Medicine* 324:889–95; George J. Annas, "The Health Care Proxy and the Living Will," *The New England Journal of Medicine* 324:1210–13.

181 "Twelve leading physicians published . . .": Sidney H. Wanzer and others, "The Physician's Responsibility Toward Hopelessly Ill Patients: A Second Look," *The New England Journal of Medicine* 320:844–49 (1989).

181 " 'that it is not immoral for a physician . . .' ": ibid., p. 848.

181 "research in the Netherlands . . . on euthanasia": Carlos F. Gomez, *Regulating Death: Euthanasia and the Case of the Netherlands* (New York: Free Press, 1991).

182 "Doctors . . . not always well skilled in pain management": This is now recognized as a serious failing of American physicians. See, for example, Warren E. Leary, "U.S. Urges Doctors to Fight Surgical Pain (and Myths)," *The New York Times*, March 6, 1992, which discusses guidelines suggested by the Agency for Health Care Policy and Research of the U.S. Congress and supported by then–Secretary of Health and Human Services, Dr. Louis W. Sullivan; and Sam Allis, "Less Pain, More Gain," *Time*, October 19, 1992, pp. 61–64. For a very thoughtful analysis of this failing in its historical and cultural context, see David B. Morris, *The Culture of Pain* (Berkeley, Calif.: University of California Press, 1991). It would seem obvious that inadequate pain control increases the temptation to suicide.

182 " 'the claim to a right to death at the hands of a physician . . .' ": Gomez, *Regulating Death*, p. 134.

182 " 'Moreover, it needs to be shown . . .' ": ibid., p. 137.

182 "emotionally very painful for some physicians": Miles J. Edwards and Susan W. Tolle, "Disconnecting a Ventilator at the Request of a Patient Who Knows He Will Then Die: The Doctor's Anguish," *Annals of Internal Medicine* 117:254–56 (1992).

182 " 'Callahan . . . opposes euthanasia": Callahan, *Setting Limits*, p. 194.

182 "Cassel . . . calls it 'misleading and even dangerous' ": Christine Cassel, "The Limits of *Setting Limits*," in Homer and Holstein, *A Good Old Age*, p. 196.

182 "*Lives Devoid of Value*": Stephan L. Chorover, *From Genesis to Genocide: The Meaning of Human Nature and the Power of Behavior Control* (Cambridge, Mass.: The MIT Press, 1979), p. 97. See also Robert Proctor, *Racial Hygiene: Medicine Under the Nazis* (Cambridge, Mass.: Harvard University Press), p. 178.

183 " 'it is one thing to let people die . . .' ": Cassel in Homer and Holstein, p. 204.

183 " 'Even if biological life span is limited . . .' " ibid., p. 199.

183 " 'The current aging of society is . . . a success' ": ibid., pp. 204–5.

184 " 'knocking on the door' ": Filmed interview with Dr. Lauren Turley, Walter D. Boswell Memorial Hospital, Sun City, Arizona, BBC Science/Features, 1991.

186 " 'Older people need to be loved' ": Filmed interview with Mary Coyne, Clifden, Ireland BBC Science/Features, Jan. 1992.

186 " 'Oh, she's better to me, I think . . .' ": Filmed interview with Bridget and John Connealy, Clifden, BBC Science/Features, Jan. 1992.

187 " 'They are also entitled to equipment . . .' ": Filmed interview with Nurse Mary Syron, Clifden, BBC Science/Features, Jan. 1992.

188 "too few coronary bypass operations": Julian Tudor Hart, "Measurement of Omission," *British Medical Journal* 284:1686–89 (1982).

189 " 'My personal philosophy . . .' ": Filmed interview with Dr. Farid Ghebleh, Boswell Hospital, Sun City, BBC Science/Features, Dec. 1991.

190 "These are the kinds of services . . .": Many thoughtful proposals have been made for expanded care of the elderly in this country, including day-care centers and home companion care. See, for example, Fazlur Rahman, "Care Options for the Elderly," *The Christian Science Monitor*, October 22, 1990.

190 " 'I made up my mind I would help . . .' ": This and other quotes in this section are from a filmed meeting of the Sun City Hemlock Society, BBC Science/Features, Dec. 1991.

192 "Hamlet's 'calamity of so long life' ": Act 3, scene 1, line 77, in the *Folger Library General Reader's Shakespeare* (New York: Washington Square, 1961), p. 64.

192 "practical advice about . . . suicide": Derek Humphry, *Final Exit: The Practicalities of Self-Deliverance and Assisted Suicide for the Dying* (Eugene, Oreg.: The Hemlock Society, 1991).

192 "Legislative initiatives have been mounted": Robert J. Misbin, "Physicians' Aid in Dying," *The New England Journal of Medicine* 325:1307–11 (1991).

192 "Kevorkian has aided in the suicide": Isabel Wilkerson, "Rage and Support for Doctor's Role in Suicide," *The New York Times*, October 25, 1991, p. A1.

193 "a Michigan court . . . dismissed murder charges": "Murder Charges Against Kevorkian Are Dropped," *The New York Times*, July 22, 1992. In Nov. 1992, Michigan prohibited assisted suicide.

193 "exoneration closed the case of Dr. Timothy Quill": Lawrence K. Altman, "Jury Declines to Indict a Doctor Who Said He Aided in a Suicide," *The New York Times*, July 27, 1991, p. 1.

193 "his admission . . . in a leading medical journal": Timothy E. Quill, "Death and Dignity—A Case of Individualized Decision Making," *The New England Journal of Medicine* 324:691–94 (1991). For an extended account, together with an analysis of the options for dying patients and their doctors, see Timothy E. Quill, *Death and Dignity* (New York: Norton, 1993). His proposed guidelines have been published in Timothy E. Quill, Christine K. Cassel, and Diane E. Meier, "Care of the Hopelessly Ill: Proposed Clinical Criteria for Physician-Assisted Suicide," *The New England Journal of Medicine* 327:1380–84 (1992).

193 "twelve prominent U.S. physicians": Wanzer et al., *The Physician's Responsibility Toward Hopelessly Ill Patients.*"

193 "Poll after poll of ordinary citizens": Susan Waller, "Trends in Public Acceptance of Euthanasia Worldwide," *The Euthanasia Review* 1:33–47 (1986). Summarizes poll data from the Harris, Gallup, and other organizations. For an account of the legal situation in eight countries, see Masaya Yamauchi and others, "Euthanasia Around the World," *British Medical Journal* 304:7–10 (1992).

194 "According to Hindu belief": Jean Filliozat, *India: The Country and Its*

Traditions; Foreword by Jawarharlal Nehru, trans. from the French by Margaret Ledesert (Englewood Cliffs, N.J.: Prentice-Hall, 1962).

195 "For one family, the dying of their . . . mother": Sequence filmed for BBC Science/Features, Banaras, 1991.

195 " 'a good death'. . . even an American one": For a moving account of such a death, see Richard B. Sewall, "A Sense of the Ending," *Williams Alumni Review*, Fall 1975, pp. 2–4. For an analysis of the modern physician's role in attending the dying and enabling a good death, see Eric J. Cassell, "Being and Becoming Dead," *Social Research* 39:528–42 (1972).

CHAPTER 8: PANDEMIC

197 "rising rapidly in almost all countries": Erik Eckholm, "AIDS, Fatally Steady in the U.S., Accelerates Worldwide," *The New York Times*, June 28, 1992, "News of the Week in Review," p. 5.

198 "some recent private projections": Lawrence K. Altman, "Researchers Report Much Grimmer AIDS Outlook," *The New York Times*, June 4, 1992, p. A1. For the full picture, see Jonathan Mann, Daniel J. M. Tarantola, and Thomas W. Netter, eds., *AIDS in the World 1992* (Cambridge, Mass.: Harvard University Press, 1992).

198 "a heterosexual epidemic looming": Anne M. Johnson, "Home Grown Sexually Acquired HIV Infection: Still Difficult to Predict," *British Medical Journal* 304:1125–26 (1992).

199 " 'partners do not come with a log book' ": ibid., p. 1126.

199 "tuberculosis has been on the rise": Barry R. Bloom and Christopher J. L. Murray, "Tuberculosis: Commentary on a Reemergent Killer," *Science* 257:1055–64 (1992); Dixie E. Snider and William L. Roper, "The New Tuberculosis," *The New England Journal of Medicine* 326:703–5 (1992). See also Geoffrey Cowley, "Tuberculosis: A Deadly Return," *Newsweek*, March 16, 1992, pp. 53–57; and Michael Specter, "Neglected for Years, TB Is Back with Strains That Are Deadlier," *The New York Times*, October 11, 1992; first of five articles on five consecutive days in a series, "Tuberculosis: A Killer Returns."

200 "The AIDS virus . . . is remarkably hardy and adaptable": Michael S. Saag, "Extensive Variation of Human Immunodeficiency Virus Type-1 In Vivo," *Nature* 334:440–44 (1988).

201 "A number of legitimate voices": Troyen A. Brennan, "Public Health Policy and the AIDS Epidemic: An End to HIV Exceptionalism?" *The New England Journal of Medicine* 324:1500–1509 (1991); with accompanying editorial by Marcia Angell, pp. 1498–1500.

202 "Thailand is a case in point": Nicholas Ford and Suporn Koetsawang, "The Socio-Cultural Context of the Transmission of HIV in Thailand," *Social Science and Medicine* 33:405–14 (1991). See also Philip Shenon, "After Years of Denial, Asia Faces Scourge of AIDS," *The New York Times*, November 8, 1992, p. A1, and Richard Rhodes, "Death in the Candy Store: The Prostitution Capital of the World, Thailand Is Committing Sexual Suicide by HIV Infection," *Rolling Stone*, November 28, 1991.

204 "Thus Thailand in three or four years . . .": This account is based on filmed interviews with Dr. Praphan Phanuphak, BBC Science/Features

and Australian Broadcasting Corporation, 1992, and on Bruce G. Weniger and others, "The Epidemiology of HIV Infection and AIDS in thailand," *AIDS 5* (suppl. 2):S71–S85 (1991).

204 "the government economizes by not giving out jelly": Personal communication from Susan Turner, July 1992.

204 " 'We're probably the first in the world . . .' ": Filmed interview with Dr. Werisit Sititrai, BBC Science/Features and Australian Broadcasting Corporation, 1992.

205 "Women here have always played a key role . . .": Marjorie A. Muecke, "Mother Sold Food, Daughter Sells Her Body: The Cultural Continuity of Prostitution," *Social Science and Medicine* 35:891–901 (1992).

205 "A remarkably dedicated and compassionate man": This account is based on filmed interviews with Dr. Wat Uthaivoravit, Chiang Rai, Thailand, BBC Science/Features and Australian Broadcasting Corporation, 1992.

206 "the Thai government is about to do an end run": Alison Clements, "Thailand Stifles AIDS Campaign," *British Medical Journal* 304:1264 (1992).

207 "AIDS is catalyzing a revolution in health care": Jonathan Mann, "The New Health Care Paradigm," *Focus: A Guide to AIDS Research and Counseling* 6:1–2 (February 1991), p. 1; adapted from a speech made in June 1990 at the Sixth International Conference on AIDS (published by the University of California, San Francisco, AIDS Health Project).

207 " 'The key to the new paradigm . . .' ": Mann, "The New Health Care Paradigm," p. 1.

207 " 'an increasingly global linkage' ": ibid., p. 2.

208 "Australia has not had a second phase": J. Wolk, A. Wodak, A. Morlet, et al., "HIV-Related Risk-Taking Behavior, Knowledge and Serostatus of Intravenous Drug Users in Sydney," *Medical Journal of Australia* 152:452–58 (1990).

209 "A 1992 study of poor black youth": Motivational Educational Entertainment, Research Division, *Reaching the Hip-Hop Generation: The MEE Report* (Princeton, N.J.: Robert Wood Johnson Foundation, 1992). The report, based on focus groups and ethnographic research by authorities on African-American culture, reads in part (p. viii) as follows: "Inner city teens would be delighted to meet their favorite NBA star. . . . But they would discount the appearance as 'playing the game'— performing one of the obligations of being a celebrity. They would feel he had little to tell them about living their lives. To be effective, a spokesman would have to possess a 'reputation' within this community, which he would be endangering by espousing a mainstream message. . . . A chilling disbelief in the future also undercuts efforts to address this audience. Magic Johnson's admission of HIV infection and his sincere campaign to warn youngsters of the risk of unprotected sex may have a tragically small effect among African-American urban teenagers. Many of the disadvantaged teens we encountered cannot envision their lives extending any distance into the future."

209 " '. . . not enough to look after individual patients' ": This and subsequent quotes are from filmed interviews with Dr. Alex Wodak, Sydney, 1992, BCC Science/Features and Australian Broadcasting Corporation.

210 "John Snow's water-pump handle": John Snow, "The Cholera near Golden Square," in Ann G. Carmichael and Richard M. Ratzan, eds.,

Medicine: A Treasury of Art and Literature (New York: Macmillan/Hugh Lauter Levin, 1991), pp. 152–55.

211 "practice the new kind of medicine": This account is based on filmed interviews with Dr. Rachael Buckley and Dr. Ingrid Van Beek, Sydney, BBC Science/Features and Australian Broadcasting Corporation, 1992.

212 "the potential to carry the AIDS epidemic": The role of prostitution in the epidemic throughout the world is increasingly clear: Michael J. Rosenberg and Jodie M. Weiner, "Prostitutes and AIDS: A Health Department Priority?" *American Journal of Public Health* 78:418–23 (1988).

212 *"harm minimization* or *harm reduction"*: John Strang and Michael Farrell, "Harm Minimisation for Drug Misusers: When Second Best May Be Best First," *British Medical Journal* 304:1127–28 (1992).

212 "AIDS cases in Australia begin to level off": J. Wolk et al., "HIV-Related Risk-taking Behavior, Knowledge and Serostatus."

213 "A prison version of the comic": Streetwize Comics Present *Gaolwize* (Sydney, New South Wales: Department of Community Services and Heal/Youth Rights Comics).

213 "halted the spread . . . in Liverpool": Steve Lohr, "There's No Preaching, Just the Clean Needles," *The New York Times*, February 29, 1988, p. 4. For description of the program and its founding, see John Marks and Allan Parry, "Syringe Exchange Programme for Drug Addicts," *The Lancet* 1:691–92, March 21, 1987. For the contrast with Scotland, see E. Follett, L. Wallace, and E. McCruden, "HIV and HBV Infection in Drug Abusers in Glasgow," *The Lancet* 1:920–21, April 18, 1987.

214 " 'ample data are available . . .' ": Ernst Buning, "Effects of Amsterdam Needle and Syringe Exchange," *The International Journal of the Addictions* 26:1303–11 (1991), p. 1303.

214 "3 percent in the United Kingdom . . .": Arnold S. Trebach and Kevin B. Zeese, *Drug Prohibition and the Conscience of Nations* (Washington, D.C.: The Drug Policy Foundation, 1990), p. 142.

214 "New York, our largest center of drug abuse": Mireya Navarro, "Needle Swap Programs Gaining Favor," *The New York Times*, October 30, 1991; S. Estepa, M. Pierre-Louis, and R. Newman, "Needle-Swap Programs Found to Reduce H.I.V. Transmission" (letter), *The New York Times*, June 17, 1992.

214 "reduced the spread of AIDS by 33 percent": "Needle Exchange Program Reduces the Spread of AIDS," *AORN Journal* 55:754 (1992).

214 "Back in New York, Judge Gustin L. Reichbach": Ronald Sullivan, "Prostitutes Get Condoms with Sentences," *The New York Times*, March 29, 1991, p. A14. See also Douglas Martin, "Assisting Prostitutes with AIDS," *The New York Times*, August 8, 1992.

215 "our health leaders . . . prefer moralizing": Harold M. Ginzburg, "Needle Exchange Programs: A Medical or Policy Dilemma?" *American Journal of Public Health* 79:1350–51 (1989).

215 "a particular subgroup of the Dade County poor": Pedro J. Greer, Jr., "Medical Problems of the Homeless: Consequences of Lack of Social Policy—A Local Approach," *University of Miami Law Review* 45:407–16, 1990–91.

216 "More than 12 percent . . . HIV positive": ibid., p. 412.

216 "The population of homeless nationally . . .": Numbers are exceedingly difficult to estimate, but for an excellent overview see Ellen L. Bassuk, "Homeless Families," *Scientific American* 265:66–74 (1991).

216 " 'We showed no difference statistically . . .' ": Filmed interview with Dr. Pedro J. Greer, Jr., Miami, BBC Science/Features and Australian Broadcasting Corporation, 1992.

216 "Many other diseases are rampant": Greer, "Medical Problems of the Homeless."

217 " 'In effect, a third-world country . . .' ": ibid., p. 413.

217 " 'Now a body floats by . . .' ": Filmed interview with Dr. Pedro J. Greer, Jr., Miami, BBC Science/Features and Australian Broadcasting Corporation, 1992.

218 "A number of recent analyses": Sylvia Nasar, "However You Slice the Data, the Richest Did Get Richer," *The New York Times*, May 11, 1992, p. C1. Children have proved particularly vulnerable: see Victor R. Fuchs and Diane M. Reklis, "America's Children: Economic Perspectives and Policy Options," *Science* 255:41–46 (1992); and National Center for Children in Poverty, *Five Million Children: A Statistical Profile of Our Poorest Young Citizens* (New York: Columbia University Press, 1990).

218 "The disparity between black and white . . .": Andrew Hacker, *Two Nations: Black and White, Separate, Hostile, Unequal* (New York: Scribners, 1992).

218 " 'the danger of a conflict . . .' ": Alexis de Tocqueville, quoted in Hacker, *Two Nations*, p. x. De Tocqueville thought it "the most formidable of the ills that threaten the future of the Union" (p. ix).

219 " 'By the end of the 1980s . . .' ": Kevin P. Phillips, quoted by Nasar, "However You Slice the Data," p. C5.

220 "70 percent of premature deaths": Amler and Dull, *Closing the Gap.*

220 " 'federal spending for AIDS was $1.6 billion . . .' ": Robert M. Wachter, "AIDS, Activism, and the Politics of Health," *The New England Journal of Medicine* 326:128–32 (1992).

221 "Other gaps in prevention": George A. Kaplan, Mary N. Haan, S. Leonard Syme, Meredith Minkler, and Marilyn Winkleby, "Socioeconomic Status and Health," in Amler and Dull, pp. 125–29. For an example of a discontinued program, see Milton Kotelchuck, Janet B. Schwartz, Marlene T. Anderka, and Karl S. Finison, "WIC Participation and Pregnancy Outcomes: Massachusetts Statewide Evaluation Project," *American Journal of Public Health* 74:1086–92 (1984).

221 "As for the rest, the underdeveloped world . . .": Andrew Learmonth, *Disease Ecology* (Oxford: Basil Blackwell, 1988). For an overview of social and cultural factors in infectious disease, see Marcia Inhorn and Peter Brown, "The Anthropology of Infectious Disease," *Annual Review of Anthropology* 19:89–117 (1990).

221 "Tuberculosis . . . the old standby killer . . .": J. Chretien, W. Holland, P. Macklem, J. Murray, and A. Woolcock, "Acute Respiratory Infections in Children: A Global Public Health Problem," *The New England Journal of Medicine* 310:982–84 (1984).

221 "Schistosomiasis . . . likewise a hopeless obstacle . . .": Learmonth, *Disease Ecology*, chapter 11.

222 "half a million women . . . die each year . . .": United Nations Children's

Fund (UNICEF), *The State of the World's Children, 1990* (New York and Oxford: Oxford University Press, 1990), p. 26.

222 "350,000 tobacco-related deaths . . .": Amler and Dull, p. 184.

222 "500,000 in Europe": Richard Lorant, "WHO Conference Draws Up No Smoking Bill of Rights," *Associated Press*, International News, November 11, 1988, A.M. Cycle. The estimate was given by Richard Peto of Oxford University.

222 " 'Winston, Style of the U.S.A.' ": Charles P. Wallace, "New Trade Issue Smoldering: U.S. Tobacco Firms' Push to Sell Cigarettes in Thailand Seen as Attempt to Export Health Risk to Asia, Third World," *Los Angeles Times*, April 17, 1989, home edition, Business Part 4, p. 3.

222 " 'Asian lungs [are] more expendable . . .' ": Rep. Mel Levine (D-Cal.), quoted by Wallace, "New Trade Issue Smoldering." See also Michelle Barry, "The Influence of the U.S. Tobacco Industry on the Health, Economy, and Environment of Developing Countries," *The New England Journal of Medicine* 324:917–20 (1991). Barry cites former Surgeon General C. Everett Koop as saying that "at a time when we are pleading with foreign governments to stop the export of cocaine, it is the height of hypocrisy for the United States to export tobacco."

223 "starvation—the full-blown clinical syndrome": Learmonth, p. 294.

223 "More than 10 million of these . . . deaths": UNICEF, *The State of the World's Children, 1990*, p. 5. See also cause-specific analyses, pp. 16–45.

224 " 'In the years from 1977 . . .' ": Filmed interview with Annie Crowe, Sydney, BBC Science/Features and Australian Broadcasting Corporation, 1992.

226 "places that have never had any . . . health care": For an account of the WHO AIDS funding controversy, see Sharon Kingman, "AIDS Brings Health into Focus," *New Scientist*, May 20, 1989, pp. 37–42.

EPILOGUE: A NEW KIND OF DOCTOR

227 "Where the doctor's conceptions of the illness": Arthur Kleinman, *The Illness Narratives: Suffering, Healing, and the Human Condition* (New York, Basic Books, 1988). See also Thomas M. Johnson and Carolyn F. Sargent, eds., *Medical Anthropology: Contemporary Theory and Method* (New York: Praeger, 1990).

228 "imaginative new strategies and tactics for outreach": Jesse Steinfeld and others, "Intervention Strategies: Reports of the Working Groups," in Amler and Dull, *Closing the Gap*, pp. 188–201. See also the references for chapter 8, and Anne R. Somers, "Why Not Try Preventing Illness as a Way of Controlling Medicare Costs?" *The New England Journal of Medicine* 311:853–56 (1984). Strategies for outreach must be rural as well as urban; for a successful program see Tim Friend, "Health Care That's Also Fiscally Fit," *USA Today*, December 5, 1991, p. D1. The program is led by Dr. James Hotz, who according to physician-author Neil Shulman is the real-life hero of his book and film *Doc Hollywood*.

230 "humane intervention in the community and the home": Fazlur Rahman, "Care Options for the Elderly." The illogic of the present system is illustrated by Robert Lebow, "Medicare Discourages House Calls by Doctors" (letter), *The New York Times*, December 10, 1991.

231 "an idea whose time has come": Arnold S. Relman, "Universal Health Insurance: Its Time Has Come," *The New England Journal of Medicine* 320:117–18 (1989).

231 "Leading physicians . . . agree": Dr. C. Everett Koop and Dr. Marcia Angell, on *The MacNeil/Lehrer NewsHour*, October ? ; transcript by Strictly Business, Overland Park, Kansas.

231 "the American College of Physicians": H. Denman Scott and Howard B. Shapiro, for the Health and Public Policy Committee (Dr. Clifton R. Cleaveland, Chair), with the approval of the Board of Regents. "Universal Insurance for American Health Care: A Proposal of the American College of Physicians," *Annals of Internal Medicine* 117:511–19 (1992), with an accompanying editorial signed by six top leaders of the ACP, pp. 528–29.

231 "the American Nurses' Association": The American Nurses' Association and the National League for Nursing, "Nursing's Agenda for Health Care Reform" (New York: National League for Nursing, 1991).

231 "More than 12 percent . . .": United States General Accounting Office, "U.S. Health Care Spending: Trends, Contributing Factors, and Proposals for Reform," Report to the Chairman, Committee on Ways and Means, House of Representatives (GAO/HRD-91-102), June 1991.

231 "doctors are growing ever more bitter": Astrachan and Weissman, "The Hassle Factor"; See also Weissman, *The Doctor Dilemma: Squaring the Old Values with the New Economy* (Knoxville, Tenn.: Whittle Books, Grand Rounds Press, 1992).

231 "this most litigious of societies": David Gergen, "America's Legal Mess," *U.S. News and World Report*, August 19, 1991, p. 72; and Walter K. Olson, *The Litigation Explosion* (New York: E. P. Dutton, 1991). See also the comments on Olson's book by former Chief Justice Warren E. Burger, *The New York Times Book Review*, May 12, 1991, pp. 12–13.

232 "prevention . . . is rarely covered at all": Elisabeth Rosenthal, "Hurdle for Preventive Medicine: Insurance."

232 "even though these measures save money": Three examples: Jane S. Willems and Claudia R. Sanders, "Cost-Effectiveness and Cost-Benefit Analyses of Vaccines," *The Journal of Infectious Diseases* 144:486–93 (1981); Arnold S. Relman, "Mild Hypertension: No More Benign Neglect," *The New England Journal of Medicine* 302:293–94 (1980); Kotelchuck et al., "WIC Participation and Pregancy Outcomes." See also Somers, "Why Not Try Preventing Illness?" *New England Journal of Medicine* 311:153–56 (1984).

232 " 'The competent physician . . .' ": Marcus Tullius Cicero, *De Oratore II.* As quoted by Bergen Evans, ed., *Dictionary of Quotations* (New York: Delacorte Press, 1968), p. 524.

233 "Over half the doctors in Britain . . .": Judy Allsop, *Health Policy and the National Health Service* (London: Longman, 1984) (a history, with a collection of relevant historical documents); and Hart, *A New Kind of Doctor*.

233 "away from every form of primary care": Colwill, "Where Have All the Primary Care Applicants Gone?" For analysis with a number of concrete proposals for change, see Barry Stimmel, "The Crisis in Primary Care and the Role of Medical Schools: Defining the Issues," *Journal of the American Medical Association* 268:2060–65 (1992).

233 "Specialists and their procedures . . . are dangerous": In one study 9 percent of patients admitted to a hospital service sustained major dele-

terious effects caused by treatment. Knight Steel, Paul M. Gertman, Caroline Crescenzi, and Jennifer Anderson, "Iatrogenic Illness on a General Medical Service at a University Hospital," *The New England Journal of Medicine* 304:638–42 (1981).

233 "to invoke interventions less dramatic . . .": Peter Franks, Carolyn M. Clancy, and Paul A. Nutting, "Gatekeeping Revisited—Protecting Patients from Overtreatment," *The New England Journal of Medicine* 327:424–29 (1992).

233 "nurse practitioners are an elite corps": Judith S. Dempster, "The Nurse Practitioner and Autonomy: Contributions to the Professional Maturity of Nursing," *Journal of the American Academy of Nurse Practitioners* 3:75–78 (1991). For a survey of the current roles of some six thousand nurse practitioners, see Jan Towers, "Report of the National Survey of the American Academy of Nurse Practitioners, Part V: Comparison of Nurse Practitioners According to Practice Setting," ibid., pp. 42–45. In an important article, no difference was found between the quality of care provided by nurse practitioners and that provided by physicians in a primary care practice: Walter O. Spitzer and others. "The Burlington Randomized Trial of the Nurse Practitioner," *The New England Journal of Medicine* 290:251–56 (1974). Reprinted in the *Journal of the American Academy of Nurse Practitioners* 2:93–99 (1990).

235 "not the slightest hint of . . . privately organized medicine": Rudolf Klein, "Labour's Health Policy: The Conflict Between the Two Main Parties Is Now over Means, Not Ends," *British Medical Journal* 304:517–18, (1992).

235 "the British people love the National Health Service": Robert Maxwell, "Aneurin Bevan on the NHS," *British Medical Journal* 304:200 (1992); Rudolf Klein, "NHS Reforms: The First Six Months," *British Medical Journal* 304:199–200 (1992). Also see Sharon Kingman, John Bain, Jane Smith, Paula Whitty, Ian Jones, and Tony Delamothe, "The New NHS: First Year's Experience"; series of five articles, *British Medical Journal* 304:907–9; 971–73; 1036–39; 1039–41; 1109–11 (1992).

235 "As for the Canadian system": United States General Accounting Office. "Canadian Health Insurance: Lessons for the United States," Report to the Chairman, Committee on Government Operations, House of Representatives (GAO/HRD-91-90), June 1991; Robert G. Evans, " 'We'll Take Care of It for You': Health Care in the Canadian Community," *Daedalus* 117:155–89 (1988). Canada has also avoided the decline of primary care: see Michael E. Whitcomb and J. P. Desgroseilliers, "Primary Care Medicine in Canada," *The New England Journal of Medicine* 326:1469–72 (1992).

236 "stringently regulated the private insurance business": United States General Accounting Office, "Health Care Spending Control: The Experience of France, Germany, and Japan," Report to Congressional Requesters (GAO/HRD-92-9), November 1991. Proposals for the United States that preserve private insurance have also received considerable attention: see, for example, Alain C. Enthoven and R. Kronick, "A Consumer-Choice Health Plan for the 1990s," *The New England Journal of Medicine* 320:29–37 (1989), and Paul Starr, *The Logic of Health Care Reform: Transforming American Health Care for the Better* (Knoxville, Tenn.: Whittle Books, Grand Rounds Press, 1992), for two influential but distinct proposals in this vein. Starr opposes employer-based plans.

236 "regulating medical malpractice . . .": Marilyn Rosenthal, *Dealing with Medical Malpractice*.

236 "reined in medical greed": Robert G. Evans and others, "Controlling Health Expenditures—The Canadian Reality," *The New England Journal of Medicine* 320:571–77 (1989); and Victor R. Fuchs and James S. Hahn, "How Does Canada Do It?: A Comparison of Expenditures for Physicians' Services in the United States and Canada," *The New England Journal of Medicine* 323:884–90 (1990).

236 "like a stock market trading floor": Dave Lindorff, *Marketplace Medicine: The Rise of the For-Profit Hospital Chains* (New York: Bantam Books, 1992). See also Paul Starr, *The Social Transformation of American Medicine* (New York: Basic Books, 1982).

237 "I helped to resuscitate . . .": For a fuller account, see Konner, *Becoming a Doctor*, pp. 264–66; and Fazlur Rahman, "Why Pound Life into the Dying?: CPR Can Be Cruel," *The New York Times*, February 20, 1989.

237 "the state of Oregon has pioneered them": David M. Eddy, "Oregon's Plan: Should It Be Approved?" *Journal of the American Medical Association* 266:2439–45 (1991); Robert Steinbrook and Bernard Lo, "The Oregon Medicaid Demonstration Project—Will It Provide Adequate Medical Care?" *The New England Journal of Medicine* 326:340–44 (1992).

237 "we have got to learn to say no": Norman Daniels, "Why Saying No to Patients in the United States Is So Hard: Cost Containment, Justice and Provider Autonomy," *The New England Journal of Medicine* 314:1380–83 (1986).

237 "a picture of Coby Howard": Melinda Beck, with Nadine Joseph and Mary Hager, "Not Enough for All: Oregon Experiments with Rationing Health Care," *Newsweek*, May 14, 1990, pp. 53–55.

238 "an epidemic that never should have happened": Rick Weiss, "U.S. Epidemics: The Price of Neglect?" *Science* 258:547 (1992). See also Robert Pear, "Bush Defers an Emergency Plan to Provide Vaccines for Children," *The New York Times*, June 23, 1991, and Centers for Disease Control, "Measles—United States, 1990," *Morbidity and Mortality Weekly Reports* 40:369–72, 1991.

238 "a 1987 Harris Poll": Louis Harris and Associates, *Making Difficult Health Care Decisions: A National Public Opinion Survey* (Deerfield, Ill.: Louis Harris and Associates, 1988).

238 "a straightforward imitation of the Canadian system": See David U. Himmelstein, Steffie Woolhandler, and the Writing Committee of the Working Group on Program Design, "A National Health Program for the United States: A Physicians' Proposal," *The New England Journal of Medicine* 320:102–8 (1989); also Kevin Grumbach, Thomas Bodenheimer, David U. Himmelstein, and Steffie Woolhandler, "Liberal Benefits, Conservative Spending: The Physicians for a National Health Program Proposal," *Journal of the American Medical Association* 265:2549–54 (1991).

238 "a single-payer system does not have to be . . .": See Richard B. Saltman, "Single-Source Financing Systems: A Solution for the United States?" *Journal of the American Medical Association* 268:774–79 (1992) for a brief recent comparative account of the varied options and different European experiences with single-payer systems. Paul Starr, in *The Logic of Health Care Reform*, attempts to reach a compromise between single-payer organization and managed competition. Starr's plan, which properly jet-

tisons employer-based coverage, goes beyond managed competition in establishing Health Insurance Purchasing Cooperatives through which clients would exercise collective buying power, generating competition among plans in an efficient and decisive way. Although it is certainly preferable to managed competition as presented by Enthoven (and the Clinton campaign), it falls far short of the streamlining offered by a single-payer plan, because it leaves the private insurance bureaucracy intact. Ironically, it also leaves both doctors and patients with less freedom of choice and of interaction than does the allegedly more "socialistic" Canadian plan.

239 "the rapid growth of for-profit medicine": Arnold S. Relman, "What Market Values Are Doing to Medicine," *Atlantic Monthly*, March 1992, pp. 99–106. See also Leon Eisenberg, "Health Care: For Patients or for Profits?" *American Journal of Psychiatry* 143:1015–19 (1986).

239 " 'the growth of the medical-industrial complex . . .' ": Relman, "What Market Values Are Doing to Medicine," p. 102.

239 "flourishes best in the private sector . . .": ibid., p. 106.

239 "Patient dumping . . .": George J. Annas, "Your Money or Your Life: 'Dumping' Uninsured Patients from Hospital Emergency Wards," *American Journal of Public Health 76*:74–77 (1986). See also Perl, " 'Patient Dumping.' "

239 "many others . . . subtle and manifest": Joel S. Weissman, Constantine Gatsonia, and Arnold M. Epstein, "Rates of Avoidable Hospitalization by Insurance Status in Massachusetts and Maryland," *Journal of the American Medical Association 268*:2388–94 (1992), and Helen R. Burstin, Stuart R. Lipsitz, and Troyen A. Brennen, "Socioeconomic Status and Risk for Substandard Medical Care," ibid., pp. 2383–87; with accompanying editorial by Andrew B. Bindman and Kevin Grumbach, "America's Safety Net: The Wrong Place at the Wrong Time?" pp. 2426–27.

240 "such a corps could be built . . .": Weissman, *The Doctor Dilemma*.

241 " 'No society can legitimately call itself civilized . . .' ": Aneurin Bevan, as quoted by Maxwell, "Aneurin Bevan on the NHS."

241 "Hawaii has one that . . . works very well": Timothy Egan, "Hawaii Shows It Can Offer Health Insurance for All," *The New York Times*, July 23, 1991, p. A1.

242 "the respected, valued, and noble profession . . .": Burnham, "American Medicine's Golden Age."

Select Bibliography

Allsop, Judy. *Health Policy and the National Health Service*. London: Longman, 1984.

Amler, Robert W., and H. Bruce Dull, eds. *Closing the Gap: The Burden of Unnecessary Illness*. New York: Oxford University Press, 1987.

Annas, George J. "The Health Care Proxy and the Living Will." *New England Journal of Medicine 324:* 1210–13, 1991.

———. "Your Money or Your Life: 'Dumping' Uninsured Patients from Hospital Emergency Wards." *American Journal of Public Health 76:* 74–77, 1986.

Astrachan, Anthony, and Gerald Weissman. "The Hassle Factor." Series of six articles in *MD* magazine, May–December 1991. Based on a survey of 1,700 physicians.

Bassuk, Ellen L. "Homeless Families." *Scientific American 265:* 66–74, 1991.

———. "The Homelessness Problem." *Scientific American 251:* 40–45, 1984.

Battistella, Roger M., and Richard McK. F. Southby. "Crisis in American Medicine." *The Lancet 1:* 581–86, 1968.

Beeson, Paul. "Changes in Medical Therapy During the Past Half Century." *Medicine 59:* 79–99, 1980.

Benner, Patricia E., and Judith Wrubel. *The Primacy of Caring: Stress and Coping in Health and Illness*. Menlo Park, Calif.: Addison-Wesley, 1989.

Brazelton, T. Berry. "Why Is America Failing Its Children?" *New York Times Magazine*, September 9, 1990.

Burnham, John C. "American Medicine's Golden Age: What Happened to It?" *Science 215:* 1474–79, 1982.

Burstin, Helen R., Stuart R. Lipsitz, and Troyen A. Brennan. "Socioeconomic Status and Risk for Substandard Medical Care." *Journal of the American Medical Association 268:* 2383–87, 1992.

Callahan, Daniel. *Setting Limits: Medical Goals in an Aging Society.* New York: Simon and Schuster, 1987.

———. *What Kind of Life: The Limits of Medical Progess.* New York: Simon and Schuster, 1990.

Carmichael, Ann G., and Richard M. Ratzan, eds. *Medicine: A Treasury of Art and Literature.* New York: Macmillan/Hugh Lauter Levin, 1991.

Cassell, Eric, J. *The Nature of Suffering and the Goals of Medicine.* New York: Oxford University Press, 1991.

Chassin, M. R. et al. "Variations in the Use of Medical and Surgical Services by the Medicare Population." *New England Journal of Medicine 314:* 285–90, 1986, with accompanying editorial by John Wennberg, "Which Rate Is Right?," p. 310.

Cohen, Mitchell L. "Epidemiology of Drug Resistance: Implications for a Post-Antimicrobial Era." *Science 257:* 1050–55, 1992.

Cousins, Norman. *Anatomy of an Illness as Perceived by the Patient.* New York: Norton, 1979.

———. *Head First: The Biology of Hope.* New York: Dutton, 1989.

Daniels, Norman. "Why Saying No to Patients in the United States Is So Hard: Cost Containment, Justice and Provider Autonomy." *The New England Journal of Medicine 314:* 1380–83, 1986.

Eddy, David M. "Clinical Decision Making: From Theory to Practice." A series of articles (approximately monthly) in the *Journal of the American Medical Association,* vols. 263–66, 1990–91.

Eisenberg, Leon. "Rudolf Karl Ludwig Virchow: Where Are You Now That We Need You?" *American Journal of Medicine 77:* 524–32, 1984.

Esselstyn, Caldwell, B. "Beyond Surgery: Presidential Address to the American Association of Endocrine Surgeons." *Surgery 110:* 923–27, 1991.

Evans, Robert G. " 'We'll Take Care of It for You': Health Care in the Canadian Community." *Daedalus 117:* 155–89, 1988.

Fields, Howard L., and Jon D. Levine. "Biology of Placebo Analgesia." *American Journal of Medicine 70:* 745–46, 1981.

Frank, Arthur. *At the Will of the Body: Reflections on Illness.* Boston: Houghton Mifflin, 1991.

Franks, Peter, Carolyn M. Clancy, and Paul A. Nutting. "Gatekeeping Revisited—Protecting Patients from Overtreatment." *New England Journal of Medicine 327:* 424–29, 1992.

Friedman, Emily. "The Uninsured: From Dilemma to Crisis." *Journal of the American Medical Association 265:* 2491–95, 1991; part of a special issue of the journal devoted to "Caring for the Uninsured and Underinsured."

Gomez, Carlos F. *Regulating Death: Euthanasia and the Case of the Netherlands.* New York: Free Press, 1991.

Greenspan, Allan M., et al. "Incidence of Unwarranted Implantation of permanent Cardiac Pacemakers in a Large Medical Population." *New England Journal of Medicine 318:* 158–63, 1988.

Greer, Pedro J., Jr. "Medical Problems of the Homeless: Consequences of Lack of Social Policy—A Local Approach." *University of Miami Law Review 45:* 407–16, 1990–91.

Hahn, Robert A., and Atwood D. Gaines, eds. *Physicians of Western Medicine: Anthropological Approaches to Theory and Practice*. Boston: Reidel, 1985.

Haley, Robert W., et al. "The Nationwide Nosocomial Infection Rate: A New Need for Vital Statistics." *American Journal of Epidemiology* 121: 159–67, 1985.

Hampton, J.R. et al. "Relative Contributions of History-taking, Physical Examination, and Laboratory Investigation to Diagnosis and Management of Medical Outpatients." *British Medical Journal* 2: 486–89, 1975.

Hart, Julian Tudor. *A New Kind of Doctor: The General Practitioner's Part in the Health of the Community*. London: Merlin Press, 1988.

———. "Two Paths for Medical Practice." *Lancet* 340: 772-75, 1992.

Himmelstein, David U., Steffie Woolhandler, and the Writing Committee of the Working Group on Program Design. "A National Health Program for the United States: A Physicians' Proposal." *New England Journal of Medicine* 320: 102–8, 1989.

Homer, Paul, and Martha Holstein, eds. *A Good Old Age?: The Paradox of Setting Limits*. New York: Simon and Schuster, 1990.

Johnson, G. Timothy. "Restoring Trust Between Patient and Doctor." *New England Journal of Medicine* 322: 195–97, 1990. See also Burnham, John C., 1982.

Kassirer, Jerome P., and Stephen G. Pauker. "The Toss-Up." *New England Journal of Medicine* 305: 1467–69, 1981.

Kaufman, Caroline L. "Informed Consent and Patient Decision Making: Two Decades of Research." *Social Science and Medicine* 17: 1657–64, 1983.

Kevles, Daniel, and Leroy Hood, eds. *The Code of Codes: Scientific and Social Issues in the Human Genome Project*. Cambridge, Mass.: Harvard University Press, 1992.

Kingman, Sharon. "AIDS Brings Health into Focus." *New Scientist*, May 20, 1989, pp. 37–42.

Klein, Rudolf. "Labour's Health Policy: The Conflict Between the Two Main Parties Is Now Over Means Not Ends." *British Medical Journal* 304: 517–18, 1992.

Kleinman, Arthur. *The Illness Narratives: Suffering, Healing and the Human Condition*. New York: Basic Books, 1988.

Konner, Melvin. *Becoming a Doctor: A Journey of Initiation in Medical School*. New York: Viking, 1987.

———. *Why the Reckless Survive, and Other Secrets of Human Nature*. New York: Viking, 1990.

Krause, Richard. *The Restless Tide: The Persistent Challenge of the Microbial World*. Washington, D.C.: National Foundation for Infectious Diseases, 1981.

Learmonth, Andrew. *Disease Ecology: An Introduction*. Oxford: Basil Blackwell, 1988.

Lin, Keh-Ming, and Arthur M. Kleinman. "Psychopathology and the Clinical Course of Schizophrenia: A Cross-Cultural Perspective." *Schizophrenia Bulletin* 14: 555–67, 1988.

Localio, A. Russell et al. "Relation Between Malpractice Claims and Adverse Events Due to Negligence: Results of the Harvard Medical Practice Study III." *New England Journal of Medicine* 325: 245–51, 1991.

Louis Harris and Associates. *Making Difficult Health Care Decisions: A National Public Opinion Survey*. Deerfield, Ill.: Louis Harris and Associates, 1988.

Mandell, Harvey, and Howard Spiro, eds. *When Doctors Get Sick*. New York: Plenum Books, 1987.

Mann, Jonathan, Daniel J. M. Tarantola, and Thomas W. Netter, eds. *AIDS in the World 1992*. Cambridge, Mass.: Harvard University Press, 1992.

Manning, Willard G., et al. *The Costs of Poor Health Habits*. Cambridge, Mass.: Harvard University Press, 1991.

Manuel, Barry M. "Professional Liability—A No-Fault Solution." *New England Journal of Medicine 322*: 627–31, 1990; with accompanying editorial by Arnold S. Relman, pp. 626–27.

Maxwell, Robert. "Aneurin Bevan on the NHS." *British Medical Journal 304*: 200, 1992.

McCord, Colin, and Harold Freeman. "Excess Mortality in Harlem." *New England Journal of Medicine 322*: 173–77, 1990.

McCue, Jack D. "The Distress of Internship: Causes and Prevention." *New England Journal of Medicine 312*: 449–52, 1985.

McGrew, Roderick E. *Encyclopedia of Medical History*. London: Macmillan Press, 1985.

McHugh, Paul R., and Phillip R. Slavney. *The Perspectives of Psychiatry*. Baltimore: Johns Hopkins University Press, 1983.

McKeown, Thomas. *The Role of Medicine: Dream, Mirage, or Nemesis?* 2nd ed. Princeton, N.J.: Princeton University Press, 1979.

McKinlay, J. B., and S. M. McKinlay. "The Questionable Contribution of Medical Measures to the Decline of Mortality." *Milbank Memorial Fund Quarterly/Health and Society 55*: 405–28, 1977.

Mechanic, David, and Linda H. Aiken. "Improving the Care of Patients with Chronic Mental Illness." *New England Journal of Medicine 317*: 1634–38, 1987.

Mizrahi, Terry. *Getting Rid of Patients: Contradiction in the Socialization of Physicians*. New Brunswick, N.J.: Rutgers University Press, 1986.

Morris, David B. *The Culture of Pain*. Berkeley, Calif.: University of California Press, 1991.

Murray, Raymond H., and Arthur J. Rubel. "Physicians and Healers: Unwitting Partners in Healing." *New England Journal of Medicine 326*: 61–64, 1992.

Ornish, Dean, et al. in the Lifestyle Heart Trial. "Can Lifestyle Changes Reverse Coronary Heart Disease?" *The Lancet 336*: 129–33, 1990.

Osler, William. *A Way of Life and Selected Writings of Sir William Osler*. New York: Dover Publications, 1958.

Payer, Lynn. *Medicine and Culture: Notions of Health and Sickness*. London: Victor Gollancz, 1990.

Perry, Seymour. "Technology Assessment: Continuing Uncertainty." *New England Journal of Medicine 314*: 240–43, 1986.

Quill, Timothy E. *Death and Dignity: Making Choices and Taking Charge*. New York: Norton, 1993.

Rahman, Fazlur. "Why Pound Life into the Dying: CPR Can Be Cruel." *New York Times*, February 20, 1987.

Relman, Arnold S. "Shattuck Lecture—The Health Care Industry: Where Is It Taking Us?" *New England Journal of Medicine 325*: 854–59, 1991.

———. "What Market Values Are Doing to Medicine." *Atlantic Monthly*, March 1992, pp. 99–106.

Reynolds, Richard, and John Stone, eds. *On Doctoring*. New York: Simon and Schuster, 1991.

Rosen, George. "What Is Social Medicine?: A Genetic Analysis of the Concept." *Bulletin of the History of Medicine 21*: 674–733, 1947.

Rosenberg, Charles E. *The Care of Strangers: The Rise of America's Hospital System*. New York: Basic Books, 1987.

Saltman, Richard B., "Single-Source Financing Systems: A Solution for the United States?" *Journal of the American Medical Association 268:* 774–79, 1992.

Schieber, George J., Jean-Pierre Poullier, and Leslie M. Greenwald. "Health Care Systems in Twenty-Four Countries." *Health Affairs 10:* 22–38, 1991.

Snider, Dixie E., and William L. Roper. "The New Tuberculosis." *New England Journal of Medicine 326:* 703–5, 1992.

Snow, John. "The Cholera Near Golden Square." In Carmichael and Ratzan, eds., *Medicine: A Treasury of Art and Literature*, pp. 152–155.

Somers, Anne R. "Why Not Try Preventing Illness as a Way of Controlling Medicare Costs?" *New England Journal of Medicine 311:* 853–56, 1984.

Spitzer, Walter O., et al. "The Burlington Randomized Trial of the Nurse Practitioner." *New England Journal of Medicine 290:* 251–56, 1974. Reprinted in the *Journal of the American Academy of Nurse Practitioners 2:* 93, 1990.

Starr, Paul. *The Logic of Health Care Reform: Transforming American Health Care for the Better*. Knoxville, Tenn.: Whittle Books/Grand Rounds Press, 1992.

————. *The Social Transformation of American Medicine*. New York: Basic Books, 1982.

Steel, Knight, et al. "Iatrogenic Illness on a General Medical Service at a University Hospital." *New England Journal of Medicine 304:* 638–42, 1981.

Stimmel, Barry. "The Crisis in Primary Care and the Role of Medical Schools: Defining the Issues." *Journal of the American Medical Association 268:* 2060–65, 1992.

Stone, John. *In the Country of Hearts: Journeys in the Art of Medicine*. New York: Delacorte Press, 1990.

————. "Characteristics of the Complete Physician." *The Pharos of Alpha Omega 44:* 16–20, 1981.

Sulmasy, Daniel P. "Physicians, Cost Control, and Ethics." *Annals of Internal Medicine 116:* 920–26, 1992.

Taylor, Shelley E. *Positive Illusions: Creative Self-Deception and the Healthy Mind*. New York: Basic Books, 1989.

Towers, Jan. "Report of the National Survey of the American Survey of the American Academy of Nurse Practitioners, Part V: Comparison of Nurse Practitioners According to Practice Setting." *Journal of the American Academy of Nurse Practitioners 3:* 42–45, 1991.

Trillin, Alice Stewart. "Of Dragons and Garden Peas: A Cancer Patient Talks to Doctors." *New England Journal of Medicine 304:* 699–701, 1981.

Ulrich, Roger S. "View Through a Window May Influence Recovery from Surgery." *Science 224:* 420–21, 1984.

United Nations International Children's Emergency Fund (UNICEF). *The State of the World's Children, 1990*. New York and Oxford: Oxford University Press, 1990.

United States General Accounting Office. "Canadian Health Insurance: Lessons for the United States." Report to the Chairman, Committee on Government Operations, House of Representatives (GAO/HRD-91-90), June 1991.

Valenstein, Elliot S. *Great and Desperate Cures: The Rise and Decline of Psychosurgery and Other Radical Treatments for Mental Illness*. New York: Basic Books, 1986.

Vayda, Eugene, William R. Mindell, and Ira M. Rutkow. "A Decade of Surgery in Canada, England and Wales and the United States." *Archives of Surgery* 117: 846–53, 1982.

Veatch, Robert M. "Voluntary Risks to Health: The Ethical Issues." *Journal of the American Medical Association 243:* 50–55, 1980.

Wachter, Robert M. "AIDS, Activism, and the Politics of Health." *New England Journal of Medicine 326:* 128–32, 1992.

Wanzer, Sidney H., et al. "The Physician's Responsibility Toward Hopelessly Ill Patients: A Second Look." *New England Journal of Medicine 320:* 844–49, 1989.

Weatherall, M. *In Search of a Cure: A History of Pharmaceutical Discovery.* New York: Oxford University Press, 1990.

Wechsler, Henry, et al. "The Physician's Role in Health Promotion: A Survey of Primary-Care Practitioners." *New England Journal of Medicine 308:* 97–100, 1983.

Weissman, Gerald. "Against Aequanimitas." *Hospital Practice,* June 1984, pp. 159–69.

Weissman, Gerald. *The Doctor Dilemma: Squaring the Old Values with the New Economy.* Knoxville, Tenn.: Whittle Books/Grand Rounds Press, 1992.

Weissman, Joel S., Constantine Gatsonis, and Arnold M. Epstein. "Rates of Affordable Hospitalization by Insurance Status in Massachusetts and Maryland." *Journal of the American Medical Association 268:* 2388–94, 1992.

Weniger, Bruce G., et al. "The Epidemiology of HIV Infection and AIDS in Thailand." *AIDS 5* (suppl. 2): S71–S85, 1991.

Whitcomb, Michael E., and J. P. Desgroseilliers. "Primary Care Medicine in Canada. *New England Journal of Medicine 326:* 1469–72, 1992.

White, Kerr. *Healing the Schism: Epidemiology, Medicine, and the Public's Health.* New York and Berlin: Springer-Verlag, 1991.

White, Kerr. *The Task of Medicine: Dialogue at Wickenburg.* Menlo Park, Calif.: Kaiser Family Foundation, 1988.

Wilkes, Michael S., Bruce H. Doblin, and Martin F. Shapiro. "Pharmaceutical Advertisements in Leading Mecical Journals: Experts' Assessments." *Annals of Internal Medicine 116:* 912–19, 1992; with accompanying editorials by David A. Kessler and by Robert and Suzanne Fletcher.

Willems, Jane S., and Claudia R. Sanders. "Cost-Effectiveness and Cost-Benefit Analyses of Vaccines." *Journal of Infectious Diseases 144:* 486–93, 1981.

Wolfe, Sidney M., et al. *Worst Pills, Best Pills: The Older Adult's Guide to Avoiding Drug-Induced Death or Illness.* Washington, D.C.: Public Citizen Health Research Group, 1988.

Wolk, J., et al. "HIV-Related Risk-taking Behavior, Knowledge and Serostatus of Intravenous Drug Users in Sydney." *Medical Journal of Australia 152:* 452–58, 1990.

Woolhandler, Steffie, and David Himmelstein. "The Deteriorating Administrative Efficiency of the U.S. Health Care System." *New England Journal of Medicine 324:* 1253–58, 1991.

Yamauchi, Masaya, et al. "Euthanasia Around the World." *British Medical Journal 304:* 7–10, 1992.

Young, James Harvey. *American Health Quackery: Collected Essays of James Harvey Young.* Princeton, N.J.: Princeton University Press, 1992.

ACKNOWLEDGMENTS

IN A PROJECT of this kind, the author's indebtedness is of an unusual range and degree. When Martin Freeth and Stefan Moore,
executive producers of the *Medicine at the Crossroads* television series, brought up the prospect of writing a related book, it seemed
a match made in heaven. I had written a critical book about medical
education, as well as many magazine and newspaper articles about
one or another peculiar feature of medical practice. I was moving
toward writing a book about the larger problems of medical care
just at the time when the series was in development. It soon became clear that Freeth and Moore saw the major issues very similarly to the way I did, which was not entirely surprising since
some of the leading physician advisors to their series were also
among my long-standing heroes.

So I came to the project with well-formed ideas and many relevant personal and professional experiences. Yet to say that this
book in its present form would not have been possible without
the help of the television series production team is to put the matter

mildly. Their enormous talent and long, hard work—four years of it—generated the structure and substance of many of the remarkable materials at my disposal. While they graciously assure me that my own knowledge and ideas have found a way into their films, and while they bear little or no responsibility for any errors in my book, I know that my debt to them is far greater than theirs to me.

The series is a coproduction of the BBC Science and Features Department, the PBS station Thirteen/WNET–New York, the Australian Broadcasting Company, Sydney, and TV Española. I thank Martin Freeth and Stefan Moore, co–executive producers of the series, who oriented me to the project, read my entire manuscript twice, and provided extensive ongoing criticism and discussion. Freeth was also producer-director of "The Magic Bullet," and Moore was producer-director of "Temple of Science" and coproducer-director of "Pandemic." Their contributions to the corresponding chapters were especially great.

Producer-directors of individual episodes were also exceptionally generous with their time and criticism: Stephen White ("Code of Silence"); Jane West ("Random Cuts"); Peter Montagnon ("Disordered States"); Henry Singer ("Life Support"); Tim Clark ("Conceiving the Future"); and Susan Lambert ("Pandemic"). Michele Renay, Kate Akerman, and Catherine Drew served as coordinators between the book and the films from the British side, as did Kerry Herman and David Wolff from the American. Jack Sameth and George Page, production executives at WNET, also helped facilitate the book's development; Carlos Martinez Ramos, Iñigo Yrizor, Luis Agudo, and Paco Garrido Lonzano represented TV Española. Patients, physicians and other health workers and health authorities around the world consented to be filmed and interviewed. Many found their way into this book and are named as they appear; others influenced the text indirectly. I thank them all for giving of their time and knowledge.

David Wolff, WNET's book editor, was responsible for arranging my participation in the project, and has since provided much welcome support and encouragement. My agent, Elaine Markson, and her capable staff were also crucial to these arrangements. Since a somewhat different British version of this book has preceded this one to press, I owe a debt to those at BBC Books whose enthusiasm and hard work have indirectly influenced the American edition as well: Ann Wilson (a superb copy editor), Heather Holden-Brown, Christine Shuttleworth, and especially Martha Caute, the book's supervising editor. Her equanimity as I imposed one delay after another on a very tight schedule, and her enthusiasm for the project, were invaluable.

But the American edition had to be quite different in a variety of ways—reconceived, really—and I owe a great debt to those at Pantheon who supported me throughout this difficult process. Dan Frank helped decide the structure and tone of the book at the outset, and provided crucial feedback at every stage of the writing, from the first draft of the first chapter through the last typographical corrections. My fussiness, combined with a variety of distractions in my life, led to really unconscionable delays that put a great strain on Dan and his staff. He was as patient, as helpful, and as tolerant as could be. I also owe thanks to Alan Turkus, his assistant, to Joan Benham, the copy editor of the Pantheon edition, and to Grace McVeigh, the production editor.

My research assistant, Nancy Lee, provided extensive, cheerful, capable help, creatively managing my relationship to the Emory University libraries; David Reisman and Lisa Laurie at WNET provided additional assistance at crucial junctures. Kate Akerman, Rosie Allsop, Sunita Berry, Terence Bradley, Jennifer Crone, Catherine Drew, Evonne Francis, and Michele Renay at BBC Science and Features provided both background research for the series, without which the book would not have been possible, and specific research for the book when that was needed. I am grateful to all of them.

Advisers to the series were indirectly advisers to the book whether or not I personally consulted with them. I benefited from reading not only their published writings but also unpublished ones, as well as transcripts of conversations that took place during advisory meetings before I joined the project. Though in no way responsible for my views, their own are fundamental to the book. They include Drs. Christine Cassel, David Eddy, Harvey Fineberg,

Cecil Helman, Anne Kern, Arthur Kleinman, George Lundberg, Roy Porter, Octavi Quintana Trias, Frederick Robbins, Wendy Savage, Victor Sidel, Mary Tudor Hart, and John Wennberg, as well as Jean Robinson of the Patients' Association/General Medical Council.

Among the advisers, Drs. Julian Tudor Hart and William Foege must be singled out for their exceptional generosity in consulting with me directly. Others who shared their expertise include Drs. Henry Kahn, Boyd Eaton, Sally McNagny, John Stone, Herbert Karp, Ian MacColl, Steven Cohen-Cole, Timothy Mastro, Mark Rosenberg, Margaret Mermin, Andre Nahmias, Stuart Seidman, Timothy Harlan, and Jennifer Weil; Sir Walter Bodmer; and Professors Carol Worthman, Wenda Trevathan, James Gustafson, Robert Hahn, Arthur Shostak, Fred Kroger, Richard Saltman, and Paul Starr. Drs. Roger Larsen, Ira Schwartz, Julian Gomez, Carlos Gomez, and Sylvia Cerel, and Professor Peter Brown read the manuscript in its entirety. Their comments were especially helpful.

The department of anthropology and the administration of Emory University generously accepted the burden of my absence on short notice for a full academic year. I particularly thank Professors Peter Brown and Peggy Bartlett, President James T. Laney, and Provost William Frye. Anthropology department staff members Judy Robertson, Shirley Sabo, and Anne Nugent facilitated my work on the book while I was on leave.

My first images of what a doctor is helped shape the consciousness that underlies this book. Early influences include our local general practitioner in Brooklyn, New York, Milton Finkel; my uncle Abraham ("Bobby") Fink; and my cousins Leon Fink and Martin Silbersweig—all dedicated primary-care physicians. Drs. Paul Pavel, Stefan Stein, and Julian Gomez encouraged and guided my strange career in medicine at crucial junctures. Teachers who played important roles in my medical education were Drs. Hans Bode, Joseph Lipinski, Walter Abelmann, T. Berry Brazelton, Norman Geschwind, Daniel Federman, Edward Gross, Ross Neisuler, Richard Wurtman, Shah Khoshbin, Philip Savitsky, Robert Green, H. Thomas Ballantine, David Hamburg, Francis Moore, and Leon Eisenberg. Drs. John Stone, Herbert Karp, Boyd Eaton, Ronald

Barr, and Jerome Walker have been influential models, as well as friends, in the time since. My participation in a seminar at the Center for Advanced Study in the Behavioral Sciences during 1986–87, with Drs. Lawrence Crowley, P. Herbert Leiderman, Robert Rose, and Albert Rothenberg, and Professors Robert Scott and Julius Moravcik, helped me to see that others more experienced than I share my doubts about the way medicine is practiced.

Kathy Mote, Joseph Beck, Dudley Clendinen, Irven DeVore, Herbert Perluck, and Steven Cohen-Cole have been valued advisers and friends. Robert Liebman provided supportive friendship as well as insight into the British health-care system. Ronnie Wenker Konner, Hannah Konner, and Irving Konner shared their experiences of illness, and Beth Kroger helped solve a puzzle about India. My brother, Larry Konner, is also my closest friend; we have weathered many trials together, including major illnesses. The same is true of my wife, Marjorie Shostak. Her support for my work on this book during a difficult time in her own life has been crucial indeed. Finally, my children, Susanna, Adam, and Sarah, are all old enough now to understand what goes into making a book, what the purposes are of this book, and what my preoccupation with it may have cost them. Their generosity has been both informed and real, and I am both apologetic and grateful.

INDEX